Otto Hietsch

Bavarian into English

A Lexical and Cultural Guide

Bavarian into English

A Lexical and Cultural Guide

By

Otto Hietsch

Dr. phil., Dott. in Lett., M. Litt.
Professor Emeritus of English Philology in the University of Regensburg

Andreas Dick Verlag

Acknowledgements

A lexico-cultural venture that reaches out over largely uncharted ground can do with many helpmates. In our case, these have indeed come forward with alacrity, good cheer, and competence. Professors Gerald Cohen (Rolla, Mo.) and George T. Riggs (Whispering Pines, NC) in the United States, Susan Rear (Lichfield), Corinna Meßmann (Dublin), and Norman E. Hoey (Landgarve Manor, Ulster) in the British Isles, offered many useful suggestions to an earlier version of the manuscript. The pictorial side was well taken care of by Heinrich Spanner (Straubing), our artist-in-residence, as well as by four generous donors, Anton Schlicksbier (Sulzbach; pp. 31, 41, 126, 190, 195), Erika Eichenseer (Regensburg; pp. 49, 57), Familie Georg Höltl (Museumsdorf Bayerischer Wald, Tittling; pp. 118, 153), and Hermann Daiminger (Burglengenfeld; p. 139). The Bayerische Verwaltung der Staatlichen Schlösser, Gärten und Seen, at Nymphenburg Castle, Munich, kindly placed at our disposal a photograph of Lola Montez (p. 123). And we shudder to think what the computerized printout would have looked like if it had not been for the specialist skill and loyal patience of Maximilian Stempfhuber (Geisenfeld).

To them all, a hearty *Dankschön* for their splendid cooperation!

Andreas Dick   Otto Hietsch

1. Auflage 1994
Andreas Dick Verlag
Lilienthalstraße 8, D-94315 Straubing
© 1994 by Andreas Dick Verlag
Gesamtherstellung Druckerei Himmer, Augsburg
Gesamtgestaltung Andreas Dick, Maximilian Stempfhuber
Umschlaggestaltung und Illustration Heinrich Spanner
Printed in Germany
ISBN 3-9801769-5-9

Contents

Publisher's Foreword 7
Preface 8
The Bavarian Anthem in English 11

The Glossary 13

Appendix 215
   Analogues of Proverbial Lore 216
   Landlubbers and Seafarers 218
   Bavarian Popular Poetry in English 220

Hints for Further Reading 224
Abbreviations Used 228

About the Author

Otto Hietsch, a native of Vienna born in 1924, is a man of many professional incarnations. In his upbringing, from early on, pragmatic and scholarly elements have been happily mixed. A graduated translator and interpreter at twenty-one, and a certificated teacher cum Dr. phil. at twenty-four, he went into tertiary education work in Austria, England, and Italy. For odd stretches of academic freewheeling, the young lecturer and lexicographer sallied forth to study elsewhere, at such cultural centres and dictionary offices as Edinburgh, Ann Arbor, and Sydney.

In 1952, Dr. Hietsch was appointed Professor of German and English at Padua's venerable Bò; and eleven years later accepted a call to the first chair of English Philology at Braunschweig Technical University, the oldest of its kind in Germany. In 1967, the newly established *alma mater Ratisbonensis* invited him to return to the banks of the Danube. There "Bavarian English", to the students' delight, has soon become one of his favourites, and that *cavallo di battaglia*, the reader can see, is proudly prancing still.

Vorwort des Verlegers

Wer sich als Autor mit einem flächenmäßig fest umrissenen Thema beschäftigt, kann der Dimension Tiefe größeres Augenmerk schenken. Dieses gilt hier dem Bemühen, das Bairische (oder eine ähnlich bedeutsame Mundart unserer Muttersprache) dem Englischen im zweisprachigen Kulturvergleich an die Seite zu stellen.

Der hier eingeschlagene Weg ist ein absolutes Novum, und die Vorteile, die der Benutzer von *Bavarian into English* daraus zu ziehen vermag, werden auf jeder Seite offenbar. Zum ersten Mal ja findet er Bodenständiges, das ihm im Landesalltag immer wieder begegnet, auf englisch einwandfrei erklärt und stiladäquat übersetzt.

Zahlreich geboten sind aber auch die im Englischen verwurzelten Analoga; sie passen oft haargenau, und sie verblüffen und erfreuen.

Wörter in ein Kontinuum einzubetten und so unauffällig zum gewandten, idiomreichen Sprachgebrauch hinzuleiten, ist ein weiterer Wesenszug dieser Sammlung.

Erfährt der Nachschlagende also nun endlich, wem im Englischen (sagen wir) ein *Adam Riese*, ein *Bierdimpfl*, ein *Wolpertinger* entspricht, so darf er jetzt auch sicher sein, keiner Fehlinformation zu erliegen, etwa der, daß die *Dampf*nudeln mit ihren Verwandten, den *Rohr*nudeln, gleichgesetzt werden oder daß die Leber als ein unabdingbarer Bestandteil unseres *Leberkäses* gilt.

Der Weg in die Verständnistiefe führt indes nicht nur zum Beseitigen von Irrtümern, sondern deckt auch - sonst ungeahnte - geistige Verflechtungen auf, die dann prompt in sprachlichen Parallelen zutage treten: bei einer Unzahl von bildhaften Vergleichen und Spruchweisheiten etwa gehen das Bairische und das Englische sehr wohl konform; es besteht daher kein Grund (wie bisher von Wörterbuchmachern mitunter leichtfertig geübt), statt einer kraftvollen Metapher der Umgangssprache oder der Mundart ein blasses Wort der Hochsprache als Alibidefinition anzubieten.

Die zweisprachige Lexikographie schlägt mit *Bavarian into English* ganz neue, eminent nutzbringende Bahnen ein. Möge das Glossar dem sprachlich wie kulturell und landeskundlich interessierten Leser, ob dieser nun hüben oder drüben danach greift, ein freundlicher und munter unterhaltsamer Leitfaden durch das Land und das Leben der Bayern in Gegenwart und Vergangenheit sein!

Preface

Human speech is a subtly orchestrated affair. It can be loud and gentle, harsh and sweet, in all being capable of carrying (or only intimating) an infinity of messages that, as a rule, are meant to be taken up and reacted to by one's fellow-beings. Even a short utterance in which one sound sequence is exchanged for another one, or a word pronounced with a variant pattern of intonation, is almost certainly bound to be noticed by the listener in its otherness.

Acquainting the learner with a foreign spoken language is therefore not easy; and teachers often try, perhaps with some pricks of conscience, to adopt a streamlined procedure. They substitute textbooks for the oral method, foisting on these a role that books can never really fulfil: to grab something in print, and to "theorize" along without at the same time having repeated recourse to a living native speaker (or indeed to a good many of them) is a caution nobody should really be prepared to accept for long these days.

Another and very important point about which the learner is likely to be misguided is the breadth and depth and variety, and variability, of the spoken idiom he is about to be initiated into.

Bilingual phraseologies and dictionaries tend to simplify matters, and skim the surface only. They far too often content themselves with equating speech at the standard level; and should left and right fail to match, lexicographers are quick to ignore the colloquiality or slanginess, the humour, irony, sarcasm, guardedness, or whatever, of the source phrase. But merely supplying a standard term or a definition in the target language will never do. In either case the outcome is a perversion, and a mockery for the translator-stylist who strives after literary adequacy.

Bavarian German, as every native of the land will laughingly testify, is largely a dialect rich in vigorous diction. Similes, metaphors, and hyperboles abound. Many of the objects surrounding our native speaker in everyday life, and curious incidences and circumstances occurring to him en route, will be drawn upon to make his speech witty and colourful. He keeps twiddling and twisting his verbal kaleidoscope, but hardly less so does his opposite number in the wide and similarly picture-happy Anglo-Saxon world. Bavarians and Britons, for instance, see eye to eye when jokingly pondering the anatomy, functionality, and physiology of some parts of the human body. They look upon the navel as the *Bauchknöpfl*, the "belly button"; they endow the clumsy person with *lauter Daumen*, "his fingers are all thumbs", but they praise the muscular man mountain for possessing *Irxenschmalz*, a lot of "elbow" or "axle grease". To quote one phrasal example, there is the semi-peeved query flung at someone obstructing the view, *"Is dei Vater a Glaser?"* The situation is common enough outside the pale of Bavaria, of course, and thus sets tongues a-wagging in English as well, "You make a better door than a window!", "One can't see through muddy water!" and, indeed, "Your father wasn't a glazier!" Just three out of a much bigger lot, with the gem of an almost perfect parallel - no need to become stiffly formulaic (as one dictionary does) or, which is as bad, become silent.

Talking of silence. As any Bavarian student of English will long have found out, German-English dictionaries heavily incline towards West and North German entries. Are Bavarian users deliberately being given the lexical run-around when they want to find an English equivalent for the homespun word or phrase they happen to have in mind at the moment? Or are they credited with the precocious knowledge of a host of synonymous regionalisms that promptly steers them to the right answer? Whatever those dictionary people think and lay down, there is - to give two concrete instances - no *Antlaßpfinsta* and no *Fotzenspangler* within sight, nor are there any pointers to *Gründonnerstag* and *Zahnklempner*, where the respective English analogues are indeed waiting.

The following glossary, then, tries, as far as space permits, to remedy the situation. It offers, wherever the need is felt, a quick look at the etymology of the headword and its possible relationship with the English word stock; meanings are elucidated and embedding sample phrases added in order to dispel any doubts about the proper uses. In order to show the practical interconnectedness of spoken Bavarian and English on a wider scale, this little book also includes some non-lexical pieces of prose and poetry that nearly everybody in this country knows, or even loves to quote in the original on the spur of the moment. May they often be heard in bilingual company and in rousing good-fellowship!

The Bavarian Anthem

Music by Max Kunz (1812-1875)   Words by Michael Öchsner (1816-1893)

2. Gott mit dir, dem Bayernvolke, daß wir, uns'rer Väter wert, fest in Eintracht und in Frieden bauen uns'res Glückes Herd! Daß mit Deutschlands Bruderstämmen einig uns ein jeder schau und den alten Ruhm bewähre unser Banner, weiß und blau!

2. May the Lord save you, Bavarians, make us walk our forebears' path; fortified through peace and union, steadfast build our fortune's hearth! May He will that German nations are like brothers for the view, keep the ancient glory going of our banner white and blue.

JOHANN LACHNER *Bairisch lernen*

Stinktada, stinktada, weilst nix vastehst,
bals zu da Wirtin in d' Kuchl nausgehst?

Hocktada, hocktada, weilstas net woaßt,
bal da da Knecht eppas sagt, was des hoaßt?

Rachtada, rachtada, weilstas net kennst,
was da de Madln sang, balst nachirennst?

Muaß da net stingga und muaß di net stiern,
teamas ge frisch mit da Sprachlehr probiern!

Gengama, gengama zammat in d' Lehr,
schaugts aa beim Ohfanga bluadi hart her.

Sahgada, sahgada oissamt, was feit,
werstas scho inne, sche staad mit da Zeit.

Moansteppa, moansteppa, bringstas glei zamm?
Tua di net teischn: an Ernst muaßt fei ham!

Bist du net fleißi, i blahs da koan Marsch.
Bleibst halt a Schuasta und leckst m. a. A.

Learning Bavarian

'Hoppin' mad, hoppin' mad, nothin' compree?
Landlord's wife's kitchen talk sounds like Chinee?

Moody thing, moody thing, no savvy vous?
Are Johnny Farmhand's words double-dutch, too?

Surlyface, Surlyface, ain't it like Greek
What lassies say when their presence you seek?

Fumin' 's no good, let not feelin's run high,
Make a fresh start givin' grammar a try!

Off we go, off we go swot. Two's a team.
Starters are bloody hard (leastways, they seem).

I will tell, I will tell, when you step wrong;
Steady and slow, movin' gently along.

Would you though, would you though, think it child's play?
Ee, what a thought! It's a grind all the way.

If you won't set to, now look, I don't care
You stay a tinker; go kiss me ... guess where.

☞ A ☜

abbusseln *vt/refl* [an intensive of *busseln*↓] *colloq.* **1.** *v/t* to kiss effusively: to cover with kisses, to shower (*or* smother) with kisses; *unsere kleine Juliane ist so ein goldiges Buzerl, daß wir sie am liebsten den ganzen Tag knuddeln und ~ könnten* our baby Juliana is such a sweet little darling we could cuddle and cover her with kisses all day. - **2.** *v/refl* (1) to kiss each other lovingly: to kissy-kissy, *AmE hum. also* to play post office, to play smacky lips. - (2) slightly *contp.*, if the act of osculation is performed with sovereign disregard for other people around: to smooch; *sich in der hintersten Kinoreihe ~* to be necking in the back row of the cinema.

abfieseln *v/t dial.* (*abnagen*) to pick (a bone, etc.) clean; *er hat die Boandl vom Hendl gründlich abgefieselt* he did a thorough job of picking the bones of his chicken; *gib die Knochen dem Hund zum* ~ give the bones to the dog (to gnaw), let the dog gnaw on the bones; to an overweening Northerner: *schau, wir Bayern haben schon eine echte Kultur gehabt, als deine Ahnen noch Missionarsknochen abgefieselt haben* look here, we Bavarians had a thriving civilization when your ancestors were still living in caves (*or*, were still climbing trees).

Abrahams Wurstkessel [-ʃt-] *m* - -s [for absurd effect, the venerable name of Abraham (according to John viii. 37, the progenitor of the Jewish people) here collates with something almost ludicrously mundane] *hum.* a crudely medieval picture, possibly lifted from a Biblia Pauperum, helps to describe man's estate when yet unborn - "sausage" embryos are afloat in a huge "cauldron" before being transmuted into human shape later on; the phrase is used to deflate a potential or real braggart, putting him in his place in one of two ways, **1.** he is made to look a callow youth, at least by comparison: *damals warst du noch in* ~~ you were then still living in a cabbage patch, *or* under the gooseberry bush, *or*, *AustralE*, under a gum-tree, you were then still coated with fuller's earth ‖ with a triumphantly sensual leer: *du bist ja noch in* ~~ *gelegen, wie ich schon fleißig Kinder gemacht hab* you weren't even a gleam in your father's eye while I was already busy fixing up kids; and **2.** he is given to understand that he may claim no privileges: *du bist ja auch nur in* ~~ *herumgeschwommen!* *you aren't a bit better than the rest of us coming out of Abraham's cauldron, you aren't any different from the common run of us, *NorBrE* *also* we're all Jack Thompson's bairns, *AmE* *also* you aren't number one on the hit parade, you aren't the only fish in the sea.

Abschneider *m* -s/- *colloq.* (*Abkürzung*[*sweg*]) (short[-]) cut, *AmE* cutoff; *einen ~ machen* to take a short-cut, to cut a corner; *wir haben einen ~ durch* (or *über*) *die Wiesen gemacht und uns prompt verirrt* we cut across the meadows, and promptly got lost.

Adam Riese *proper name* [the name of a Franconian arithmetician (also spelt Ries or Ryse), 1492-1559, whose books, written for the general public, gained him proverbial fame; as striking parallels from beyond the Channel, Edmund Gunter, 1581-1626, and Edward Cocker, 1631-1675, two English mathematicians, have successfully entered the Hall of Lexicalized Fame] only in the *colloq.* phrase, used to clinch the soundness of the speaker's simple, usu. mental, calculation: *das macht nach ~ ~* (e.g., *[zusammen] fünf Mark zwanzig*) this, according to Cocker (*or, more common in AmE*, according to Gunter), is (five marks twenty [all totted up]).

Advent *m* -(e)s/pl. rare: -e [< L *adventus* 'the coming (of Christ into the world)'] **1.** *R.C.* the period beginning four Sundays before Christmas: Advent (season *or* time); *(der) ~ ist eine stade Zeit gläubigen Wartens* Advent is a silent holy time of waiting; *am ersten Sonntag im ~* on the first Sunday in (*or* during) Advent, on Advent Sunday. - **2.** *folklore* pre-Christmas season (*or* time).

Advent... or **Advents...**: **~kerze** *f* -/-n *R.C.* Advent candle; *die ~n versinnbildlichen das Licht der Welt, welches in der Heiligen Nacht zu uns gekommen ist* the Advent candles are a symbol of the Light of the World which came to us in Holy Night. - **~kranz** *m* -es/...kränze *R.C.* Advent wreath *or* garland (usu. made of fir-twigs [and laurels]); *die vier Kerzen des ~es, jede Woche eine mehr, brennen dann alle am Heiligen Abend, zusammen mit denen am Weihnachtsbaum* the four Advent-wreath candles, one for each week, at last are all burning on Holy Eve, along with those on the Christmas tree. - **~zeit** *f* -/pl. rare: -en = *Advent*↑.

Alkoholvernichtungstrupp *m* -s/-s *hum.* a group of regulars drinking beer (as often as not in sizeable quantities) round their table at a pub or inn (*Stammtischrunde*): booze-fighting squad, gang of bottle-crackers, gym team of elbow-benders (*or* elbow-crookers), *AmE also* posse of bar polishers.

Allerwelts...: **~kirtag** *m* -(e)s/pl. rare: -e, **~kirchweih** *f* -/pl. rare: -en *folklore* "All-Bavarian Sunday Fair", a festive occasion, on the third Sunday in October, to engage in various merry-makings and to have roast goose as a traditional meal; established in 1869, it is also known as *großer Kirtag*, distinguishing it from the more specific, and more religious, *kleiner Kirtag*↓.

Alpenfestung *f* - *mil. hist.* Alpine Redoubt [-aʊt], the mountain area around Berchtesgaden, where Hitler intended to make his last stand in 1945, at the end of the Second World War.

Amerikaner *m* -s/- *bak.* (*rundes Mürbteigstück mit Zuckerguß*) "American (cookie)", a sponge cake, flat and round, about four inches in diameter, with sugar icing on top.

Antlaß *m* ...lasses/...lasse [< MHG *antlaz*, ModHG *Entlassung* 'release, absolution (from ecclesiastical penalty)'] *R.C. hist.* penitent's readmission to church; usu. only in compounds, and reflecting active folk customs: **~ei** *n* -(e)s/-er, *dial.* **~oa**, pl. -r "Maundy Thursday egg", one laid on that day and considered to be of special benefit if blessed and eaten on Easter Sunday; moreover, if buried in the field, crops should prosper; if kept at home, the house should be safe from fire and lightning; and if jointly eaten with another person, thinking of that companion is a guarantee to find one's way again after being lost. - **~pfinsta** *m* -(s)/- [for the etymology of that element, see *Pfinsta*↓] **1.** or **~tag** *m* -(e)s/-e (*Gründonnerstag*) Maundy Thursday, *AmE* also Holy Thursday, in former times the day on which sinners received absolution. - **2.** in the Bavarian Forest: Corpus Christi Day (otherwise known as *Fronleichnamstag* [which is just a free translation of that Latin term], or *Prangertag*↓ or *Kranzltag*↓). - **~rose** *f* -/-n, *dial.* **~ros(e)n** *f* -/- *bot.* (*Pfingstrose*) peony.

Antn *f* -/- *dial.* [< the awkwardly slow rolling gait of a duck (*Ente*)] *school sl.* dull girl: dopey duck, daffy duck. - **~jung** *n* -s *cul.* (*Entenklein*) duck giblets *pl.*, a gravy dish of the heart, liver, neck, and wing parts of a duck, usu. served with a white-bread dumpling.

anwanzlg *adj colloq.* (*aufdringlich*) clinging; *der ist aber* ~ he sticks like glue, *or* like a tick, he's a leech *or* limpet; *die ist aber* ~ she's a clinging vine.

Apfel...: **~butzen** *m* -s/- *dial.* (*Kerngehäuse e-s Apfels;* → *Butzen*) apple core. - **~kücherl** *n* -s/often pl.: - [second el., a dim. variant of *Kuchen* 'cake'] *cul.* a slice of apple dipped into batter, cooked in hot fat, and sprinkled with sugar and cinnamon: apple fritter. - **~strudel** *m* -s/- *bak.* a pastry consisting of sliced apples rolled in a blanket of paper-thin dough, and baked in the oven: apple strudel.

Apostelbereifung *f* -/pl. rare: -en *hum.* light shoes consisting of a sole of leather fastened to the foot by thongs or straps, traditionally worn by Christ and his disciples during their peregrinations in the Holy Land (*Jesussandalen*): Jesus sandals (*or* slippers, *or* boots) *pl.*, Jesus slippers *pl.*

Armdorfer or **Armsdorfer** *adj* [derivatives of fictitious place-name forms, to be suitably rendered by '(coming) from "Poorsville" or "Hungerthorpe"' (contrasting with *Reichsdorf* 'Richville')] only in a *hum.* or *sarc. dial.* warning to the children (and the rest of the family) that they will needs be kept on short commons this Christmas: *heuer kimmt's* (or, *gibt's nur 's*) ~ *Christkindl* it's an empty sack of gifts Santa Claus (*BrE also* Father Christmas) will come trudging by with this year (, mind); it's a skimpy meal we'll be sitting down to this Christmas (, mind).

Arm...: **~drücken** *n* -s *folklore* wrist-wrestling, arm-wrestling **1.** a popular entertainment and test of strength, practised in Upper Bavarian inns, etc. between two men seated opposite one another across a table; with their left hands joined on the surface between them, the opponents clasp right hands firmly and brace their right elbows on the table; at the 'go' signal, both try to force the other's hand down to achieve a victory. - **2.** *sports* an official international sport with the above rules, requiring a table of specific size and padded elbow cups. -

~drücker *m* -s/- wrist-wrestler, arm-wrestler, one engaged in the sport of wrist-wrestling (*Armdrücken*↑).

Armenhaus *n* -es/...häuser [actually, 'poorhouse', *BrE also* 'workhouse', *AmE also* 'almshouse'] *fig.*, *econ.* the area within a larger political unit which, because of its meagre productivity and comparative lack of industry, has the lowest per capita income of the whole region: poorhouse; *das ~ Bayerns* "The Poorhouse of Bavaria", a sobriquet for the Upper Palatinate (or, in the opinion of others, for the Bavarian Forest) because of its largely unproductive soil.

Aschentonne *f* -/-n [still so named for once receiving much powdery residue from domestic heating] *admin.* a container with a lid, for holding household waste: *BrE* dustbin, *AmE* ashcan, garbage can, trashcan.

Auffahrtstag *m* -(e)s *R.C. & folklore* → *fliegen* 2.

auf geht's! *interj* a cheerful invitation, sometimes to oneself, but more often for others to join the speaker in starting work, or in having fun, with zest and vigour: here we go!, off like blazes!, let's get cracking!, let's whoop it up!, let's get the show on the road!; to others also: let's go, boys [girls]! ‖ as a spirited elaboration of that phrase ("Papa" Schichtl, 1851-1911, having been a well-known showman at the Munich *Oktoberfest*↓, who for years performed "real" decapitations with his guillotine): *~ ~ beim Schichtl!* as one earwig said to another, "'ere we go!" ‖ a rallying call to join the crowd of merrymakers at the Munich *Oktoberfest*↓: *~ ~ zur Wies'n!* to the Meadow off we hie!

aufmandln *colloq.* **1.** *vt/i agr.* [second el., *Mandl* 3↓] *Getreide ~* to put sheaves together in the harvest field for drying (*Garben zur Nachreife aufstellen*): to stook [-uː-], *NorBrE also* to set (the) sheaves up in a hattock, to set up, to hattock, to stack, to stowk [-(a)ɔː-], [-əʊ-]. - **2.** *v/refl* [second el., *Mandl* 1 & 2↓] often *iron.* or *contp.* whenever said with reference to a person, usu. male, whose slight frame is at odds with his, at the moment, aggressive and overbearing manner — to become impatient and angry: to work oneself into a lather, to get one's dander (*or*, quills) up, *AmE also* to rear up on one's hind legs.

Auftreiber *m* -s/- *colloq.* **1.** *contp.* noisy, blustering person: loudmouth, rip-roarer, show-off; *if an annoying schoolchild*, little nuisance (*or* pest, *or* rascal), limb of the devil, holy terror, pain in the neck. - **2.** = *Gaudibursch* 2 & 3.

auf Wiederschauen *interj* a slightly less frequent variant than *auf Wiedersehen*: goodbye, *colloq.* see you, be seeing you ‖ a good-natured warning that the object about to be given away on a loan basis should be duly returned: *du weißt [Sie wissen] ja, da steht „ ~ ~ " drauf!* mind you, it's got a back to it!, *or* ... it's on an elastic band - it comes back!

auspapierln *v/t* [second el., < *Papierl*, here: 'tissue paper (to wrap flowers), or kraft paper (to wrap items of food, such as a snack meat loaf) in'] *colloq.* to unwrap: to undo, e.g. a bouquet of flowers before presenting it to the hostess; *er geht fürstlich ins Wirtshaus essen, und ich bleib da und kann mein Wurstbrot ~!* he lords it at the inn with knife and fork, and I am left behind to dig my teeth into a slice of bread and sausage!

Auswärts *m* -/no pl. [literally, '(season of leaves sprouting) outward', the time when the days are 'getting longer'] *dial. & poet.* (*Frühling*; opp. *Einwärts↓*): spring; *im ~* in spring; *für den naturverbundenen Menschen liegt der Schnee nicht wie ein Leichentuch auf der Landschaft, sondern als Zudecke, unter der Blumen, Gräser und Saaten schon dem ~ entgegenträumen* for nature-loving folks, the snow is not so much a deathly pall covering the landscape but rather a protective blanket, under which flowers, grasses, and seeds dreamily await the coming of spring ‖ a piece of old weather lore:

wenn's um Lichtmeß stürmt und schneibt, / ist der ~ nimmer weit! *storms and snows at Candlemas / herald springtime flowers and grass.

☞ **ß** ☜

Baaz *m* -es [< sound symbolism] *colloq.*, sometimes with a playfully pleasant undertone **1.** mud, or any other slushy mass: goo, *AmE also* gumbo, glob; *Kinder und Wildschweine spielen für ihr Leben gern im ~* children and wild boars just love to wallow in the mud. - **2.** any other sticky substance the speaker has, often inadvertently, come upon: goo, *BrE also* gunge, *AmE also* gunk; *was ist denn das für ein ~ da unten in der Tasche? ... da muß die Schokolade zergangen sein!* what's all that goo at the bottom of this bag? ... the chocolate must have melted. - **baazig** *adj colloq.* said of, or resembling, a sticky substance: gooey, *BrE also* gungy.

Backofen *m* -s/...öfen **1.** *agr.* a separate farmyard structure close to the main building, to bake the huge rye bread loaves and simple cakes in for family consumption every week: bakehouse. - **2.** *fig.*, low *colloq. hum.* a pregnant woman's uterus: oven (in reference to which a coarse English metaphor speaks of the mother-to-be as "having a bun in the oven"); *bei Obermeiers ist der ~ eingefallen* "with the Obermeiers the bakehouse has caved in", the Obermeiers have been storked (*or* blessed-evented), the Obermeiers have rung the stork bell (*or*, have had a bundle-from-heaven).

Baiern 1. *m pl., hist.* (*Baiwaren, Bajuwaren*) (ancient tribe of the) Bavarians. → **2.** *n* -s *hist. geog.* (*Altbayern*) Old Bavaria, i.e. the tribal heartlands around Munich, Landshut and Regensburg (extending at one time south to include a large part of what is today Austria and South Tyrol); cp. *Bayern*.

Bamberger *attr.* '(typical) of Bamberg', a quaint medieval town in Upper Franconia: ~ **Honigmarkt** *m - -(e)s com.* "Bamberg Honey Fair", an annual event held for the past fifty years or so on Shrove Tuesday, honey being considered a good remedy for hangovers prevailing in carnival time. - ~ **Hörnchen** *n - -s/- - bak.* "Bamberg Crescent", a rich yeast roll made from pure butter and milk. - ~ **Rauchbier** *n - -(e)s/pl. rare: - -e bev.* a special type of beer cultivated from olden times, when malt was dried in the open air and wood fires were kindled to assist the process; as with whisky-distilling in Scotland, smoke pervades the malt, adding a quaint tang of its own to the end product: "Bamberg smoked beer"; *~ ~ hat 13,5 Prozent Stammwürze (also ziemlich viel) und 4,5 Prozent Alkoholgehalt* Bamberg smoked beer has 13.5 per cent of original wort (which is rather high), and 4.5 per cent of alcohol. - ~ **Reiter** *m - -s art* in the choir of the Cathedral, on a small pedestal fairly high up against its northernmost pillar: "Bamberg Horseman", a delicate sculpture dating from early Gothic times (13th cent.), claimed to portray King Philip of Swabia (*d.* 1208), but often felt to be the supreme embodiment of royal knighthood as conceived in Hohenstaufen art.

Banzen *m -s/-* [< MHG *panze* < L *pantex* 'stomach', 'belly'; related to E *paunch* '(a man's) fat stomach'] (beer) barrel.

Bärwurz "bear root" **1.** *f -/-en, also* **Bärenwurzel** *f -/-n,* **Bärendill** *m -s/-e bot.* an umbelliferous plant (*Meum athamanticum*) whose natural habitat are the high-lying meadows (all above 3000 ft. in altitude) of the Rachel and Lusen mountains, in the Bavarian Forest; its root, shaggy in appearance, and similar in taste to celery, is dug in autumn: (true) spicknel, baldmoney, bear fennel. → **2.** *m* -(es)/-(e) *bev.* a pungent brandy distilled from this root (commonly known as *Waldlerschnaps*), sometimes diversified by the addition of various woodland berries.

Bärwurzbrennerei, Bärwurzerei *f* -/-en *indus.* "bear-root" distillery (at Zwiesel).

Batzl *n* -s/-(n) [a dim. formed from the stem *batz-* (as in *batzen* 'to cling stickily together', 'to cake' [an intensifying variant of *backen* 'to bake']) and *Batzen m* 'lump', 'clod'] *colloq.* **1.** a small lump (*Klümpchen*): twiddly-bit (of earth, mud, etc.); → *Hirnbatzl*. - **2.** *emot.*, hence also **Batzerl** *n* -s/-(n) [→ *-erl*] a very small amount (*ganz kleine Menge*): smidgin (*or* smidgen); *könnt ich bittschön noch ein ~ Kartoffelbrei haben?* could I have another smidgin of mash, please? - **3.** *med.* a pimple or other minor skin blemish (*Pickel*): hickey; *soll ich dir das ~ ausdrucken?* do you want me to squeeze out your hickey for you? - **4.** *agr.* a white, often globular root crop, the size of a fist or a baby's skull: turnip.

Batzl... *colloq.:* **~augen** *n pl.* **1.** *med.* protuberant eyes (*hervortretende Augen*): bug-eyes, goggle-eyes, pop-eyes; *der hat fei ~* his eyes stick out like organ stops (*BrE also* ... like chapel hat-pegs). - **2.** often *contp.* momentarily bulbous eyes, due to intense curiosity or greed: beady eyes, goo-goo eyes, pop-eyes; *gib Obacht, du kriegst am End vor lauter Schauen noch ~!* mind, if you don't stop staring your eyes will pop out; *er hat vor lauter Gier solche ~ gekriegt, daß man sie mit der Knopfgabel hätte putzen können* he became all agog and gawping with greed, making his eyes shine like shoe buttons ‖ in stark irony, also: *hast du deine ~ vielleicht auf einen gewissen jungen Mann geworfen?* have you by any manner of means set your beady blue eyes on a certain young man? - **~kraut** *n* -(e)s [see *Batzl* 4] *cul., colloq.* (*gehackte Rüben*) (finely) chopped turnips. - **~radi** *m* -(s)/-(s) *colloq.* [the first compound element draws attention to the neatly rounded shape of the root] *bot.* = *Batzl* 4.

Baucherer *m* -s/- *colloq.* = *Bauchplatscher*↓.

Bauch... *colloq.*: **~butzen** *m* -s/-, **~knöpfl** *n* -s/-(n) [second el., dim. of Knopf 'button'] *anat.*, *hum.* navel (*Nabel*): belly button. - **~platscher**, **~pflatscher** *m* -s/- [second el., echoic for the thud caused by the impact of a heavy object on a hard surface] *sports*, esp. in swimming and ice-skating — the awkward pancake landing of a diver or skater, whose front of the body falls flat against the water, or ice, respectively: flop(per), *BrE also* belly flapper, *AmE also* belly whop(per), belly buster. - **~stecherl** *n* -s/-(n) *hum.* [in literal translation, "little belly stabber", so called because finger-shaped noodles (1) when raw, were once used as roast-goose stuffing, and (2) are nowadays favoured as a tummy-filling side dish] **1.** usu. pl., *cul.*, also **~zweckerl** *n* -s/-(n) a prepared item that goes well with goulash and other gravy dishes but sometimes, when boiled in milk and sweetened, also serves as a dessert; the dough consists of flour, eggs, butter and salt, it is trimmed and rolled into the shape of fingers, cooked in boiling water, basted with brown butter or sprinkled with cheese or parsley: finger noodles. - **2.** *vulg.* a smart, sexually attractive girl: snappy undercut, (choice) piece of crackling. - **~weh** *n* -s **1.** *med.* abdominal pains: bellyache. - **2.** *fig.* an ironic way of expressing one's feeling of dislike: *die Hausarbeit ist mir so lieb wie* ~ housework is my pet hate (*or*, pet aversion). - **~zwicken** *n* -s *med.* (*Bauchgrimmen*) sudden and severe stomach cramps: gripes; *er hat* ~ he's got the gripes; *gegen* ~ *ist ein Stamperl gut, bei* ~ *ist ein Stamperl fällig* a little pick-me-up is good for (*or*, comes in handy with) the gripes.

Bauern...: **~bub** *m* -en/-en (*Bauernjunge*) country lad, farmer's boy, *AmE* farmboy. - **~fünfer** *m* -s/. **1.** *hist.*, *contp.* Roman numeral V which, along with other simple Roman numerals, continued to be used by the rural population long after Arabic numerals had found widespread acceptance in the seventeenth century. - **2.** *hist. jur.* (*ländlicher Hilfsschöffe*) peasant juryman, one of a group of five called by the judge in doubtful cases from the market assembly to assist at a trial. - **3.** *contp.* an invective hurled in anger at any male person

thought to have acted foolishly or clumsily: clodhopper, country yokel, *AmE also* country clod, alfalfa grower, pea picker, rube. - ⁓**gendarm** *m* -en/-en *contp.* (*Dorfpolizist*) village clown, *AmE also* hick cop. - ⁓**hammel** *m* -s/-(n) *contp.* country boor, peasant lout. - ⁓**heilige** *m & f* -n/-n patron saint for farmers, e.g. St Isidor, St Leonard (→ *Leonhard*), St Notburga, and St Wendelin. - ⁓**herrgott** *m* -s *R.C. & folklore, colloq.* "farmers' favourite saint", a popular usage for St Leonard, the patron saint of horses, who is revered as the most important saint in rural areas of Southern Germany; on the anniversary of his death, November 6, a horseback procession (→ *Leonhardiritt*) is held around the village church, often named in his honour, and the horses are blessed by the parish priest. - ⁓**lackel** *m* -s/-(n) *contp.* = *Bauernhammel*. - ⁓**maß** *f* -/...masse (after numerical data: - [e.g. zwei Maß], *dial.* pl. also: ...massen) *bev.* "farmer's *or* country-style measure", a mixed drink said to be very potent and a lively party pepper-upper at big country weddings (*Bauernhochzeiten*) and other convivial gatherings; the ingredients, to be mixed in a huge mug, are: 1 litre of bock beer, 3/10 litre of champagne (sparkling wine), 4 steinhägers, 1/4 litre of white wine (tart), 1/2 litre of wheat-beer, 2 juniper berries, as well as one whole black peppercorn and a pinch of salt. - ~**maurer** *m* -s *archit.*, *sobr.* "Peasant Bricklayer", referring to Dominikus Zimmermann, 1685-1766, a grand-master of Bavarian Rococo; the epithet indicates the artist's humble life, his preference for designing small country churches rather than imposing ones (the gem-like Wies Church is one of the few exceptions), and above all the extreme vigour of his artistry which could only have sprung from native grounds. - ~**museum** *n* -s/...museen *folklore* at Perschen (Upper Palatinate), near the Ammersee, and elsewhere: agricultural museum, displaying farm tools and other farmhouse implements that have since gone out of use, e.g., flails, horseshoes, and spinning-wheels. - ~**rose** *f* -/-n *bot.* (*Pfingstrose*) peony. - ~**schmaus** *m* -es/- (when ordering at an inn) or *joc.* ...schmäuse *gastr.* "farmer's delight", a hearty dish of sauerkraut, sausages, pork and (white-)bread dumplings. - ~**schrank** *m* -(e)s/...schränke rustic cupboard *or* wardrobe. - ~**seufzer** *m* -s/usu. pl.: - *cul.* "farmer's sigh", a smoked sausage of equal quantities of fat and lean pork, seasoned with pepper, salt, marjoram, and caraway seed; about 1 1/4 in. thick and 4 in. long; to be eaten hot; the term is some hundred years old and describes the farmer's reaction at the sight of the part-time butcher (*Brandmetzger*) taking home his "tithe" of newly-made sausages after the work is done. - ~**-Shakespeare von Kiefersfelden** *m* -s - - *sobr.* "Rustic Shakespeare of Kiefersfelden", an honorary nickname for Joseph Schmalz, a Tyrolean charcoal-burner, 1793-1845, who wrote some twenty-three plays of romance and chivalry for the peasant stage, which are still being performed at the local summer theatre; his highly dramatic art makes free use of Schiller and Shakespeare, e.g. in *Richardus König von England, oder die Ge-*

walt der Liebe, and there are borrowings from old English folk-plays. - **~theater** *n* -s/- *theat.* "peasant theatre", a small-town or village stage on which traditional comic plays in Bavarian dialect are performed by native lay actors and actresses. - **~wald** *m* -(e)s/...wälder *econ.* untended forest owned by one or several farmers, chiefly used for self-supporting ends.

Baunzerl *n* -s/-(n) *bak.* a thin piece of fruit (apple, pear, plum, etc.), sugared and dipped in wine, covered with a mixture of egg and flour and cooked in hot fat (*Beignet*): fritter.

Bavariade *f* -/-n [a blend of *Bavaria* and *-iade*, a pseudo-suffix detached from the word *Olympiade* 'Olympic Games' (and sprouting into neologisms like *Spartakiade*); cp. also *Dackel-Olympiade↓*] *folklore*, *sports* first held at Inzell, Upper Bavaria, in early June, 1993: "Bavariad", Bavarian Olympics *pl.*, a venue of young Bavarian athletes who compete in altogether fifteen events that, like finger-tug (*Fingerhakeln↓*), wrist-wrestling (*Armdrücken↑*), climbing the maypole, and tobacco-snuffing, are looked upon as traditional Bavarian feats of strength.

Bayer *m* -n/-n a native of Bavaria: Bavarian; *woher* (or *wieso*) *weißt du, daß er* (*ein*) *~ ist?* how do you know (that) he's (a) Bavarian?; *Herzog Ludwig der ~* Duke Lewis of Bavaria ‖ a brief sampling of familiar quotations on a Bavarian's reputedly simple and easy-going nature: (1) *Gott ist kein ~, er läßt sich nicht spotten* God is no Bavarian, He does not allow Himself to be made fun of (*or*, you can't make fun of Him). - (2) *Alles kann man dem ~n abkaufen, nur nicht seine Dummheit* you can get a Bavarian to part with anything except his credulous good nature. - (3) *Für den* (or, *dem*) *~n ist das Leben ein sich täglich erneuerndes Fest* a Bavarian looks upon life as a perpetual feast (*hum. also*, as a pageant of highdays, holidays and bonfire nights).

Bayern *n* -s, *polit. geog.* Bavaria; *sie stammt aus* ~ she's a native of Bavaria; *bei uns in* ~ in Bavaria, where I come from; *der Freistaat* ~ the Free State of Bavaria; cp. *Baiern*.

beinand [a short form of StandG *beieinander* 'together', brought about by haplography and end-clipping] *adv, colloq.* in (jovial) company, happily well met ‖ *phr.* **1.** hearty greetings by one joining the circle of family or friends, entering a cosy inn which is pleasantly filled, etc.: *grüß Gott ~!* (God) bless you all (in here)!; *guten Abend ~!* good evening, everybody! - **2.** a cheerful or mocking comment on seeing, or hearing of, a clique gathered together: *da ist ja eine saubere Blasn ~!* there's a fine get-together of good fellers (*AmE also* a swell bunch [*if ironical*: a happy family]) for you!

beinand... *colloq.*: **~bleiben** *v/i* **1.** to stay together. - **2.** said of two or more people who (intend to) stay loyal to each other: to stick together. - **~haben** *v/t* to have (s.th.) together *phr.* **1.** *hast du endlich das Kleingeld beinand?* (have you) got the cash ready at last? - **2.** with reference to a person's five senses: *alle fünfe ~* to be in one's right mind; *er muß nicht alle fünfe beinandgehabt haben, daß er so was gemacht hat* he must have taken leave of his senses to have done such a thing. - **~halten** *v/t* to hold *or* keep (s.th.) together. - **~liegen** *v/i* to lie together. - **~sein** *v/i* **1.** to be together; *das Geld ist Gott sei Dank beinand* thank God the sum is ready. - **2.** to be healthy of body and mind; *für einen Achtziger ist er noch gut beinand* he carries (*or* wears) his eighty years well, he's eighty and still going strong, he's in good shape for eighty. - **~sitzen** *v/i* to sit together. - **~stehen** *v/i* to stand together.

Beisel, Beisl *n* -s/-(n) [< Yid. *bajis* 'house'] *colloq.* **1.** a simple, but sometimes rather cosy little place (1) where alcoholic drinks are sold to be consumed on the premises: *BrE* pub, *AmE* bar, saloon; (2) where plain food may eaten: little inn, *AmE also* little eatery. → **2.** *contp.* such a place which, on the whole, looks poor and uncared-for (1) when offering liquor: low dive, *BrE also* crummy *or* seedy pub, *AmE also* Cheap John, snake ranch; (2) when offering things to eat: *BrE* greasy spoon, *AmE* scruffy little eatery.

Berg *m* -(e)s/-e *orogr.* mountain; hill ‖ *prov.* (1) the common man's plea for tolerance and sociability, and its echoes from across the British Isles: *~ und Tal kemma niat zsam, aba d'Leit* people meet but mountains never greet, *in Irish* castar na daoine ar a chéile ach ní chastar na cnoic ná na sléibhte ('people meet one another but the hills and the mountains don't'). - (2) an easy-going Bavarian's reputed pattern of thought when facing three of the most important features of his native place: *'n [= den] ~ von unten, d' [= die] Kirch von außen, 's [= das] Wirtshaus von innen* * I choose to look at the mountains from below, at a church from without, and at an inn from within.

Berg...: **~käse** *m* -s "alpine cheese", a hard, Emmenthal type of cheese made in the mountain dairies of the Allgäu Alps and sold only locally; its taste is more pungent than that of its near relative, a loaf is not as big and high, and the holes are somewhat smaller. - **~kirchweih** *f* - [a triple compound of but nominally religious associations (cp. *Kirchweih, Kirtag*)] *folklore* on the Burgberg N of Erlangen, Middle Franconia: "Hillside Consecration", the oldest beer festival in Germany, dating as it does from 1755; it starts on Thursday before Whitsuntide with the *Bierprobe* ('sampling the beer') and lasts for twelve days.

berglerisch *adv*: ~ (*gekleidet, etc.*) (dressed, *etc.*) mountain fashion, in the style of the hill people; *Franz von Kobell war einer der größten bayerischen Gelehrten, der aber so ~ daherkam wie ein Oberförster aus den Alpen* Franz von Kobell was one of the greatest Bavarian scholars, and yet he went around looking like a senior forester from the Alps.

In Praise and in Defence of Beer
A Bavarian Soliloquy, by Sigi Sommer

Ma sojt net gega sei' Natur o'kempfa und gscheida sei' wojn wia da Herrgott. Der werd scho gwißt ham, warum er an Durscht daschaffa hat. Im übrigen is des nachgwiesn, daß a Maß Bier mehra Nährwert hat ojs wiar a Pfund Rindfleisch. Ojso nacha - i konn aba do net zehn Pfund Rindfleisch auf oan Sitz essen! Und as Bier brauch i aa zweng an Durchramma. Oder moana Sie, daß i bloß aso zum Gschpaß siem Maß in mi nei' schütt? Und überhaupt stärkt des Bier die Nervn. Mei' Liaba, da kriagst a Ruah zsamm und a Schlaf geht hera! No ja, des bisserl Bauch, des muaßt hoit in Kauf nehma. Es hat hojt ojs sein Preis auf da Wejt.

... and its Echo from Northern Ireland

Ye shouldnae fecht again' yer ain nature an' try tae be smerter than the Lord. He be tae hae knowed why He 's gien ye a Thirst. Onywey, they hae proved that a pint o' porter diz ye mer guid than a pun' o' mate. But it stan's tae sense that A cannae ate ten pun' o' mate at yin sittin'. An' A need the porter tae clean m' guts oot. Or dae ye think A emp'y sayven pints intae me fur fun? An' anither thing, porter strengthens yer nerves. Boy, it taks yer bothers awaw an' gies ye a richt soon' sleep. Min' ye, ye can expec' tae git a li'le big aboot the middle; bit sure iverythin' hiz its price in this worl'.

Bier *n* -(e)s/-e beer, an alcoholic beverage for which, in the states of Bavaria and Baden-Württemberg, under a law dating from 1516, only malt, hops, culture yeast, and water may be used as ingredients; naturally, the merry devotee gives the drink many names, such as *Gerstensaft* 'barley juice' and *Hopfensaft* 'hop juice', and indeed generally looks upon it as *flüssige Nahrung* 'liquid food'; what is more, beer is *das fünfte Element in Bayern* 'the fifth element in Bavaria' which, in addition to the four classical elements (viz., earth, water, air and fire) is thought to be basically indispensable to the Bavarian's minimal world of existence, while humanity of large, inside our blue-and-white pales, can lustily enjoy *die fünfte Jahreszeit* 'the fifth season', between the end of winter and the beginning of spring when strong brown stout (*Starkbier*) is sold during a fortnight early in Lent. ‖ a *prov. phr.* warning against superfluous or absurd action; specifically, not to supply a commodity to a place where there is already plenty of it: ~ *nach München bringen* to carry *or* take coals to Newcastle, *AmE* to sell refrigerators to Eskimos; *Speiseeis an die Italiener (zu) verkaufen, das hieße doch ~ nach München bringen - oder?* selling ice cream to the Italians - that's carrying coals to Newcastle, isn't it?

Bier...: **~bauch** *m* -(e)s/...bäuche usu. *cont.* a greatly protruding abdomen assumed to be caused by a surfeit of beer; any man with such an unsightly excrescence: potbelly, *AmE also* beer belly. - **~-Convent** *m* -(e)s "Beer Convention", the first fraternity of beer drinkers, established in Munich in 1968, whose aim is to raise the social prestige of beer as a beverage which, apart from being drunk for pleasure, should also play a cultural role. - **~deckel** *m* -s/-, *dial.* **~filzl** *n* -s/-(n) [dim. of *Filz* 'felt'] = *Deckel*. - **~dimpfl** or, in its original, rounded form, **~dümpfl** *m* -s/-(n) [second el., *Dümpfel* 'stout person' (cp. E *dump* 'short thick object')] **1.** *colloq.* one very fond of drinking beer: beer quaffer, beer slinger, beer tippler, *contp.* guzzler; *wenn du am Freitag auf d'Nacht ins Wirtshaus neinschaust, dann siehst du sie alle drin hocken, die ~* looking in at a pub on Friday night you'll catch them going into a huddle, the whole lot of honourable froth-blowers; *die ~n schlagen sich vor lauter Freud auf den Schenkel und der Sepp der Bedienerin auf den Hintern, die ihm dafür eine langt* the beer quaffers slap their thighs with merry laughter, and Joe follows suit taking aim at the bottom of the waitress, who duly clouts (*or*, pastes) him one in return. ‖ → *schnaufen*. - **2.** *hum.* or *contp.* a habitual drinker, usu. old and destitute, who makes the round of public houses in search of leftovers in beer mugs (*Noagerl*↓): *BrE* scrounger of heel-taps, *AmE* backwash scavenger.

~krug *m* -(e)s/...krüge tankard, beer mug (often provided with a pewter lid); *if made of stoneware*: (beer) stein.

> Note: Many Bavarians are fond of making a personal collection of such mugs of different shapes and sizes.

~**metropole** *f* - *hum.* "Beer Capital", a nickname for brewery-studded Munich. - ~**noagerl** *n* -s/-(n) [see *Noagerl*] *dial.* dregs of beer: backwash, tail-end ‖ *hum.* said of a disappointingly stale joke: *abgestanden wie ein ~ am Aschermittwoch* as moth-eaten as Joe Miller's old working jacket. - ~**stüberl** *n* -s/-(n) *archit.* a cosy, usu. wood-panelled annex to a restaurant or inn, where men meet over beer and cards: snug (room), snuggery. - ~**pantscher-Walhalla** *f* -/no pl. *hum.*& *sarc.* "Beer-cheaters' Valhalla", the ruins of Stockenfels Castle, near Nittenau, on the river Regen, a place of banishment for the spirits of brewers who watered down their product, and of landlords whose filling measure was always a little below the mark (cp. *Daumen*); bad conscience makes them haunt the old castle at midnight, when they are forced to drink watery beer throughout the witching hour.

bieseln, *dial.* **bisln** [both: -z-] *v/i* [echoic] *colloq.* to urinate: to piddle, to pee, to weedle, *NorBrE* to scoot; *ich muß ~ (gehen), ich muß zum ~* I must go for (*or* do, *or* have) a pee; *ins Bett ~* to wet the bed, to pee in bed (cp. *zündeln* 1↓); *der schau(g)t aus, wie wenn er in die Hosn biselt hätt* he's looking as if he'd wet his britches. - **Bieselwasser** *n* -s *colloq.* urine: piddle; *Mami, wo soll ich das Potschamberl mit dem ~ hinschütten?* Mummy (*AmE* Mommy, *or* Momma), where do you want me to pour my piddle potty on to? ‖ *fig.* in an ungracious comparison (cp. also *Pfeiferlwasser*↓): *die Limo schmeckt wie ein ~* the lemo tastes like pee-water. - **Bieserl** *n* -s/pl. rare: -(n) low or domestic *colloq.* a girl's pudend: weewee. - **biesi-biesi**, **bisi-bisi**: only in ~**machen** used esp. to and by children — to make water: to tinkle, to wee, to wee-wee, to widdle; *sie muß ~ (machen)* she wants to have (*or* do) a wee-wee, *AmE* she wants to make weewee.

Billmersschnitter, **Bilmesschneider** *m* -s *folklore* in Upper Franconia, the Upper Palatinate, and in Lower Bavaria:

"Corn Cutter", a dreaded field demon with goat's feet shaped like sharp sickles, who claims his third of the harvest by cutting swaths into the grain-field, then allowing himself to be wafted with his booty towards his den by a blustery wind; the basis for this folk belief is the damage done by animals or freakish gales mowing straight or zigzag lanes into the field at harvesting time.

Bilwißschnitter, Bilwitzreiter, Bilwitzschneider *m* -s [< MHG *pilwiß* 'witch'] *folklore* = *Billmersschnitter*.

Binsenschneider *m* -s *folklore* = *Billmersschnitter*.

blank [actually, 'shining', 'clean'] *colloq.* **1.** *adj* without money (*ohne Geld*): broke; *ich bin völlig* ~ I am flat (*or* stony) broke, I'm on my beam-ends (*AmE also* ... on the beam-ends, on the beam's ends). - **2.** *adv* (1) coatless (*ohne Mantel*): minus a (*or* one's) coat; *es ist kalt heute, geh mir nicht* ~*!* it is cold today, do wear your coat! - (2) *mus.* said of a small ensemble performing with amplifiers or any other mechanical aids (*ohne Technik*): straight, live [laɪv].

blaue Reiter, Der *art* The Blue Rider **1.** the first abstract picture painted by Russian-born Vassily Kandinsky in the Munich suburb of Schwabing, in 1910. → **2.** the expressionist group of artists around Kandinsky, Franz Marc, Paul Klee, and August Macke, active in or near Munich during the early twentieth century; their works were characterized by the use of Fauve colour and forms distorted for structural or emotive purposes - to the horror of all lovers of traditional painting, who preferred to stick to Kaulbach and Lenbach, the grand old men of Munich's art life in the nineteenth century.

Blaukraut *n* -(e)s *bot.* (*Rotkohl*) red cabbage. - **Blaukrautien** [-tsien] *n* -s [playful analogy here re-attaches the noun suffix *-ien*, denoting 'country', that has been lifted from such names as *Belgien, Italien* and *Slowenien*] *hum.* Bavaria: "Land of the Red Cabbage".

Blunze *f* -/-n *gastr.*, rare, since stilted for next. - **Blunzen** *f* -/- **1.** *gastr.* a sausage made from pig's blood, often containing small cubes of bacon: *BrE* black pudding, *AmE* blood sausage, blutwurst, *IrE* drisheen ‖ placing an order at an inn: *zwei ~n mit Sauerkraut BrE* one plate of black pudding and pickled cabbage, *AmE* two blood sausages with sauerkraut. - **2.** *contp.* a fat, unshapely person, often an elderly female: *BrE* jelly-belly, jelly-wobble, lump of lard, rubber-guts, fat slag, *AmE* blubberpot, five by five; *das ist (dir) eine ~! BrE* (look,) she [he] 's a right pudding, *AmE* ... a tub of lard.

Böhm *colloq.* **1.** *m* -(e)s/no pl. *meteor.* = *Böhmische Wind*. - **2.** *n* no decl. *geog.* (*Böhmen*) Bohemia; chiefly in phrases like *ins ~ gelangen* to reach Bohemian territory, and *aus dem ~ kommen* to come [if indicating origin, also: to hail] from Bohemia.

Böhmer...: **~wald** *m* -(e)s/no pl. *geog.* Bohemian Forest, a mountain range along the boundary between Bavaria and Bohemia, having the Arber, 4780 ft., as its highest peak ‖ a rhymed observation that speaks of the inclement weather East Bavarians have to put up with at times: *wild um und um jetzt braust es kalt, / schickst deine Wind' uns, ~!* *blustery cold your winds now blaw, Man Forest of Bohemia! - **~weg** *m* -(e)s/no pl. *geog. hist.* "Bohemian Trail", from Deggendorf to Regen, and beyond over the border.

Böhmische: 1. *adj* **~ Bettelgeige** *f* -n -/-n -n *mus. hist.* "Bohemian beggar's violin", a telltale sobriquet for the hurdy-gurdy, a small barrel organ turned by itinerant players from Bohemia travelling through the Bavarian Forest. - **~ Scheibenknödel** *m* & *n* -n -s/usu. pl.: -n -(n) *cul.* "Bohemian slices", yeast dumplings into whose dough small cubes of white bread have been mixed; served in large slices. - **~ Wind** *m* -n -(e)s/no pl. *meteor.* "Bohemian Wind", a dry and biting cold fall wind coming from the north-east; it causes vast snowdrifts in winter, and damage to seedlings in spring. - **2.** (1) *m* -n/no pl. *meteor.* = *Böhmische Wind*. - (2) *n* -n/no pl. = *Böhm*, 2; *die Steinloher Wallfahrtskapelle wurde seit jeher aus dem ~n viel und gern besucht* the pilgrimage chapel of Steinlohe was always frequently visited by pious worshippers from Bohemia.

Böhm...: **~schuhe** *m* pl. Bohemian clogs *pl.* - **~wind** *m* -(e)s/no pl. *meteor.* = *Böhmische Wind*.

brandeln *v/i* [< *Brand* 'fire' + *-eln↓*] *colloq.* **1.** (*brandig riechen*) to smell of burning, or of something burnt (e.g., food); *es brandelt* there is a smell of burning (in the air); *für mich brandelt's da wo* I can smell burning. - **2.** (*brandig schmecken*) when sampling some food that was (overly) exposed to fire: *das brandelt (ja) noch* it still has (*or*, there still is) a burnt taste.

Brät, **Brat** *n* -s *comest.* meat finely ground and seasoned, to be used for meat loaves, frying sausages, etc. (*feingehacktes [Bratwurst-] Fleisch*): sausage meat; cp. *Leberkäs*.

Bräu -(e)s/-e or -s **1.** *n* (1) (*Bier[sorte]*) (brand of) beer, *colloq.* brew; *Thomas~ ist meine Marke* Thomasbräu is my brand (of beer). - (2) (*Brauerei*) brewery [Note: The use of the word in that sense as a *neuter* noun is frowned upon by real Bavarians, who think it to be an abomination typically committed by "Prussians" only - cp. *Bräu* 2 (1).] - (3) (*Bierlokal*) beer tavern *or* restaurant (often serving only beer of a certain brand), *BrE* also pub. - **2.** *m* (1) (*Brauerei*); often to be found in proper-name compounds, e.g. (*der* [!]) *Hof~* ‖ *Bayern ist bekannt wegen seiner guten ~e* Bavaria is known for its good breweries.

Brau...: **~bursch** *m* -cn/ en brewery lad ‖ *phr.* a simile referring to one using a lot of offensive language: *fluchen* o*r schelten wie ein ~* to swear like a trooper (*AmE* ... like a soldier). - **~gaul** *m* -(e)s/...gäule, **~roß** *n* -rosses/-rösser (*Brauereipferd*) brewery horse, brewer's dray-horse. - ~**meister** *m* -s/- (*Braumeister*) master brewer. - ~**stüberl,** ~**stübl** *n* -s/-n a small room, sometimes with wainscoting, in a brewery, inn, or public house: beer (*or* ale, tap) room; if felt to be very cosy, also: snug (room), snuggery.

Brauerei *f* -/-en brewery ‖ a Bavarian's ingenuous way of describing his gargantuan thirst (and duly hearing the same metaphorical hyperbole echoed from across the Channel): *ich könnt' eine ganze ~ austrinken* (or, more coarsely, *aussaufen*)*!* I've got a thirst that would swallow a brewery, I could drink a brewery dry.

Brauerei...: ~**-Gasthof** *m* -(e)s/...höfe an inn with its own brewery: home-brewed inn, inn-cum-brewery. - ~**geschwür** *n* -(e)s/pl. rare: -e *hum.* or *contp.* beer barrel (*or* belly, *or* muscle); *sich ein ~ zugezogen* (or *zugelegt*) *haben* to have developed a beer tumour, *SouthernAmE* also to have Dunlop's disease [which (punning the name of John Boyd Dunlop, 1840-1921, the Scottish inventor of the pneumatic tyre) is explained in that dialect as "that's when your belly's *done lop*ped over your belt"]. - ~**roß** *n* -rosses/-rösser brewery horse, brewer's dray-horse ‖ a simile that comes natural to a Bavarian's lips: *feist* (or, in dialect: *foast*) *wie ein ~* (as) fat as a pig, *AmE* also (as) fat as a hog.

Brennsuppe, *dial.* **Brennsuppm** *f* -/- [first el., (*ein*)*brennen* 'to fry in fat', 'to make a brown roux [ruː]'] **1.** *cul.* a simple type of soup, once a common morning dish among the poor country population, usu. made from two finely chopped onions, two or three tablespoonfuls of flour allowed to brown in butter, one quart of water poured on and allowed to simmer, at last caraway seeds, chopped chives, parsley, and one teaspoonful of vinegar added: (1) cream soup (made of a base of flour, butter, and stock), thickened soup, - (2) when dark: brown roux soup, brown vegetable soup. - **2.** *dial. phr.*

heard in protest when one has been told an obvious falsehood or a tall tale, the message conveyed being, "I am nobody's fool!": *ich bin fei nicht auf der ~ dahergeschwommen!* I wasn't born yesterday, you know; I didn't come down with the last shower (*or*, ... fall off a Christmas tree), you know; *AmE also* I didn't just roll into town on the hay wagon.

Brett *n* -(e)s/-er board, = *Totenbrett*↓ ‖ the following usages reflect some unrefined folk parlance of today, although the custom (leading to such utterances) of resting the deceased on a board, carrying the body to its burial, and tipping it into the grave may well hark back to pagan times and has, of course, long since been discontinued: **1.** said of someone who is about to die: *der kommt bald aufs ~* *he will soon be on the board, he is aching *or* begging (*or*, is a [prime] candidate) for the board. - **2.** said of a dead person: (1) *er liegt schon auf dem ~* he's already (lying) on the board, they've already got him on the board. - (2) *er ist schon längst hinuntergerutscht* he slid into the grave ages ago.

> Note: Although the concept and the fact of "death boards" do not exist in Anglo-Saxon countries, English folk speech is similarly outspoken on the occasion of death and burial; note such phrases as "to buy the farm" and "to be pushing up (*BrE* the) daisies" - the latter idiom neatly corresponding to BavG *die Radieserl* [↓] *von unten wachsen sehen.*

Breze *f* -/-n [a rare pseudo-standard form of *Brezel*↓ and *Brezen*↓]; **Brezel** *f* -/-n [< OHG *brezitella* < It *bracciatello* 'little arm'] *bak.* pretzel, a crisp knot-shaped biscuit flavoured with salt, a favourite relish with beer: **1.** the earlier form made with water and salt, and grey in colour. - **2.** = *Laugenbrezel*; *~architekt m* -en/-en *hum.* (*Bäcker*) baker, *AmE sl.* dough roller, dough slinger; **Brezen** *f* -/- = *Brezel*; *~wochen f pl.* pretzel season, i.e. carnival time, in which pretzels are much in vogue.

Bröih [brɔːɪ] *f* -/-n [StandG *Brühe* < MHG *brüeje* 'heated liquid'; related to E *broth* 'liquid in which meat, etc. has been boiled'] Upper Palatinate *dial.* soup; broth (if containing meat, fish, rice, or vegetables); → *Erdapfel.*

Brot...: **~laden** *m* -s/...läden **1.** *agr.* bread drawer, still found in massive old farmhouse tables, wide and deep enough to hold a big (often home-made) loaf. - **2.** *sg.* only, *contp.* a person's mouth, esp. if considered as an organ of speech: (fish, clam, potato, *or* tater) trap ‖ a peremptory call for silence: *halt deinen ~!* shut your (fish, *etc.*) trap!, *AmE also* shut your grub trap *or* box!, zipper it!, *BrE also* shut your cake-hole! - **~zeit** *f* -/-en [actually, 'second breakfast'; cp. *Frühstück* 'piece of bread eaten early in the morning'] **1.** (*Zeit für einen Imbiß*) snack-time; *~ machen* to have a snack, usu. bread and sausage or cheese, with beer or another drink ‖ a semi-proverbial saying: *die ~ ist die schönste Zeit!* snack-time is the best time!; → **2.** *cul.* (*Imbiß*) mid-morning *or* afternoon snack, as a break during working-hours ‖ in the Old Sausage Inn of the City of Regensburg: *historische ~* "historical snack", i.e. small sausages roasted on an open charcoal grill, served with plenty of sauerkraut and beer; *klassische ~* "classical snack", i.e. a small Regensburg sausage and a piece of brown bread, to be eaten cold.

Bschoad [pʃɔɑt] *m* -s/-e [< StandG *Bescheid* (*geben*) '(to spread) the glad tidings (of a wedding or christening [dinner], or of some other positive event on the farm')] *dial.* a parcel of food items from the festive dinner, meant to be delivered to absent friends and relatives, so that they may have the vicarious opportunity to share in the fun: choice titbits (*AmE* tidbits) from the wedding [christening, or other celebration].

Bschoad...: **~binkerl, ~packerl, ~tüachl** *n* -s/-(n) *colloq.* **1.** piece of (ornamental) cloth or linen, often simply a large handkerchief or napkin, tied at four corners, which holds food to take home from a festive meal: take-home bag (*or* sack), *colloq.* goodie bag, *AmE esp.* doggie-bag; *für jeden Ernte-*

helfer richtete die Bäuerin, wenn er nach dem „Erntebier" den Hof verließ, ein ~ „für die Leut dahoam" after the "harvest beer", as the hired hands prepared to leave, the farmer's wife fixed each of them a goodie bag "for all the folks back home". → **2.** *fig.* angry message for others to take notice of what one thinks of them: bundle of complaints (*or* grievances); *nach seinem Vortrag gaben die Bürger der Stadt dem Finanzminister ein ~ nach München mit: bei ihnen werden nämlich bei Steuerzahlungen für jeden Tag Terminverlust neun Prozent Verzugszinsen berechnet* after his address, the townspeople gave the Minister of Finance a hefty bundle of complaints to take with him back to Munich: as it was, the citizens were required to pay a default interest of nine per cent for every day they had missed paying their taxes.

Burgstall *m* -s/...ställe [< OHG *burcstal* 'site of a castle'] **1.** *archaeol.* (site of a) prehistoric hillside fort, former earthwork or other fortification (often encountered in riverside Lower Bavaria, from the Michelsberg near Kelheim to the Zanklberg near Landau on the Isar). - **2.** *geog.* level patch of ground above the valley floor, possibly indicative of its once having been fortified.

Burschi *m* - ; when doubling the pet-ending, also **Burschilein** *n* -s [< *Bursche m* 'young man'; actually 'student' (formerly also, handicraftsman, soldier, etc.) who lives in a fraternity (MedL *bursa*)'] *dim.* a parent's form of endearing address to the son, or the family members' name for their small dog: (darling) laddie; *na, wie geht's dir denn, ~?* how are you, then, my boy (*ScotE also,* ... mylad [mɪˈlæd])? ‖ with such dual directedness, it can be a somewhat traumatic experience for the teenage son of the house (an *on dit* has it) to have his school-inspector father come home on the weekend, hear him give the ringing shout of expectancy at the doorstep, *ja, wo ist denn mein Burschilein?* 'now, where's my little laddie?', and realize that the master's own flesh and blood was n o t meant.

Bussel, also **Bußl** *n* -s/-(n) [the "common-or-garden" diminutive form in -(*e*)*l* has become rigid here and hardly conveys any warmth of feeling; *Buss*-, the stem (cp. E *buss* 'kiss'), is possibly due to nursery onomatopoeia, or < F *pousser* 'to make flirtatious advances to a woman' (whence G *poussieren*) < L *pulsare* 'to push'] *colloq.* (*Küßchen > Kuß*) kiss; *dem Kind ein ~ geben* to give the child a kiss; *dafür kriegst* [*verdienst*] *du ein ~* you get [deserve] a kiss for that ‖ *ein flüchtiges ~* a peck; *ein lautes ~* a smack.

busseln *vt/i* [< *Bussel*↑] *colloq.* to kiss (heartily); *die haben (sich) gebusselt wie nicht gscheit* they beslobbered each other as if kissing was going out of fashion.

Busserl *n* -s/-(n) [an often warmly affective variant (cp. *-erl*↓) of *Bussel*↑] *colloq.* **1.** ([*süßes*] *Küßchen*) (sweet) little kiss; *ein ~ auf die Wange* a playful kiss on the cheek ‖ *phr.* (1) *hum.* asking, in a cheerfully relaxed atmosphere, for permission to give a lady a chaste little kiss (and taking this request to be implicitly granted): *ein ~ in Ehren kann niemand verwehren!* (a) in prose: there's nothing wrong with a harmless kiss; a friendly kiss can do no harm; who could object to a friendly little kiss? (b) in rhyme: there's nothing amiss in an honest kiss. - (2) *ich möchte mir ein ~ holen, wenn's gestattet ist* and I'll steal a small kiss, if you don't mind. - (3) *jetzt möcht' ich aber ein richtiges ~, Schatzi, das erste war ja nix!* but now, darling, let's have a real sweet kiss - the first one was just an excuse (*or*, an apology) for one. - **2.** *bak.* a small hard conical biscuit (*AmE* cookie) made of egg-white, honey or sugar, and finely ground nuts: almond (hazelnut, coconut, etc.) kiss, *BrE also* rock cake.

Bussi *n* -s/-(s) [the nursery dim. variant of *Busserl*↑] *colloq.* **1.** nursery, lovers', and bird- or dog-fanciers' talk — sweet little kiss: kissie, kissie-wissie; *schau, das Hunderl will dir ein ~ geben!* look, the doggie wants to give you a kissie(-wissie). - **2.** *hum.* or *iron.* a light-hearted expression of thanks, in mock imitation of a doting parent or lover, for a minor service rendered or to be rendered: *~ aufs Bauchi!* you are a precious darling!

Butter...: **~faß** *n* -fasses/...fässer **1.** *econ.*, if somewhat small in size, or if spoken of with affective warmth, also **~faßl** *n* -s/-

(n) (butter-)churn, a container in which milk is shaken until it becomes butter; here is a cheerful ditty spoken by our grandmothers when coaxing the contents of a churn to coagulate:

> *Geh, Butter, tu dich z'sam* *Well then, cream, thicken home,
> *von Regensburg bis Rom;* From Regensburg to Rome;
> *von jeder Kuh an Löffel voll* One spoonful from each cow I'll skim,
> *macht's Butterfaßl auch noch voll!* And so my churn fills to the brim.

2. *geog. & archit. hist.* "Butter Churn", the 75-foot-high castle-keep of Burgruine Neuhaus, fittingly nicknamed because of its quaint shape; it towers over medieval Windischeschenbach, at the entrance to the romantic Waldnaab Valley, in the northern Upper Palatinate. - ~**model** *m* -s/- *econ.* (*Butterform*) butter mo(u)ld, butter pat; *hölzerner* ~ butter print. - ~**schmalz** *n* -es/pl. rare: -e *cul.* butter made less perishable by melting, and then left to settle: clarified (*or* run) butter, butterfat. - ~**semmel** *f* -/-n *bak.* (*Butterbrötchen*) buttered roll; *es gibt Kaffee und* (or, *mit*) ~*n* they [we] are serving coffee and buttered rolls.

Butzen *m* -s/- [? < Dutch adj *bot.* 'short and stumpy'; cp. E *butt* 'thicker end of a thing', 'lump'] *dial.* **1.** *bot.* also **Butz** *m* -en(s)/-en (*Gehäuse*) the heart of an apple, pear, etc.: core; *wirf den* ~ *vom Apfel grad beim Fenster raus!* why, just throw the apple core out (*BrE* out of) the window. - **2.** *art* (*Verdickung*) lump, clump, irregularity (in glass, metal, etc.).

Butzenscheibe *f* -/-n [first el., < *Butzen*, 2] *art* an old form of window glass made by blowing a globe and whirling it into a disc: crown glass, bull's eye ([window] pane), bottle-bottom glass (*or* pane).

Butzenscheiben...: ~**fenster** *n* -s/- *art* a nineteenth-century architectural feature on the frontage of timber-framed houses throughout Southern Germany, esp. in Bavaria, evocative of the Middle Ages: crown-glass window, i.e. a casement window of rather small dimensions, made up of bull's eye panes wholly or partly in colour. - ~**lyrik** *f* - *lit.* "colour-glass lyricism", an ironic label given by Paul Heyse, a German playwright and novelist, 1830-1914, to a school of medievalizing

German poetry in the second half of the nineteenth century.

Buzerl *n* -s/-n [? < the base of *putzig* 'amusing', 'cute' + dim. suffix *-erl*] → *-erl*. - **Buziwackerl** *n* -s/-n, **Buziwacki** *n* -s/-(s) [second el., a twin diminutive tacked onto the base of *wackeln* 'to waggle one's head' and/or 'to walk with short unsteady steps'] *hum.* a parent's or an auntie's affectionate form of endearment for a small child (though some mothers tend to protract the word's use into, or even beyond, the child's adolescence): toddlekins, toddles, tumble boy [lady], fiddledeflumps, polliwog.

☞ **C** ☜

Carmina burana (or **Burana**) *n pl.* -- L *mus.* (*Vagantenliedersammlung aus Benediktbeuern*) "Songs from Benediktbeuern", a unique Middle Latin and German collection of some 200 goliardic songs from the early thirteenth century in praise of wine, women and company, compiled by a monk of and long preserved in that Benedictine monastery of Upper Bavaria (now at the Bavarian State Library, Munich, Cod. Lat. 4660); they were first edited by Andreas Schmeller in 1847, and set to music by Carl Orff in 1936.

Castra Regina *f* - *place-name* Castra Regina **1.** *hist.* the principal military seat of the Roman province of Rhaetia, completed in 179 A.D. on the site of a pre-Roman, Celtic settlement; → **2.** *journ.* = *Ratisbona* (under *Ratisbonerl*)↓; *die alte ~* good old Ratisbon.

Charivari *m* -s/-(s) [< F *charivari* [ʃɑrɪvəˈriː] 'mock serenade of discordant noises made with pans, horns, etc. after a wedding'] *folklore* a distinctive feature of a male Bavarian's regional costume: ornamental fob chain; *an der Trachtenweste darf der mit Silbertalern, Sauzähnen, Hirschgrandeln usw. behängte ~ nicht fehlen* the ornamental fob chain is a must with a Bavarian's festive waistcoat, and from it dangle sundry trinkets like silver thalers and the eye-teeth of a boar and a stag.

Christkind *n* -(e)s [< Jesus Christ, as a new born child] **1.** *relig.* & *art* the representation of the Infant Jesus, a happy, smiling baby with plump cheeks and blond curls: Christchild, Holy Child; *das liebe ~* (the) Baby Jesus ‖ said on or after December 25: *gehen wir (in die Kirche) das ~ anschauen in der Krippe* let's go (to the church) and have a look at (*AmE* the) Baby Jesus in the manger. - **2.** *colloq.* & *folklore* also in the dim. form, **Christkindl** — the legendary bearer of gifts on Christmas Eve, usu. depicted as a curly-haired child (in the Bavarian tradition, often a girl) in shining robes: Santa Claus, Santa, *BrE also* Father Christmas, *AmE also* St Nicholas (a fat and jolly, white-bearded old man in a red coat, who comes in a sleigh drawn by reindeer).

C+M+B *R.C.* & *folklore* the initials, in popular peasant belief, of The Three Holy Kings, or The Three Wise Men (or Magi), G *die Heiligen Drei Könige*, *C*aspar, *M*elchior, and *B*althasar, who came to Bethlehem on Epiphany (January 6) to worship the new-born Jesus Christ; actually, the abbreviation stands for "*C*hristus *M*ansionem *B*enedicat" (or, "*C*ustodiat *M*ansionem et *B*enedicat [Deus]"), according to which, on Twelfth Night, every room of the house and the stable are sprinkled with incense, and the sequence, say for 1995, of *19 C+M+B 95* is chalked on door lintels.

> Note: This practice, purporting to show that The Three Holy Kings have called, is also found in certain German and Austrian communities in the United States of America.

The Silence of Christ's Holy Night
Ludwig Thoma's Masterpiece in Bavarian German and in Scottish English

Im Wald is so staad,
Alle Weg san vawaht,
Alle Weg san vaschniebn,
Is koa Steigl net bliebn.

The wuds are sae still,
A' the weys wi' snaw fill,
A' the weys in snaw tint -
Fient a loan leeft ye kent.

Hörst d' as z'weitest im Wald,
Wann da Schnee obafallt,
Wann si' 's Astl o'biagt,
Wann a Vogl auffliagt.

Through the wuds scarce a blaw,
Saft 'n still fa's the snaw.
Ye can hear miles aroon'
Ae bird whihher, a grain boo'n.

Aba heunt kunnts scho sei,
Es waar nomal so fei,
Es waar nomal so staad,
Daß si' gar nix rührn tat.

But the nicht nae a stir,
Nae a snaw-flaich or whirr:
There's a wonner aboot
A' profound in its root.

Kimmt die Heilige Nacht,
Und da Wald is aufgwacht,
Schaugn de Hasn und Reh,
Schaugn de Hirsch übern Schnee.

For it's Christ's Haly Nicht.
The wuds wauk tae the sicht;
An' the bawd, hart an' raa
Keek wi' awe frae the snaw.

Ham sie neamad net gfragt,
Hat 's eahr neamad net gsagt,
Und kennan s' do bald
D' Muatta Gottes im Wald.

There is nane wha coud tell,
Yet they ken very well:
The wuds knaw and they nod
Tae the Mither o' God.

D

Dackel-Olympiade *f* -/-n [second el., actually 'the space of four years' after which all-round competitive athletic games, originally held at Olympia, Greece, were (and to this day, since 1896, are) due again] *zo.*, *folklore* "Dachshund Olympics", a gargantuan gathering, since 1968, of dachshunds ['dækshɒndz], *AmE also* ['dæʃhaʊndz], and then spelt, occasionally, dashhounds, *colloq.* daxies, from a number of countries in Europe and overseas, at Gergweis, near Vilshofen, Lower Bavaria, every fourth Whitsuntide; groomed and cuddled by their owners, and admired by a milling crown of dog-fanciers, they compete for the title of "world champion" in their respective classes, long-haired, short-haired, and wire-haired dachshunds.

Dampferl *n* -s/pl. rare: -(n) [a mannered dim. of *Dampf* 'steam'] *cul.* slightly stilted, to be found in some cookery books, for the following. - **Dampfl** *n* -s/pl. rare: -(n) [the everyday dim. of *Dampf* 'steam'] *cul.* (*Vorteig*) yeast dissolved in lukewarm milk: leaven ['le-]; *ein ~ ansetzen* or *vorbereiten* to set the sponge; *fix, heut geht das ~ wieder gar net!* oh heck, my leaven won't budge at all today.

Dampf...: **~nudel** *f* -/-n *cul.* a sweet yeast dumpling cooked in milk and sugar (*in Milch gedämpfter Hefeteigwürfel*): stewed dumpling; such sticky sweet rolls are usu. served on Fridays as a main dish with hot vanilla sauce ‖ *fig.* said on an appropriate occasion of a short-tempered person; *er ist aufgegangen wie eine ~* he blew his top, he had steam coming out of his ears. - **~plauderer** *m* -s/- *contp.* or *hum.* (*Schwätzer*) a person who talks too much, esp. about uninteresting things: chatterbox, windbag; *er ist ein alter ~ BrE* he's a proper Peter Waggie, he has been inoculated with a gramophone needle, *AmE* he talks a blue streak; *das waren (dir) ~ (, ich sag dir's)!* they were chatting away nineteen to the dozen (, I can tell you).

Datschi *m* -(s)/-(s) [< *dätschen, datschen* < MHG *tetschen* 'to press down' - reference is both to the dough which is being pressed onto the baking tray, and to the halved or sliced fruits, usu. plums, then being duly forced into the dough] *bak.* (*Blechkuchen*) yeast cake cooked on a baking tray.

Datschi...: **~burg** *f* - *hum.* a nickname for Augsburg, the capital of Bavarian Swabia, whose inhabitants are said to have a predilection for eating yeast cakes: *City of Cakes ‖ the local rallying-call in carnival time: ~ heu-hoi!* *three cheers for the City of Cakes! - **~burger** *m* -s/-, **~burgerin** *f* -/-nen *hum.* a nickname for a native, or a citizen, of Augsburg: *City of Cakes boy [girl].

Daube *f* -/-n *curl.* (*Zielklotz*) target, mark, i.e. a ten-centimetre square piece of wood sticking up from the ice at the end of a curling lane; *auf die ~ schieben* or *schießen* to shoot for the mark.

Daumen *m* -s/- [< OHG *dumo* < IE **tum-*, one of several extensions of **tu* 'to swell'; cp. E *tumour, tumult, tumulus*] *anat.* thumb; in *colloq.* phrases: **1.** a semi-proverbial sarcasm on how the landlord of an inn, or a waitress, can cheat customers of their rightful amount of beer through sticking the thumb well in while the mug is filling up: *hundert ~ sind auch eine Maß!* *one hundred thumbs will also fill the mug. - **2.** a reproach, or self-reproach, about using one's hands awkwardly or being unable to control them: *lauter ~ haben* to be all thumbs; *du hast heute früh wieder lauter ~!* your fingers are all thumbs (*or*, you're a real butterfingers) this morning; *jetzt ist mir das liebe Haferl runtergefallen, heut hab ich schon lauter ~!* now I dropped that darling little cup of mine - my fingers are all thumbs (*BrE* also I am [*or* I feel] all fingers and thumbs, *AmE* also I'm all thumbs today).

Deckel *m* -s/- [short for *Bierdeckel*] *colloq. BrE* beer mat, *AmE* coaster ‖ a man standing his friends a round of drinks tells the waitress to mark his beer mat with a pencil stroke: *mach das auf meinen ~!* put it on my mat (*AmE* coaster)!

deftig *adj* [< Du *deftig* < IE *dhabh* 'fitting'] *colloq.* **1.** of food: simple and substantial, plain and filling; *ich mag halt einen Eintopf, wie's der Pichelsteiner ist - das ist was ~es, da kannst du richtig reinhauen* give me a hot pot like the Büchelstein stew any time - that's something hefty to really sink one's teeth into. ‖ → *Obatzte.* - **2.** of behaviour, jokes, etc. (*grob*): coarse ‖ → *krachledern* 2.

der-, *dial.* **da-** an intensifying prefix, based on StandG *er-*, with an excrescent initial consonant for added 'body', and therefore added strength, conveying the aspect of finality, e.g. *beißen* 'to bite': *derbeißen* '(to manage) to bite through', 'to worry to death (with one's teeth)', *schießen* 'to shoot': *derschießen* 'to shoot and kill', *schrecken* 'to frighten': *derschrecken* 'to frighten no end'.

derblecken *v/t* [*der-*↑; *blecken* is the causative of *blicken*, hence 'to make s.o. see (*scil.*, one's teeth or tongue as an act of jest or mockery)'] *dial.* (*hänseln*) to tease, *colloq.* to rag, to pull s.o.'s leg; ([*j-n*] *verulken*, [*j-m*] *einen Streich spielen*) to play a prank on; *die Eingeborenen ~ gern einen Nichtbayern, indem sie ihn um Mitternacht zum Wolpertingerfangen in den Wald schicken* natives love to play a practical joke on a non-Bavarian by setting him to catch a mysterious forest animal (in *AmE*, a cryptically elusive snipe) around midnight.

Dezimal *n* -s/-(e) *husb.* "decimal", an old area measure (*Feld-*

maß) of 33.3 square metres, still used when buying a plot of ground (for building, etc.); cp. *Tagwerk* 2.

Diezl *m* -s/-, as a nursery word also **Diddi** and **Dizzi** *m* -/- [cognate with StandG *Zitze* and StandE *teat*] *dial.* = *Luller*.

Diridari *m* - [? < *Diradey*, an old word denoting 'grain and barley mixed' (cp. *Gerstl* 2)] *hum.* money: the wherewithal, what it takes (to get along), *AmE also* bees and honey, mint sauce, do-re-mi [this one from a pun on dough 'money', plus the second and third notes of the diatonic scale].

Dirn *f* -/rarely -en *husb.* (*Bauernmagd*) female farm-hand, farmer's maid; *Stall⁓* milk-maid, dairy maid. - **Dirnderl** *n* -s/-(n) *emot.* very young girl: (sweet) little lassie *or* chippie. - **Dirndl** *n* -s/-(n) **1.** chiefly in rural use: (teenage) girl, lass; → **2.** a peasant dress traditionally worn by girls and women, usu. a dress and apron whose form and colour vary from region to region: Bavarian costume, dirndl (costume).

Distelscheißer *m* -s/- *vulg. hum.* "thistle crapper", a border patrolman on his beat (maliciously described here as stopping in his tracks to answer a call of Nature amid the sylvan solitude of the Bavarian-Bohemian frontier).

Docke *f* -/-n [< MHG *tocke* 'plaited length of yarn'] *art* & *folklore* also known as *Wickelkind* and *Fatschenkind*↓ a simple, crudely painted wooden toy, rather like a skittle or chessman, representing a child in swaddling clothes: wooden dolly; *von den armen Bauern einst für ihre Kinder gedrechselt, sind die Berchtesgadener ~n heute als Ausfuhrware und Christbaumschmuck sehr begehrt* once made on wood-turning lathes by the poor peasants for their children, Berchtesgaden baby dolls are now much in demand as an article of export and a Christmas-tree decoration.

D͟o͟der..., in its dialect spelling also **D͟o͟ader...** [onomatopoeically related to E *to dither, to dodder, to totter* 'to rock to and fro on its base'] *comp. el.*: **~mandl** *n* -s/-(n), **~weibl** *n* -s/-(n) *folklore* "wedding dummy", the effigy of a bridegroom or bride, which is maliciously placed opposite, sometimes even on top of, the house of a former partner of the person to be married; further insult is added to the injury by leaving a trail of sawdust or lime which connects the house of the "ex" to that of the wedding party.

Dorf...: **~depp** *m* -en/pl. rare: -en, **~trottel** *m* -s/pl. rare: -n *contp.* in former times, a physically or mentally handicapped person who was often held responsible for any misfortune that had befallen the community: village idiot.

Drei...: **~m͟äderlhaus** *n* -es/...häuser *colloq.* (*Gruppe von drei Mädchen* [or *Frauen*]) the Three Graces, the (Holy) Trinity; in *hum.* surprise, when encountering a group of three females: *was, ein ~!* rub-a-dub-dub, three maids in a tub! - **~männerwein** *m* -(e)s/-e *bev., hum.* or *sarc.* "three men's wine", a wine of such high acidity as to require the muscular performance of three men to bring about the act of drinking - one, the unwilling imbiber-to-be; two, the man holding the struggling victim in check and forcing his mouth open; and three, the man who does the pouring. - **~quartlprivatier** [-ˈtjeː] *m* -s/-s *colloq.* **1.** *hist.*, mildly *contp.* a pensioner who orders the beer mug brought with him from home to be filled "three quarters full" (cp. *Quartl*), in the furtive hope that the landlord will obligingly "top him up": *penny-pinching beer scrounger. → **2.** openly *contp.* any niggardly male proceeding on that assumption in a similar situation: cheapskate, old scrimp, *AmE also* dough pincher, nickle nurser.

☞ **E** ☜

Eggenschmiere *f* -/pl. rare: -n; **Krebsschmalz** *n* -es/no pl.; **Maikäferfett** *n* -(e)s/no pl. *hum.* on April Fools' Day, or whenever potential pranksters are on the prowl: "harrow grease", "crayfish lard", "cockchafer fat", three of a long row of fictitious items of "practical" use on the farm which the potential victim, naive and unsuspecting (often an apprentice or other youngster), is asked to go and buy from the local grocer; native speakers of English are known to have been sent by their elder countrymen on even more bewildering errands, such as procuring bumblebee feathers, a pint of pigeon's milk, a pie opener, a four-foot yardstick, a room stretcher, a sky-hook, and a left-handed monkey wrench.

Eierlein *n* -s/- [the SouG diminutive *-lein* is firmly at home in Middle Franconia, and has indeed long been attached to civic features in its capital, like *Chörlein* in architecture] *mech. eng.* a cultural feat and landmark: *Nürnberger* ~ "Nuremberg Egg", the first portable watch, invented and produced in series by Peter Henlein, a gifted locksmith, around 1504; the metaphor derives from its curious bulgy shape, inviting comparison with "artichoke" and "turnip", names for elaborate old-fashioned watches in English.

Einöd *f* -/pl. rare: -en [cp. OE *ānad* 'solitude', 'lonely place'], also **Einödhof** *m* -(e)s/...höfe *agr.* a single homestead surrounded by an expanse of arable land: isolated *or* lonely farm.

Einschicht, *dial.* **Oaschicht** *f* - [? < on the analogy of *Einfalt* 'single-ness', which is a loan translation of L *simplex* and *simplicitas*, respectively] *geog.* a very distant and lonely spot or area, often surrounded by extensive fields or forests: isolated (*or* out-of-the-way) place; *in diese ~ verliert sich selten ein Fremder* there is hardly a stranger finding his way to this lonely place; *die beiden hausen irgendwo in der ~ auf einem Bauernhof* the two live on a farm somewhere off the beaten track (*or* path), somewhere at (*or* in) the back of beyond; *ein Urlaub in der ~ eines bayerischen Bergtals* a holiday in a Bavarian mountain valley, away from it all. - **einschichtig** *adj* **1.** *geog.* (*abgelegen*) isolated; *eine ~e Gegend* a lonely region. - **2.** *colloq.* (*unverheiratet*) single, unmarried ‖ an impromptu quip: *immer noch ~, du Weiberfeind?* still going it alone (*or,* still in single harness), you old celibate?

Einser, *dial.* **Oansa, Oasa** *m* -s/- (NorG *die Eins*) **1.** *math.* (figure) one; *ein arabischer [römischer]* an Arabic [a Roman] one ‖ with reference to public transport: *er sollte lieber mit dem ~ fahren* he had better take (*or,* go on) the number one bus [tram]. - **2.** *school* the number indicating the highest quality of a pupil's work in a course, examination, or special assignment: full marks, (mark [*AmE* grade]) A; *sie hat im Aufsatz einen ~ gekriegt* she got full marks (*or,* an A) for the essay.

Einser...: ~bremse *f* -/-n *school sl.* a difficult question, or a hidden trick (inserted usu. in a written test), to trap a pupil and keep him from obtaining the highest mark: "achievers' judder bar". - **~schüler** *m* -s/-, **~schülerin** *f* -/-nen *colloq.* pupil with a first-class report, *AmE* grade-A student.

Einwärts *m* -/no pl. *dial.* & *poet.* the time of year when the days are getting shorter (*Herbst*; opp. *Auswärts*↑): autumn, *NorE* the back-end (of the year), *AmE* also fall (of the leaves); *so geschätzt die Schlüsselblume im Auswärts, so verachtet ist die giftige Herbstzeitlose im ~* the cowslip is highly prized in spring, and the poisonous meadow saffron is as sincerely despised in autumn.

Eiweckerl, sometimes also **Eierweckerl** *n* -s/-(n) [so called after its shape which, to the fanciful mind, resembles two eggs joined as if by melting] *bak.* a small oval cake whose dough contains butter, sugar, and milk (but no egg!): twin bun.

Eiweiß *n* -s/- *cul.* (*Eiklar*) the white or colourless part of an egg: white of egg, egg white; *drei ~ steifschlagen* beat three egg whites until stiff.

-eln a bound morpheme used to form intransitive verbs, with a colloquial and often disparaging slant, to denote sense impressions [→ *brandeln, fischeln*], human activities [→ *flacheln, garteln*], or both [→ *schwäbeln*]; its occurrence in transitive verbs is rare [→ *krampfeln*].

Emmaus, SouG also **Emaus** *n* place-name [a village, according to the Bible (St Luke 24: 13-31), "about threescore furlongs", i.e. some twelve kilometres, from Jerusalem, to which two disciples undertook a walk on the day after Jesus had risen from the dead; suddenly He was by their side, "expound[ing] unto them in all the scriptures the things concerning himself"] *relig. & folklore* in constructions like *~ gehen* and *der ~gang* 'walking to Emmaus' [eˈmeɪəs], always with reference to Easter Monday, a day set aside for visits to friends and relatives, or for pilgrimages to nearby centres of worship; *eine solche Wallfahrt geht tunlichst über ebenes Gelände, weil die fromme Einfalt das Wort „Emmaus" mundartgerecht als assimiliertes „ebnaus" deutet* such a pilgrimage is preferably made along ground that is level because pious simplicity interprets *Emmaus* (or rather *Emaus*), quite legitimately from a dialectal point of view, as an assimilated form of *eben aus*.

Englische Garten *m* -n -s [created in 1790 by Sir Benjamin

Thompson, a native American who, during the War of Independence, showed marked loyalty to the old country and its ruling classes (for some biographical details, see under *Rumfordsuppe*↓) - hence, too, his natural choice of the epithet "English"] *hist.* and *landscape gardening* in Munich, on the site of what used to be a wild and neglected hunting area: "English Garden", one of the most beautiful parks in the world, laid out on the English pattern (and surrounded by a six-mile road), with pleasure grounds, streams, waterfalls, promenades, grottoes, a small lake, and a Chinese pagoda; moreover, there was a model farm to demonstrate the best methods of raising produce and cattle.

Englmarisuchen *n* -s [first el., gen. *sg.* of *Englmar* (E *Engelmer*), the son of a poor Bavarian labourer who, after leading a sainted life as a hermit, died a violent death on January 14, 1096; he was later beatified by a popular cult] *relig.* & *folklore* at St Englmar, a well-known hillside resort north-east of Straubing, on Whit Monday: "The Quest of St Engelmer", a religious folk play acted out by a long cast of parishioners both on foot and on horseback; the central theme focuses on the tradition that the body of the blessed martyr remained unaccounted for until a priest, passing through the forest, saw a miraculous splendour of angels hovering over the site where the victim lay buried.

Enzian *m* -s/-e [< MHG *encian*, *entian*, a borrowing from LateL *jentsiana* < L *gentiana*; said to be named after *Gentius*, an Illyrian king] **1.** *bot.* a usu. blue mountain plant: gentian. → **2.** *bev.* a spirit distilled from the roots of that plant: gentian brandy.

Erdapfel *m* -s/...äpfel **1.** (*Kartoffel*) potato, *poet.* earth apple, *colloq.* tater, *dial.* spud, *IrE* murphy, Irish apple *or* apricot - various names on various levels of usage for one and the same food item which, in past centuries, is said to have "graced" the Upper Palatinate farmhouse dinner table with cloying regularity; here is a dialect quatrain which mourns such eternal recurrence:

Erdäpfl in der Fröih;	*Taters when crows the cock;
Mittags in der Bröih,	Noons, soaking in the stock;
Af d'Nacht in die Häut;	Nights, unpeeled they're a sore -
Erdäpfl in Ewigkeit!	Taters for evermore!

2. *hum. phr.* the confessions of one who can well dispense with potatoes: (1) *die Erdäpfel sind mir lieber, wenn sie zuerst die Sau gefressen hat* (or, *wenn sie zuerst durch die Sau getrieben werden*) *potatoes taste better to me (*or,* taste best) after they've been eaten by the pig, and the pig has become pork. - (2) *die Erdäpfel sind eh im Schweinernen drin* *taters are part of pig-turned-pork, anyway.

-erer [-ərə] this popular duplicative suffix is, of course, agentival in origin (*Bahnerer*, for instance, easily linking up with *AmE* railroader); at times, though, the morphemic structure of *-erer* is apt to bring out inherent echoic properties (*Hupferer*, one of the many, suggesting a sequence of bumps, or jumps, and rebounds, in real life), while in others end-of-word repetitiousness conjures up the picture of a flabby dewlap, and thus adds a faintly disparaging note (cp. *Hauterer, Krauterer, Landerer, Stadterer*).

-erl [-əl] a diminutive suffix which, in contrast with *-l*↓, often either expresses smallness, youth, sometimes also their very opposite (e.g. *Enterl* 'duckling', *Katzerl* 'pussy[cat]', *Weilerl*, meaning both 'a little while' *and* 'quite a while'), or more often affection (e.g. *Herzerl*, *Schatzerl* 'lovey-dovey', 'sweetie-pie', *Weiberl* ScotE 'wifiekie'), or indeed both (e.g. *Buzerl* 'babykın', 'ibsy-wibsy', 'kiddie-winkie', *AmE* 'kiddie-widdie' [all referring to a sweet little child], *Deanderl, Dirnderl*↑ ScotE 'wee lassie' [sweet little girl], *Laderl* ScotE 'wee bit shopie' [tiny little shop], *Zahnerl* 'toosie-peg' [tiny little tooth]); as can be seen from these few samplings even, English shows great versatility in forming terms of endearment.

Etui de la titte [tɪt] *n* -s - - - [pseudo-French] low *colloq. hum.*, typical of male-to-male talk and joking — a brassière: tit hammock, *AmE also* double-barreled slingshot, flopper-stopper, over-shoulder boulder-holder.

Fangamandl *n* -s [actually, a substantivized imperative phrase, 'catch a man', „*fang a Mandl* (↓)!", a type of construction that has been common in our two languages since the Middle Ages], also **Fangsterl** *n* -s [similarly, the remnant of an inviting question, „*fangst du mich* [*uns*]?" + *-erl*↑] a children's game in which one player chases the others (*Fangen*): tag, tick, tig; *spielen wir ~!* let's play tag!

Fasching *m* -s/-e and, at times, -s [< MHG *vaschanc, vastschang* 'dispensing the Lenten drink', i.e. a beverage permitted in that season of fasting and penitence in preparation for Easter; later, with thoughts of rigour and abstemiousness, the word was re-etymologized as *vastganc* 'carnival procession'] *folklore* **1.** the period of public enjoyment and merry-making, with eating, dancing, drinking, and often processions and shows, held in the weeks before Lent, at the latest from January 7 to Shrove Tuesday (*Karnevalszeit*): carnival; *im ~* in the carnival (season); *auf den ~ gehen* to go to a carnival ball; *in München und in anderen größeren Städten geht es mit dem ~ schon früh los, und zwar am 11.11. um 11 Uhr 11, denn dann besteigt das dortige Faschingsprinzenpaar den*

Thron in Munich and in other major cities, the carnival season starts quite early, indeed at 11.11 a.m. on the eleventh day of the eleventh month of the year, when the local royal carnival couple ascend the throne to begin their rule.

Fasten *n* -s *R.C. relig.* fast, fasting, an abstinence, esp. as a religious observance, from all solid food; liquid food is exempt, as tipplers are quick to spread the semi-proverbial message: *Flüssigkeit bricht ~ nicht* "drink won't break your fast". - **~bier** *n* -(e)s/-e *brew.* a strong beer with an original wort (*Stammwürze*) of at least 16 per cent, brewed as a special treat for habitual froth-blowers in the period between Ash Wednesday and Easter: "fasting-season beer".

Fatsche *f* -/-n [< It *fascia* 'bandage'] *med.* (*lange Binde*) (roller) bandage, elastic *or* gauze bandage. - **fatschen** *v/t* **1.** *med.* ([*mit einer Fatsche*] *fest umwickeln*) to bandage, to swathe with bandages. - **2.** *hist. folklore* with reference to a baby: to wrap tightly in many coverings, to swaddle.

Fatschenkind *n* -(e)s/-er, warmly also **Fatschenkinderl** *n* -s/-(n) **1.** *med. hist.* & *folklore* baby (wrapped) in swaddling clothes. - **2.** *art* & *folklore* wooden dolly, painted in a way as to represent a baby in swaddling clothes; = *Docke*↑. - **3.** *R.C. art* to be seen at Christmas, since baroque and rococo times, in churches, and now also in folklore museums: Christ Child as a manger figure, dressed in elaborate knitwear adorned with thin gold wire.

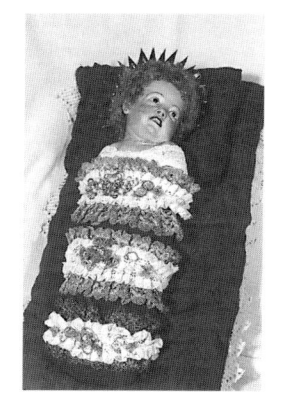

fei *adv* [by apocope, < *fein* 'nice(ly)'; like G *mei* < *mein* and E *my* < OE *min* (and ModE *mine*, the possessive form of *I*)] an unassuming element in colloquial speech (hence invariably unstressed), but conveniently ready to lend weight or emotive colour to the utterance immediately following; it may connote **1.** sheer emphasis, or at least inviting attention: *das gibt's ~ oft!* that's quite often the case (*or*, this happens quite often), you know; *die Suppe war ~ heiß* the soup was good and hot; *auf den Bergen ist 's ~ sonnig* it's nice and sunny on the hills; *es ist ~ windig heut!* BrE it isn't half windy today; *ihr habt's ~ rote Gesichter!* you've got rare red faces; *die Kathi find't die neue Arbeit ~ bärig* Cathy's new job suits her down to the ground, AmE also ... suits her to a T (*or* tee); *das Schaun ist ~ kein schlechter, es ist ein schöner Brauch* looking at things is surely not a bad habit, it's a good one; *du, dem sein Vater ist ~ wirklich ein Baron gewesen* listen, his father was really and truly a baron, I'm telling you; *der glaubt ~ alles* he'll believe any mortal thing. - **2.** pleased surprise, praise or self-praise: *weißt (du) was, das Grablichtl brennt ~ immer noch!* well, what do you know! the grave-light's still burning; *du bist ~ ein tüchtiges Bürscherl!* ScotE you're a brave good laddie, I say!; *das hab ich ~ selber gemacht!* I did this all by myself, mind. - **3.** a plea: *gib ~ Obacht!* do be careful!; *laß das ~ bleiben!* leave that well enough alone!; *sag ~ nix, von wem du das (gehört) hast!* don't let on please who told you!; *komm mir ~ nicht zu spät!* don't you be late, I'm asking you. - **4.** a note of humorous or gentle warning to come up to the speaker's expectations: *daß du mir ~ was Gutes bringst!* be sure to get me something good!; *daß du mir ~ brav bist!* I want you to be a good boy [girl], d'you hear me?; *den Regenschirm borg ich dir ~, aber Wiedersehen macht Freude!* I'll be glad to lend you my umbrella, but it's on an elastic band - it comes back!; *so was Grobes mag ich aus deinem Mund ~ nimmer hören!* next time I hear such a thing I'll tell you to rinse your mouth out with soap-water! -

5. disappointment or criticism: *das is ~ a Schlauch!* my, that's a very trying thing!; it takes it out of you, no kidding!; *erzähl mir ~ nicht, daß ...* don't you (dare) tell me that ...!; *eine gute Zigarn is das ~ net, hast d' mi'?* that's an apology for a cigar, you get me? - **6.** grudge, past or present: *das hat sie ihm ~ lang nicht vergessen!* oh, she's held this against him for quite a while! - **7.** a negative value judgment (here, in broad dialect): *des is ~ nix!* that ain't any good! - **8.** a protest of one's innocence, or an apology for an oversight: *das hab ich ~ net gsehn* gee, I didn't see that.

Feitel, the syllabic spelling of **Feitl** [< dialectal p.p. *gefeitelt*, through vocalization of the *l* before a dental in Central Bavarian (cp. *Geid < Geld*) < *gefaltet* 'folded', + syllabic *-l*], also **Taschenfeit(e)l** *m* -s/- *colloq.* a cheap knife with usu. two blades that fold into the handle, often carried in the pocket ([*billiges*] *Klappmesser*): pocketknife, penknife; if large, and with only one blade: jackknife.

Felbe *f* -/-n [a back-formation, current in the Allgäu dialect, due to the structural analogy of many other tree names, like *Buche*, *Erle*, and *Espe*], or **Felber** *m* -s/- [< MHG *velwer* < OHG *felwar*], also **Felberbaum** *m* -(e)s/...bäume *bot.* (*Weide[nbaum]*) white willow, swallow-tail willow. - **Felberbandl** *n* -s/-n *vinic.* (*Weidenrute*) willow twig, osier ['ɔʊʒə] switch, used in wine-growing areas for tying vines to the stick.

Felchen [< MHG *felche*] also, **Bodenseefelchen** *m* -s/- *ichth.* a fish of the family *Coregonidae*, similar to the trout but having a smaller mouth and larger scales, eaten for food in the Lake Constance region: lake whitefish.

Feldherrenhalle *f* - in Munich: **1.** *archit.* "Hall of Generals", a freely translated copy of the Loggia dei Lanzi at Florence (1376), an attraction for visitors because of its hugely scaled frescoes of ferocious battle scenes. - **2.** *polit. hist.* on November 9, 1923: *Marsch auf die* ~ "March on the Hall of Generals", better known in English as the "beer-hall putsch" of November 8, a spectacular but abortive attempt by Adolf Hitler and General Erich Ludendorff to bring Germany under national control with support of the army.

Fenster... *archit.* [three words ending in -*l*↓, a suffix here evoking merely an aura of colloquial ease, but not suggesting that the technical feature mentioned is small]: ~**bankl**, ~**brettl** *n* -s/-(n) (*Fenstersims*) window-sill. - ~**reiberl** *n* -s/-(n) (*Fensterriegel*) (rotary) window catch ‖ *fig.* in allusion to the Alpine custom of "window courting", but taboo in polite use: *sie hat ein loderes* (or *lockeres*) ~ she is ready for promiscuous love-making: she plays around, she plays the field, she shakes a loose leg, *BrE also* she is an Essex girl.

fensterln *v/i* [this present-day form of affective morphology (< *Fensterl n* '[dear] little window') is as yet absent in its earliest documentation, sixteenth-century G *fenstern* (showing but the verbal suffix -*n* added to the noun form)] *folklore, colloq.* only possible in a rural setting, with the girl courted having her bed in an upstairs closet (*Menscherkammer*) of the farmhouse — to pay a secretive visit to one's lady love (by climbing a ladder, after nightfall); *darf ich bei dir heute abend* ~ (or, *zum* ~ *kommen*)*?* may I go knock-knock (*or*, tappety-tap) at your window tonight?

fieseln *vt/i* [an ablaut variant of *fuseln* 'to work ineffectively','to trifle'] *colloq.* **1.** *v/t* often also **abfieseln**↑ (*sauber abnagen*) with reference to a bone of cooked meat: to gnaw bare; *ich tu(e) leidenschaftlich gern Knochen* ~ I really enjoy chewing on the bones, I love picking bones clean. - **2.** *v/i* (*mühsam hinarbeiten*) (to have) to work at an often uninteresting task, employing excessive time and effort over inconsequential details: to niggle.

Fieselarbeit, Fieselei *f* -/-en *colloq.* a piece of work demanding (but occasionally also catering to a person's penchant for) excessive care, attention, time, etc.: niggling chore; nitpicking grind (*or* drudgery).

Filser-Bairisch *n* - *ling.* the type of Upper Bavarian dialect used by Ludwig Thoma, 1867-1921, in his prose and plays featuring Josef Filser, a shrewd yet woefully unlettered figure of a farmer-cum-deputy-to-the-provincial-diet at Munich; modern journalists have revived the type and fed dozens of newspaper columns, one also written in an atrociously Germanized English: "Filser's Bavarian", a down-to-earth vernacular, rough and racy of speech, but whimsically defiant of all spelling rules when seen on paper.

Filz *m* -es/-e [< MHG *vilz* < OHG *filz*; like E *felt*, actually 'wool and fur (or hair) worked into a compact substance'; cp. G *walken* and E *to walk* 'to full', i.e. to thicken cloth by a special process in manufacture] *geog.* a tract of open, peaty waste land in Upper Bavaria and in the Bavarian Forest, common in places where drainage is poor (*Hochmoor*): highland moor; *in einigen ~en kann die Torfmächtigkeit sechs und mehr Meter erreichen* in some of the moors, the peat can reach down to a depth of seven yards or more.

Finger...: ~**hakeln** *n* -s finger-wrestling, finger-tug **1.** a popular entertainment and test of strength, practised in Upper Bavarian inns, etc. involving a middle finger tug-of-war between two male opponents across a table; - **2.** a traditional sport, formally organized since about 1950 with championship matches for the Alps, for Bavaria, and for the whole of

Germany: both players sit on opposite sides of a table, one finger hooked into a leather ring (*Hakelriemen*), and try to pull their opponent's hand past the 'out' mark near the edge of the table; any finger except the thumb may be used. - ~**hakler** *m* -s/- finger-wrestler, finger-tugger, i.e. one who engages in the sport or contest of *Fingerhakeln*↑; in official games, classed by weight. - ~**hut** *m* -(e)s/pl. rare: ...hüte [actually, 'thimble'] *bot.* (*Wiesenglockenblume, Campanula patula*) spreading bell-flower.

Finsing [-z-] *n* -s/pl. rare: -e or -s [there are at least three villages or hamlets of that name throughout Bavaria, but widespread fame, if of a dubious kind, goes to the one mentioned in the writings of Hans Sachs, 1494-1576: in them, the well-known Nuremberg Mastersinger pokes fun at its inhabitants being *"tölpet ... toll und unbesonnen"*] *place-name, hum.* or *sarc.* an imaginary Bavarian village renowned for the foolishness of its inhabitants, and the subject of many jokes and anecdotes; comparable to G *Schilda(u)*, Saxony, and E *Gotham* ['gəʊtəm], Nottinghamshire: Finsing; *ja, bist du denn aus ~?* why, are you Simple Simon from Finsing?

Finsinger [-z-] *attrib. adj* typical of, and foolish like, a man from Finsing↑; *das war ein ~ Stückl, ... ein Stückl wie von den ~ Bauern* that was worthy of a man [of the men] of Gotham, that was not a very bright thing to do.

fischeln *v/i* [< *Fisch* 'fish' + *-eln*↑] *colloq.*, often with an implied critical note on the sense impressions received. - **1.** olfactory: *es fischelt* there is a smell of fish (in the air). - **2.**

gustatory: *die Suppe fischelt (aber) arg* (my [AmE also gee],) this soup tastes strongly of fish.

flacheln *v/i* [< *flach* 'flat' + the agentive morpheme *-eln*↑] *colloq.* a pastime in which flat stones are made to skip across the surface of water several times before sinking (the English metaphor suggests a fancied likeness to a waterfowl's movements): to play *or* make ducks and drakes; *tun wir* (dial.: *deamma*) ~! let's play ducks and drakes. - **Flachl** *m* -s/-(n) [cp. -*l*↓] *colloq.* flat stone: flattie.

Flascherl *n* -s/-(n) [< *Flasche* 'bottle' + -*erl*↑] *colloq.*, nearly always used appreciatively — a little bottle of something delicious, usu. of the alcoholic persuasion: baby, bottle of goods; *machen wir noch ein ~ auf, grad weil's so grüabig is!* let's crack another wee bottle just 'cause things are so nice and cosy now ‖ a fictitious commodity (one from a long list) an unsuspecting child or adult is sent for as a practical joke, preferably on April Fools' Day: *ein ~ Fischblut* a pint (*or*, AmE, can) of pigeon's milk.

Fleckerlteppich *m* -s/-e [first el., *Fleck* 'patch (of cloth)' + -*erl*↑] **1.** (*Flickenteppich*) rag rug *or* carpet, crazy carpet. - **2.** often *hum.* or slightly *contp.* (*Flickwerk, bunte Sammlung*) patchwork, omnium gatherum; *vom Flugzeug aus bieten sich die Felder wie ein ~ dar* the aerial view presents a patchwork (*or*, resembles a huge patchwork quilt) of fields; *unsere grammatische Terminologie ist ein ~, an dem zwei Jahrtausende gearbeitet haben* our grammar terminology is an odd mishmash which has been worked over for two thousand years.

Fleisch... *gastr.:* **~käse** *m* -es (rare, but the official term) = *Leberkäs*. - **~küchel** *n* -s/- [second el., a dim. variant of *Kuchen* 'cake'], **~pflanzerl** *n* -s/-(n) [an endearing variant of the next, cp. -*erl*↑], **~pflanzl** *n* -s/-(n) [a blend of OBav *Fanzel* 'pulp', 'mash', and *Pfanne* 'stew-pan', both being required for preparing the dish] a small round loaf of minced pork and beef, plus bread rolls (well soaked), eggs, and spices, all patted into shape and cooked in hot fat (*Frikadelle*, *Bulette*, *Deutsches Beefsteak*): meat ball, meat croquette, *BrE also* (meat) rissole, *AmE also* ground meat patty, hamburger. - ~**schlegel** *m* -s/- (*Fleischklopfer*) meat mallet, steak hammer.

Fletz, **Flez**, **Flötz**, **Flöz** *f* -/-, also *m* & *n* -es/-e [< MHG *vletze* < OHG *flezzi*, *flazzi* 'levelled ground', '(barn-)floor'; cp. ScotE *flet*] *dial.* chiefly in farmhouses of the Bavarian Forest (*Hausflur*): (paved) entrance-hall, *AmE also* hallway; *der Rinderstall lag im Haus und war durch die ~ zu erreichen* the cow stable, forming part of the main building, could be reached from the hall. - ~**kammer** *f* -/-n *archit. hist.* in old farmhouses: servants' small bedroom (usu. adjoining the hall and the stable).

fliegen *v/i* to fly; in *R.C. folklore*: the verb is found at the core of two popular expressions used by the pious, who like to keep the memory of our Saviour's former presence on earth very much alive: **1.** between the Gloria on Maundy Thursday and Easter Sunday, when the churchbells remain silent for the Passion of Jesus Christ (and rattles or clappers take over as makeshift devices): *jetzt ~ die Glocken nach Rom* now the bells fly to Rome. - **2.** on Ascension Day, a holy day on which Jesus Christ is celebrated to have returned to Heaven (and when, to symbolize this during the service, an effigy of Him is often pulled through the church ceiling): *am Auffahrtstag soll man ~des Fleisch essen* you are supposed to eat 'meat on the wing' (i.e. fowl) on Ascension Day.

Floriansjünger, less often **Florianijünger** *m* -s/- [first el., < *St Florian*, d. 304, a high Roman officer in Noricum, now Upper Austria, who as an early Christian was killed by drowning in the River Enns, near Lorch, under Diocletian, venerated as the patron saint of fire fighters, the martyr is commonly pictured as a knight in armour who pours a bucket of water on a house in flames] gently *hum., journ.* a sobriquet for a fireman: "disciple of St Florian", *AmE* also smoke-eater, Smoky; *als voriges Jahr ein Brandstifter hier sein Unwesen trieb, mußten unsere ~ wiederholt ausrücken* when an arsonist was up to mischief in the area last year, our stalwart men of the fire brigade repeatedly had to go out on emergency calls.

Fo̱**am** [foɑm] *m* -s [< MHG *veim* 'froth' - extinct in StandG except in *ausgefeimt* 'devoid of any frothy head forming in the glass once the beer has been freshly poured out', hence 'subject to suspicion', 'arrant'; the English cognate of G *Foam* is, of course, *foam* [fəʊm], but the word, one of the notorious "false friends", is inapplicable to beer] *dial.* (*Schaum* [*in e-m Glas Bier*]) froth; *des Bier hat koan ~* there's no froth on this beer, this beer has no head, this beer is flat.

Fö**hn** *m* -(e)s/-e [< OHG *phonno* < ? VulgL *faonius* < L *favonius* 'gentle west wind', 'vernal breeze'; akin to L *fovere* 'to warm'] *meteor.* chiefly in Upper Bavaria: (*warmer, trockener Fallwind*) foehn (wind), föhn (wind), a warm, dry wind blowing down a mountainside.

> Note: A similar type of wind occurs in some mountainous regions of the English-speaking world, e.g. the *chinook*, on the eastern side of the Rocky Mountains in Canada and the USA, and the *nor'wester*, in New Zealand.

Fo̱**tze** *f* -/-n, usu. *dial.* **F**o̱**tzn** *f* -/- [< MHG *vut* 'mouth (of an animal)'] low *colloq. & vulg.* **1.** a person's mouth: gob ‖ *phr.* (1) usu. imperative: *halt dei' ~!* shut up!, shut your gob (*or* trap)!, *ScotE* steek yur gab! - (2) *j-m die ~ recht herhauen* to box s.o.'s ears left and right. - **2.** a person's eloquence: gift of (*BrE* the) gab ‖ said in praise, but as often also in derision, of an orator's, politician's, or lawyer's verbal performance: *der hat dir eine ~!* there's a spieler (*or* spouter) for you!

- **3.** (*Ohrfeige*) (1) slap (in the face), box on the ear; *j-m eine ~ geben* to slap s.o.'s face, to box s.o.'s ears. - (2) *fig.* a humiliating remark or action: slap in the face, facer, kick in the teeth. - **fotzen** *v/t* low *colloq.* & *vulg.* (*ohrfeigen*) *j-n ~* to slap s.o. in (*or* on) the face, to box (*or* cuff) s.o.'s ears.

Fotzenschmied *m* -(e)s/-e rare = **Fotzenspangler** *m* -s/- [second el., < *Spange* 'metal clasp', one of the common articles produced in a tinsmith's workshop; the standard SouG occupational term is now *Spengler*, an umlaut variant preferred by seventeenth-century grammarians who were no longer aware of the word being derived from *Spange*] low *colloq.*, *hum.* or *contp.* dentist: *BrE* fang-farrier, *AustralE* fang-carpenter, gum-digger, gum-puncher, *AmE* tooth plumber.

Fotzhobel *m* -s/- [the musical instrument is held close to the mouth, and being moved from side to side resembles the to-and-fro of a cabinet-maker's plane] *mus.*, *hum.* (*Mundharmonika*) harmonica: mouth-organ, *AmE also* corn-on-the-cob, French harp, mouth Steinway.

Fraunhofersche Linien *f* pl. [named after Joseph von Fraunhofer, 1787-1826, an ingenious optician and physicist, and inventor of the telescope, whose birthplace at Straubing, Lower Bavaria, is commemorated by a bust] *phys.* any of the dark lines in the spectrum of sunlight: Fraunhofer lines.

Friedhofs...: **~frau** *f* -/pl. rare: -en *colloq.* (*Friedhofswärterin*) (1) if the burial site lies around, and belongs to, a church in which dead members of that church are buried, e.g. at St Peter, Straubing. female churchyard keeper, *colloq.* churchyard woman. - (2) if the burial site usu. does not belong to a church: female cemetery (*or* graveyard) keeper, *colloq.* cemetery (*or* graveyard) woman. - ~**jodler**, also **Gottsackerjodler** *m* -s/- mainly *joc.* a severe cough: churchyard cough. - ~**mann** *m* -(e)s/pl. rare: ...männer [see above, under *Friedhofsfrau*] (1) churchyard keeper, *colloq.* churchyard man. - (2) cemetery (*or* graveyard) keeper, *colloq.* cemetery (*or* graveyard) man. - ~**spargel** *m* -s/- *hum.* or *sarc.* a cigarette or cigar: coffin-nail.

Frosch... [typical of the anatomy of an amphibian of the family *Ranidae*, and by disparaging metaphor applied to a human being who is only sparsely endowed with facial beauty]: ~**auge** *n* -s/usu. pl.: -n *colloq.*, mostly *contp.* protuberant eye (*hervorquellendes Auge*): bug-eye, goggle-eye; *er hat ~n* he's pop-eyed, his eyes stick out like organ stops (*BrE also* ... like chapel hat-pegs). - ~**maul** *n* -s/pl. rare: ...mäuler *colloq.*, mostly *contp.* a broad, flattened mouth: frog's mouth.

Fuchsie ['foksɪə] *f* -/-n [named after Leonhart Fuchs, 1501-1566, a physician and botanist who, in his clever description of domestic plants alphabetically arranged, laid the foundation of a permanent botanical nomenclature; his picturesque little birthplace, on the market-square of Wemding, north-northwest of Donauwörth, is adorned with the emblem of a fuchsia] *bot.* a shrub of drooping flowers: fuchsia ['fjuːʃə].

Fünfer *m* -s/- (*die Fünf*) **1.** *arith.* (*Ziffer*) (the number) five; *in unserer Telefonnummer sind* (or *gibt es*) *drei ~* our phone number has three fives. - **2.** *educ.* the next-to-lowest mark when evaluating any scholastic achievement: *BrE* pass (mark), *AmE* (grade) D; *wer am Gymnasium im Juli in zwei Fächern einen ~ bekommt, muß das Jahr wiederholen* a grammar-school pupil receiving two pass marks in July has to repeat the year (*or*, to stay back for one year).

Fürtuch *n* -(e)s/...tücher [< MHG *vortuoch*], *dial.* **Firta**, **Fiada**

fürwährend 68

n -/- [with unrounding of the vowel in the first syllable (plus vocalization of the *r* in *Fiada* before the dental), and vowel weakening as well as consonantal loss in the second syllable; semantically, the headword and the Germanic English equivalent both point to a common cultural past - the protective piece of garment was originally "pinned" over the dress "in front"] *colloq.* apron, pinafore: pinny.

fürwährend *adj* [*für-* 'ahead', 'beyond' > generally intensifying prefix] *hist.*, in contemporary documents, on gravestones, etc.: everlasting, sempiternal; *Der Fürwährende Reichstag = Der Immerwährende Reichstag*.

Fuß *m* -es/usu. pl. Füße, *dial.* Fü(a)ß *anat.* (*Bein*) leg; *die hat fei schöne Fü(a)ß!* BrE her legs aren't half pretty, AmE & AustralE ... are real beauts, AmE also her gams aren't half bad.

☞ **G** ☜

Gackerl *n* -s/-(n) [dim. of echoic *gack* 'cluck', the low short sound a hen makes when sitting on her eggs or when calling her chickens] *colloq.*, esp. in baby talk — egg: eggie; *willst du ein weiches ~ oder ein hartes ~?* would you like your eggie boiled soft or hard? - ²**gelb** *adj* [the compound refers to the vivid yellow, the typical colour of the yolk of a hen's egg] *colloq.* intensely yellow: bright-yellow, AmE also punkin yellow; *die ~en Singerln, sind die nicht süß?* the chickabiddies, all brightly yellow, aren't they sweet?

Gams *f* -/-en; in hunters' jargon, with reference to the male animal, **Gams** *m* -/- [< MHG *gam(e)z*, a variant of *Gemse*] *zo.* chamois ['ʃæmwɑː], Alpine goat; *flink wie eine* ~ nimble as a (mountain) goat.

Gams...: **~bart** *m* -(e)s/...bärte *folklore* the bristly black hair on a chamois buck's withers (*Widerrist*), often worn as a decoration in the Alps by men in their hats of green or black felt as part of the regional costume: tuft of chamois' hairs, chamois tuft (*or* brush), gamsbart; cp. *Wachler.* - **~bock** *m* -s/...böcke chamois buck. - **~geiß** *f* -/-en chamois doe. - **~hüter** *m* -s/- *hunters' jargon* "chamois keeper", mountain fog shielding the stalked animals from view.

gamsig *adj* **1.** *colloq.* (*sehr flink*) nimble as a (mountain) goat. - **2.** low *colloq.*, said of people — lecherous (*geil*): randy, horny.

Gams...: **~krickel** *n* -s/-(n) horn of the chamois; (pair of) chamois horn. - **~läuten** *n* -s *hunters' jargon* "chamois ringing", the jangling noise accidentally made on rock by a mountaineer's iron-shod alpenstock. - **~rudel** *n* -s/- herd of chamois. - **~wild** *n* -(e)s chamois-deer, chamois *pl.* ['ʃæmwɑːz]

Gankerl ['gaŋkəl] *m* -s [< the fusion of the nominal elements *Gan f* -/-en 'fiery spark' (a by now obs. UpG dial. word (related to ModHG *knistern* 'to crackle [as said of fire]') + *Kerl m* -s/-e 'fellow' (related to E *churl* 'low base fellow', 'rude person')] *colloq.* an imaginary evil spirit (sometimes described as a little devil) brought into play by adults to scare children (*Kinderschreck*): bogey (man), child-bogey ‖ a dialect speaker's baleful warning: *etz kimmt na glei da* ~*!* you (just) wait, the bogey man's on the prowl to get you!

Ganserer ['ganzərə] *m* -s/- **1.** *zo.* (*Gänserich*) gander, i.e. a male goose. - **2.** *contp.* a term of abuse for a stupid male: silly goose, ass, blockhead.

Gansjung *n* -s *cul.* the traditional light hot meal at an annual fair, eaten late in the day (*Gänseklein*): goose giblets *pl.*, a gravy dish of the heart, liver, neck, and wing parts of a goose, marked by dark thickening, and usu. served with a white-bread dumpling.

Gant *f* -/-en [< MHG *gant*; from the auctioneer's shouted query, It *incanto* < LateL *in quantum* 'to which (sum are you ready to go)?'] *jur.* (*öffentliche Versteigerung*) (sale by) auction, public sale; *sein Hof ist auf die ~ gekommen* his farm was sold at (*or*, by) auction.

gar *colloq.* **1.** *adj* [< MHG *gar* < OHG *garo* 'prepared', 'finished', 'complete(d)'] (1) said of food consumed (*aufgezehrt*): eaten up, all gone, at an end; *das Brot ist ~, kein Bröserl ist mehr da* the bread is all gone, not a crumb's left ‖ *phr.* found in a cheerfully resigned four-line ditty to echo a Bavarian Old Mother Hubbard's sentiment who, on trying "to fetch her poor dog a bone", discovered that "the cupboard was bare":

Aus is 's	*All o'er,
und gar is 's,	What a bore -
und schad is 's,	Ain't we sore
daß 's wahr is!	There's no more!

(2) said of material, merchandise, etc. given away or sold out (*aufgebraucht*): used up, all gone, at an end (*or* spent); *unser Geld ist ~* our money is at an end, we are broke. - (3) said of something immaterial, e.g. a theatre performance (*vorbei*): at an end, over; *das Stück ist ~* the play is over. - **2.** *adv* [a sense development of the former] an intensifier (1) preceding negatives (*überhaupt*): at all; *~ nie* never at all, never ever ‖ the opening couplet of a famous dialect lyric by Franz Stelzhamer (1802-1874):

Allweil kreuzlusti	*All the while merry
und trauri gar nia,	and no whit in gloom:
I steh da wia da Kerschbam	here I stand like a cherry
in ewiga Blüah.	tree ever in bloom.

(2) preceding adverbs and indefinite pronouns (*sehr*): very; *das schmeckt ~ gut* that tastes delicious; *so ~ schwierig ist das*

ja nicht, gell? it isn't that difficult, is it?; ~ *mancher hat das auch gemeint* many a man thought so too.

gärteln, *dial.* **garteln** *v/i* [see -eln↑] *colloq.* (*gärtnern*) **1.** to garden: to do gardening. - **2.** to be a hobby gardener, to do gardening in one's spare time (*or*, in a small way): to potter in (*AmE* to putter around) the garden. - **Gartler** *m* -s/- *dial. colloq.* hobby gardener, spare-time (*or* weekend) gardener.

Gassen...: **~bub** *m* -en/-en *colloq.*, often slightly *contp.* a small untidy boy who roams the streets (*Straßenjunge*): street urchin, *BrE also* street-boy, *AmE also* dead-end kid. - **~schenke** f -/-n off-licence counter, *AmE also* package store.

Gäu, *dial.* (through unrounding) **Gai**, **Gei** *n* -(e)s/-e [the SouG variant of unumlauted StandG *Gau*, also found in *Allgäu* 'Alpine region', the official name for a district in SW Bavaria; OE has the analogous form *gē*, repeatedly documented as a compound element in SE England (testifying to the fact that Kent was, at an early period, divided into administrative areas incorporating that word, e.g. *Denge* 'valley district' and *Lyminge* 'district on the River Lympne', and Cambridgeshire had an *ælgē* 'eel district' where many eels were once caught in the fens around *Ely*)] **1.** *geog.* = *Gäuboden*. - **2.** *colloq.* (*Gehege*) one's territory, i.e. a field of occupational or amatory activity, by tacit rather than written consent felt to be one's own: reserve; *der Metzger hat früher jede Woche sein Gäuwagerl herausgeholt und ist mit ihm ins ~ gefahren* in former times, a butcher got out his horse-and-buggy every week and did his purchasing round. - **3.** *colloq., fig.* a person's assumed or real prerogative in regard to a rival: (1) (*BrE* Tom Tiddler's) ground jealously held, or attempted to be held, by the incumbent claimant to a girl's favours; *der Hiasl geht dem Hans ins ~* Matt is out to wheedle Jack's girlfriend away from him; a telltale *Schnadahüpfl*↓, already recorded by Schmeller, has it:

> *De Traunstoaner Metzger,*
> *dee hom a groß Gai,*
> *hom überall Menscha*
> *und Kinder dabei.*

> *The butchers of Traunstein
> Are getting around;
> Their wenches are many,
> And kiddies abound.

(2) a politician's ranking position in a regional party organization: top stance; *in ihrem weiß-blauen ~ hat es jüngst Renate Schmidt gut verstanden, den Basis-Rebellen besänftigenden Zucker zu geben* on her blue-and-white ground, Renate Schmidt did pretty well lately to mollify the rank-and-file rebels in the Party.

Gäu...: **~bauer** *m* -n/-n *geog., agr.* = *Gäubodenbauer.* - **~boden** *m* -s *geog.* "bottomland district", the fertile Danubian plain S of the Bavarian Forest, between Regensburg and Vilshofen (with Straubing for a centre), the deep loessial deposits making it the *Kornkammer Bayerns* 'The Granary of Bavaria'; *~bauer m* "bottomland farmer", a usu. very affluent agriculturalist in Danubian Lower Bavaria. - **~wagerl** *n* -s/-(n) [second el., < the stem of MHG *wagen* < OHG *wagan*, actually 'the thing that moves' (cp. ModHG *sich bewegen* 'to move' as well as E *wain* and *wag(g)on*, respectively) + *-erl*↑] *com.* a light, four-wheel, one-horse service vehicle for one person, with a small loading surface (cp. *Gäu 2*): buggy.

Gaudi *f* - [this is the unsuffixed base of *Gaudium*, prob. a student-slang borrowing (< L *gaudium* 'joy', 'merriment'), with the gender following G *Freude, Ausgelassenheit, Fröhlichkeit*] *colloq.* **1.** (*Spaß*) lark, (bit of) fun, sport; *aus* or *zur ~, zwecks der ~* for fun, for a lark; *nur so zur ~* just for fun, just as *or* for a joke, just for a giggle; *er hat es aus* (or *zur*) *~ gemacht* he did it for a lark; *aus* (or *zur*) *~ soll man beim Bergsteigen Geröll nie lostreten* when climbing, stones (*AmE* rocks) should never be set scattering (*or* kicked loose) for sport; *bei dem Fernsehratespiel geht es uns hauptsächlich um dle ~, aber sollte wirklich ein Gewinn herausschauen,* *dann wollen wir ihn für einen guten Zweck spenden* we do the TV quiz mainly for the fun of it, but should a prize really come our way we'll give it to charity ‖ *auf ~ aussein* to be out for kicks; *das* (or *es*) *war eine ~* it was (great) fun [cp. *Mordsgaudi*]; *Buben machen gern eine ~* boys are fond of having a lark. - **2.** (*Lärm*) a loud noise: racket, hullabaloo; *~ machen* to kick up a racket, to raise (merry) hell; *macht's net so eine ~!* stop making such a racket! - **3.** (*Schabernack*) prank; *das Maibaumstehlen ist eine landbekannte ~* in this neck of the woods, robbing the maypole is a well-known practical joke. - **4.** *sarc.* (*Ärger*) trouble; (*Durcheinander*) mess ‖ in annoyance, when noticing something unpleasant recurring: *jetzt geht die ~* (*von vorn*) *wieder los* (or *an*)*!* (ah, well,) here we go again! - **5.** ([*Ehe-* etc.]*Streit*) marital (*etc.*) quarrel: row, rumpus, fall-out; *bei denen hat's heute fei wieder eine richtige ~ gegeben* they had a royal fight (*or*, a regular set-to) again today.

Gaudi... *colloq.:* **~blech** *n* -s *colloq.* (*Faschingsorden*) carnival tin medal. - **~bursch** *m* -en/-en **1.** any innocently cheerful young man: glad lad, happy duck. - **2.** a young man who is the cause of enjoyment or activity in a group: party pepper-upper; *er ist unser ~* he's the life and soul of our party. - **3.** a young man out for a wild time of irresponsible fun: hell-raiser, *AmE also* whoop-it-upper; cp. *krachledern* 2 (1). - **4.** any male member of a carnival procession: carnival caroller, *AmE & CanE also* carni guy. - **5.** a fairground crier: barker, spieler, *AmE also* ballyhoo man. - **~-Lindwurm** *m* -(e)s/ ...würmer = *Gaudiwurm*. - **~macher** *m* -s/- = *Gaudibursch* 2-5. - **~mannschaft** *f* -/-en *apprec.* a harmonious group of habitués of an inn that meet for various social activities: team of fun-lovers; *wenn man so bedenkt, waren wir eine echte ~, eine, die von Anfang an zusammengepaßt hat* come to think of it, we were really a merry bunch of regulars, one that clicked from the word go. - ~**nockerl(n)** *n* pl. low *colloq.* & *joc.* a woman's breasts, esp. if small: bubbies, titties, *AmE also* muffins, boosiasms [a word partly based on the word enth*usiasm*]. - ~**programm** *n* -(e)s/-e carnival program(me), carnival celebration. - ~**wagen** *m* -s/...wägen (*Festwagen*) carnival float. - ~**wurm** *m* -(e)s/...würmer **1.** in Munich and elsewhere (*Faschingszug*): carnival procession, on the Sunday preceding Lent. - **2.** Indian file of merrymakers (linking hands with shoulders). - ~**zeit** *f* -/-en fun-time, party-time; *Fasching ist bei manchen nicht nur Gaudi-, sondern auch Raufzeit* to some people, carnival is open season not only for fun but also for fistfights.

Geldbeutel... [in medieval and early modern times, any ready cash the common man had about him was carried in a "money-bag" strung to his girdle (hence also the descriptive name of G *Beutelschneider* and E *cutpurse* for a money-seizing thief of stealthy violence)]: ~**waschen** *n* -s, less often ~**wäsche** *f* - *folklore* in Regensburg and elsewhere in the Upper Palatinate, in the morning of Ash Wednesday, by the side of a river, brook, or pond: "purse rinsing", a hilarious gathering of men who, as "rueful" Carnival bankrupts, now "clean" their purses to make room for "better" money.

Geldige *m* or *f* -n/-n [an adjective used as a noun, *geldig* 'moneyed', 'wealthy'] *colloq.* a person who is in a very comfortable financial situation: *er* [*sie*] *ist ein ~r* [*eine ~*] he [she] 's a rich one, ... is well-heeled, he [she] has no end of money, *BrE also* he [she] 's warm.

Geldsau *f* -/...säu *dial.*, often *contp.* wealthy person: money-bags *sg.*, pig in clover, *AmE also* bum on the plush; *scheinbar haftet dem Besitz eines Motorboots automatisch an, eine „~" sein zu müssen* owning a motorboat seems to carry the fixed notion of being one who has money to burn (*or,* who is filthy rich, *AmE also* who is wallowing in dough).

Georgi *n* [< *Georgii*, L gen. sg. of *Georgius* 'George (the Great)', *d*. ca. 300 A.D., who having been martyred in Palestine was venerated as the model of knighthood (as such also the legendary hero slaying a dragon) and protector of soldiers; he is the acknowledged patron saint of both Germany and, since the mid-seventeenth century, of England] *n* only in use with prepositions: *an* ~ on St George's Day, March 23 (cp. *Georgitag*↓); *von* ~ *bis Michaeli hist.* "between St George's Day and Michaelmas" (September 29), i.e. the span of six months during which farm labourers, because of the more intensive call then on their time and range of activities, drew increased "summer wages" (*Sommerlohn*).

Georgi...: ~**ritt** *m* -(e)s/-e *relig. & folklore* "St George's Procession", a time-honoured ceremony on horseback, dating from the sixth century and based on the Germanic springtime rides, old fertility rites, through the fields. - ~**ritter** *m* -s/- Knight of St George, a member of distinguished orders both in Bavaria and in England, the insignia of the respective order showing a figure of St George killing the dragon. - ~**tag** *m* -(e)s/pl. rare: -e *hist.* St George's Day, an important date for payments, changes of employment, and sundry legal transactions in agricultural life. - ~**taler** *m* -s/- *numis.* still holding pride of place, occasionally, on the fob chains of Bavarian peasants: "St George's Dollar", a nineteenth-century coin with the image of the Saint, kept on one's body in the belief (as happened, for instance, when Bavarian troops took the field against France in 1870) that its bearer is thus made safe from bodily harm.

Germ *m* -(e)s; rarely *f* - [< *Gerbm* < *Gerbe*(*n*) 'activating agent' (cp. the verb *gerben* 'to tan', actually 'to change [animal skin] into leather', and *gar* 'done', 'cooked')] *cul.* (*Backhefe*) (bakers') yeast. - ~**teig** *m* -(e)s/pl. rare: -e *cul.* dough made with yeast, yeast dough.

Geröstete *f pl.* [< *geröstet* p.p. of *rösten* 'to roast', i.e. to cook by dry heat, either in front of an open fire or in an oven; 'to fry', i.e. to cook in hot fat or oil; 'to sauté', i.e. to cook quickly in a little hot oil or fat] *cul.* (*Röst-* or *Bratkartoffeln*) roast potatoes *pl.*; fried potatoes *pl.*; sauté potatoes *pl.*

Gerstl [usu. pron.:-ʃtl] *n* -s [dim. of *Gerste* 'barley'] **1.** *cul.* (kernel of) hulled barley, pearl barley; ~*suppe* barley soup. - **2.** *sl.* money [since riches in barley at one time conferred the prestige of affluence]: dough, beans *pl.*; *die* (*Leut*) *müssen viel ~ haben* they [the people] must have lots of dough; *er ist sein letztes* (or *das letzte*) *~ los und kann dir gwiß nichts geben* he hasn't a penny (*AmE* a dime) left, so he can't give you a thing.

geschert, often pronounced and spelt **gschert** *adj* [actually, the p.p. of the weakly conjugated verb *scheren* 'to shear': 'shorn', 'close-cropped'; historically, reference is to the bullet-shaped head of hair once compulsorily worn by bonded underlings and villeins as a conspicuous symbol of subservience to their land-owning overlords (note in the English Civil War the Puritan party of the "Roundheads", who wore their hair cut short)] *colloq. dial.* **1.** *adj* **a.** a rural attribute of more or less good-natured abuse, echoing the fact that once not only lowly farm labourers but also knackers, millers, gravediggers, hangmen, travelling journeymen, and even schoolmasters (who at inns all had to keep to segregated tables) were branded by the signal ignominy of crop-eared beardlessness; the word is often part of a greeting bandied among young peasant cronies, but also in other juvenile circles: *servus, ~e Nuß* (or *Ruam* [StandG *Rübe*])*!* hey, mucky Joe (*or* Farmer John)!, *IrE* also hey, bog-hopper!, *AmE* also hi, country hick! - **b.** boorish, coarse-mannered, uncouth; *daß sie dir nicht gratuliert haben, ist einfach ~* it's right bad manners that they failed to offer you their congratulations. - **2.**

adv speaking broad (*or* plain) dialect; *wir reden hier oben fei arg* ~ we don't half talk our broad dialect up here; *"Toilette" und "Nichteinheimischer" werden auf* ~ *bairisch zu "Scheißhaisl" und "Zuagroasta"* "Toilette" and "Nichteinheimischer" become "Scheißhaisl" and "Zuagroasta" in plain Bavarian.

Geselchte *n*, with *adj decl.*: -n *cul.* (*geräuchertes Schweinefleisch*) smoked salt pork.

Gewichtl, *dial.* **Gwichtl** *n* -s/ -(n) [an irregular diminutive, not to be derived from *Gewicht* 'weight' but from a unique past-participle noun *Gewicht* (with vowel gradation, to go with the pseudo-verb (*ge*)*weihen* 'to furnish with antlers [*Geweih*]'), to avoid the regular diminutive form **Geweiherl*, which is somewhat awkward to pronounce] *hunt.* antlers *pl.* (or horns *pl.*) of the roebuck.

Gigerl *m* -s/-(n) [< MHG *giege* 'fop', 'dandy' and MHG *giegel* 'vain', 'proud' (-*el* is here fused with the diminutive ending -*erl*↑ to bring out the derisive connotation); possibly influenced also by *Giggerl* 'cockerel, one that inflates itself with pride when standing on its own dunghill'] *colloq.*, often *iron.* any flashily dressed young man (*Modenarr*): spiv, swank pot, posh guy, Gaudy Georgey, Bobby Dazzler.

gipfeldürr *adj* [the metaphor is, of course, that of a mountain summit where every growth of vegetation, if it ever existed, has disappeared] *hum.* or *iron.* bald (*glatzköpfig*): bald as an egg, sporting an unthatched roof, *AmE* also barefooted on top of the head.

Glaser, *colloq. also* **Glaserer** *m* -s/- glazier; glass-worker ‖ *phr.* used in good-humoured or caustic annoyance to someone obstructing the view: *ist dein Vater ein ~?* your father wasn't a glazier, you make (*or* are) a better door than a window; *AmE* you know, it's hard to (*or* one can't) see through muddy water.

Glasscherbenhändler, *dial.* **Glasschermhandler** *m* -s/- *contp.* **1.** *hist.* (Bohemian) glassware pedlar: *contp.* hawker of trashy (*or* kitschy) glassware. → **2.** any destitute person: *colloq.* poor (old) devil, poor (old) tramp, *AmE also* bum.

Glasscherbenviertel, *dial.* **Glasschermviertel** *n* -s/- *colloq.* slum area of a city: Poverty Row, Skid Row *or* Road, *AmE also* gas-house district, hell's (half) acre, East Side, *in N.Y. City also* hell's kitchen; *er ist im ~ groß geworden* he was born on Poverty Row, *AmE also* ... on the wrong side of the tracks; *auch in dieser idyllischen Altstadt gibt es ein ~, in dem so manche Familie von der Fürsorge lebt* even this idyllic part of the town has its Poverty Row, where many a family is on welfare.

Glaubensbote *m* -n/-n *eccles.* missionary; *die ersten ~n in Bayern waren Wandermönche aus Irland und Schottland* the first heralds of Christianity in Bavaria were wandering Irish and Scottish friars.

gmaht *p.p.* [the unumlauted participle form, with vowel elision in the prefix, of StandG *mähen* 'to mow'] *dial.* said of grass, grain, etc.: mown ‖ *phr.* a pleased comment on an opportunity readily offering itself, or on a task that is easy to perform (conjuring up the picture of oneself strolling in comfort across a closely cut meadow, and not having to struggle through overgrown grass): *ein ~es Wiesl* (or *Wieserl*), *eine ~e Wiesn* a walkover, a pushover; *die Prüfung war ein ~es Wiesl* (also:) the exam was a cinch (*or,* was as easy as pie).

Gmoa... *dial.* [< 'rural *or* church community' (StandG *Ge-*

meinde) < MHG *gemeine* 'common (life of a rural or religious body of people)']: **~depp** *m* -en/pl. rare: -en **1.** *agr.* (*Dorfdepp*↑) village idiot. - **2.** *educ.* bottom boy (of the class), *AmE also* low man (*or*, bottom guy) on the totem pole. - **~stier** *m* -(e)s/pl. rare: -e **1.** *agr.* a potent breeding bull kept for service to the whole bovine community of the village or area: parish bull, town bull, village bull. - **2.** *hum.* or *contp.* a local man who has sex a lot and who thinks he is very good at it: parish bull, village stud, cock of the heap, *AmE also* stallion; *er moant, er is da der* ~ he reckons he's the cock-o'-the-walk in this place.

Goldene (rarely also **Güldene**) **Steig** *m* -n -es, L semita aurea [the epithet stands in praise of the lucrative business transacted through its existence; linguistically, G *golden* and *gülden*, as well as E *golden* and *gilded* (or *gilt*) are rival adjectives, both meaning 'made of gold', the latter variants, umlauted derivatives of the noun (ultimately stemming from Goth *gulþ* 'gold'), being much older] *transport hist.* "Golden Trail", for centuries a major trade link between Bavaria and Bohemia, with salt moving up and glassware down, all on the backs of heavily-laden sumpters (→ the related word *säumen*), some 1200 or 1300 such horses trotting their course every week around the middle of the sixteenth century; the route led from Passau by way of Röhrnbach, Waldkirchen and Leopoldsreuth, or by Röhrnbach, Freyung and Mauth, across the border to Prachatitz. - **Goldene Straße** *f* -n - *transport hist.* "Golden Road", a similar sobriquet for a slightly more recent line of trade communication, leading from Nuremberg via Weiden and Eger (now Ohře) to Prague.

Gottsackerjodler *m* -s/- mainly *joc.* = *Friedhofsjodler*.

Grammel *f* -/usu. pl. -n [< *gram(m)eln* 'to make a crunching noise (as when biting crisp bits of food)'] *cul.* (*Griebe*) a small bit of fat bacon rendered down: scrap, crackling; *ich* *weiß, ich sollte auf die Linie achten, aber ~n mag ich halt für mein Leben gern* I know I should be watching my waistline, but I just love eating scraps.

Grand *m* -(e)s/-e [< MHG *grant* 'trough'], also **Wassergrand** rural *archit.* an indestructible feature outside farmhouses as well as on pastures, to attract thirsty cattle: (stone) trough. - **Grandl** *n* -s/-(n) [dim. of the above], also **Wassergrandl** rural *archit.* a feature built into old farmhouse stoves of kitchen-ranges, to keep the inmates well supplied around the clock: hot-water tank.

greislich *adj* [of *Graus* '(feeling of) horror' two adjectival variants are of interest here - *grauslich* is preferred in Austria, and *gräuslich*, the umlauted form (today invariably showing dialectal unrounding of the diphthong), in Bavaria] *dial. colloq.* (*häßlich*) ugly, unsightly; *oft bleibt der ja wunderschön geschmückte Maibaum einige Jahre stehen, bis er halt „~" oder gar morsch geworden ist* often the maypole, beautifully decorated as it is, remains standing for a couple of years until, well, it isn't much to look at any more, or has even become rotten.

Griebelsuppe *f* -/-n *gastr.* in Franconia = *Kesselsuppe*.

großkopfert *adj* [-*ert* is the present-day conventional spelling of the suffix -*et*, the Bavarian, Franconian and Alemannic dialect variant of -*icht* 'being provided with', a common ending in the older stages of the language, but today found in StandG *töricht* 'foolish' only] *dial.* (1) *concr.* said of persons as well as animals: large-headed. - (2) *contp.* said of someone who has too high an opinion of his own importance: bigheaded. - **Großkopferte** *m*, with *adj decl.*: -n/-n *dial., contp.* a rich as well as influential person (who therefore often has an inflated opinion of himself): (self-important) bigwig (*or* bighead), AmE also swellhead, conceited ass.

grüabig, grüawig *adj* [< a fusion of two compound elements, in StandG *ge-* + *ruhig*] *dial.* **1.** said of time spent in an unhurried atmosphere (*geruhsam*): quiet, peaceful; *a ~er Tag* a day of restful peace; *an ~en Nachmittag verratschen* to spend a jolly good afternoon chatting. - **2.** said of an atmosphere, a person's home, etc. (*gemütlich*): easy-going, cosy, homey; *da herin find ich's fei ganz ~* I feel as snug as a bug in a rug in here; *jetzt wird's erst richtig ~* things are really getting nice and cosy now. - **3.** said of a person's placid disposition (*gutmütig*): good-natured, good-humoured, easy-going.

Grüabige, Grüawige *m* -n *dial.* (a person's) peace of mind; *in meinen vier Wänden hab ich meinen ~n* it suits me just about fine to be (*or*, I'm blissfully happy) within my four walls; *ich sag dir's* [*ich sag's enk*], *wir möchten unsern ~n habn* we want to be jolly well left in peace, I'm telling you; *der Bayer kriegt leicht einen Grant, wenn er seinen ~n nicht findet* a Bavarian soon gets his dander up if he doesn't find his bit of peace and quiet.

Grüabigkeit, Grüawigkeit *f* - jollification; *für den Bayern macht ~, also gemütlicher Spaß und Freude im Alltag, ein gut Teil seiner Lebensanschauung aus* to a Bavarian, jollification, in other words easy-going fun and enjoyment, forms a good part of his outlook on life.

Grummet, *dial.* **Groamat** *n* -s [< MHG *gruonmāt* 'green mowing': a spring meadow, when in flower, is a riot of colours, but a mid-summer or autumn meadow, by contrast, looks a uniform green] *agr.* (*letzter, oft dritter Heuschnitt*) the second or third crop of hay in the season: aftermath, *AmE also* rowen.

Gschaftl *n* -s/-(n) [dim. of *Geschäft* 'business' *colloq* little job; *vor lauter ~n nebenbei kommt man zu gar keiner richtigen Arbeit* all those jobbing twiddlybits on the side keep one from getting down to real work. - **~huber** *m* -s/- *colloq.*, slightly *contp.* (*Wichtigtuer*) meddlesome person: Jack-in-office, busybody, fusspot, *AmE also* fuss budget; *du bist mir ein ~!* you're a regular fusspot ‖ as a fictitious name: *Herr ~* Mr. Busyman, Meddlesome Mattie; *Frau ~* Mrs. Mixin. - **~huberei** *f* -/-en *colloq.*, slightly *contp.* fussiness, meddlesomeness.

gscheit, the syncopated *colloq.* variant of **gescheit** [< MHG *geschide* 'showing good judgment', 'discriminating', < MHG *schiden* 'to separate', 'to decide'] **1.** *adj* (1) of a person: clever; *er ist sehr ~ in Mathe* he's very good *or* clever at maths (*AmE* math). - (2) of a person: capable, skilled; *können Sie mir einen ~en Doktor sagen?* can you tell me the name of a good doctor? - (3) said of one's hunger or thirst: enormous, great; *ich hab einen ~en Hunger* I'm (as) hungry as a wolf, I could eat a horse. - (4) of time, a tool, etc.: suitable, convenient; *wäre fünf Uhr eine ~e Zeit?* would five o'clock be a good time? - (5) of food: plain and substantial; *zum Kesselfleisch gehört ein ~es Bauernbrot* pork titbits should be eaten with hunks of good farmhouse bread. - **2.** *adv* (1) conveniently; *wie kommt man am ~esten* (dial., *am ~er[e]n*) *nach ...?* which is the best way to ...? - (2) seriously, in earnest; *sag ~, ist er wirklich verheiratet?* joking apart, is he really married? - (3) badly; *das letzte Gipfelstück scheint ein paar der Kletterer ~ hergenommen zu haben* the summit climb seems to have taken it out of some of the climbers. - (4) in negative sentences, describing, often reproachfully, an excess of speed or other activity: *wie nicht ~* like mad, *BrE also* like the clappers; *er hat dann wie nicht ~ herumtelefoniert* he went to work making phone calls like mad ‖ → *busseln, pumpern*.

Gscheiterl, Gscheitl [dim. nouns formed from *gescheit*↑ (cp. *-erl*↑ and *-l*↓), **Gscheithaferl** [second el., < *Haferl*↓; thus, literally, 'one brimming over with conceitedness'] *n* -s/-(n) *colloq.* **1.** *hum.* said in praise, though sometimes in subtle mockery — capable person (*aufgeweckter [junger] Mensch*): cleverboots *sg.*, cleverclogs *sg.*, clevershins *sg.*, smart boy [girl], wizard, *NorBrE also* cleversides *sg.*; *ja, der Hansi ist unser ~ - wenn wir den nicht hätten!* why, Johnny is our clevershins - what would we do without him? - **2.** slightly *iron.* or *contp.* someone who annoys others by claiming to know everything and trying to sound clever (*Alleswisser*): know-all, smart aleck, smarty-pants *sg.*, smart-pants *sg.*, *BrE* clever dick, *AmE also* know-it-all, Mr. [Miss] Smarty, wise guy, wisenheimer; *er ist (und bleibt) halt ein ~* ah well, he thinks he has all the answers.

Gschwerl *n* -s [? < MHG (*ge*)*swer* 'ulcer'; or < *Schwirbel* 'heterogeneous group of people'; or < *Geschwei* 'male person, related through marriage' (*Schweher*, obsolete for 'father-in-law' + pejorative *-l*↓)] *dial.*, *contp.* a set or clique, some or all of them distantly related, for whom the speaker has little respect: breed of pups, bunch, crew, gang, tribe; *ein ~ Gassenbuben* a bunch of guttersnipes (*AmE also* ... gutter bums); *das ganze ~ kann mir gestohlen bleiben* I can't be bothered with the whole lot (*or*, all this riffraff), *AmE also* I have no use for the whole kit and caboodle.

Gspusi ['kʃpuːzɪ], variously spelt **G'spusi**, **Gschpusi**, **Gespusi**, *n* -(s)/- [< *Gespons m hum.* 'bridegroom', 'husband' < L *sponsus* 'fiancé'] *colloq.*, often slightly *iron.* **1.** regular boy [girl] friend: flame, heartthrob; *ist sie dein ~?* is she your sweet thing (*AmE also* ... your cuddlebug)?; *der Hans ist ein verflossenes ~ von mir* Jack's an old flame of mine. - **2.** a sexual relationship between two people not married to each other, esp. one that lasts for some time: affair, steady flirt; *sie hat mit dem besten Freund ihres Mannes ein ~* she's having an affair with her husband's best friend; *die haben schon jahrelang ein munteres ~ (miteinand[er])* theirs has been a steady whirl for years; *er hat alle zwei Wochen mit einer anderen ein ~* he goes with a different girl every other week; *fang dir mit der kein ~ an* don't you go and give that one a whirl.

Gstanzl [k-] *n* -s/-n [*g(e)*-, a collective prefix often elided in Bavarian, and the dim. suffix -*l* here surround and aptly modify the base -*stanz*- (< LateL *stantia* 'stay', 'habitation', which [as a loan translation < Arabic *bait* 'room'] in once Arab-occupied Sicily combined the meanings of 'room' and 'verse')] *mus.* (*neckender Vierzeiler*) a popular rhyming couplet, broken into four lines in print, often improvised and usu. making teasing fun of someone: merry ditty (*or* jingle).
- **~singen** *n* -s *mus.* communal singing of ditties (which, if strung together in a give and take, can readily become a lively contest of infectious banter and mirth):

Die Zwölfhäusler Menscher,	*A Zwölfhäusl lassie
die ham an schen Gang,	Has legs fine and gay:
mit oan Fuaß tean s' mahn	One does the mowing,
und mi'm andern heign s' zam.	The other makes hay.

ha [hə] *dial. interj* **1.** a rather impolite interrogative utterance wishing someone to repeat what he or she has just said (corresponding to StandG *wie bitte?*): eh [eɪ]; A: *mir ist kalt!* B: *~?* A: *kalt is ma, hab i gsagt!* A: I'm cold! B: eh? (*BrE also* y' what?) A: I said I'm cold! - **2.** a curt manner of asking someone to agree (corresponding to StandG *nicht wahr?*): eh, huh [hʌ]; *des taugt doch, ~?* that'll do, huh?

haa *interj* [< OHG *hweo* 'which way?'; related to E *how?*] low *colloq.* a rude way of demanding repetition of a word or phrase one has failed, or ostensibly failed, to understand: eh [eɪ]?, whazzat [< what's that]?

Hadern [-ɔː-] *m* -s/- [< MHG *hader* < OHG *hadara*] *colloq.* **1.** (1) (*Lumpen*) rag; *der Gassenbub kommt in ~ daher* the street urchin is dressed (all) in rags. - (2) ([*Putz-*]*Lumpen*) cleaning rag; *hol mir einen Öl~* get me a piece of oily rag. - (3) *second comp. el.* of its former frequency, in that position, of denoting specific items of linen (e.g., *Hand~* towel; *Prang~* cuff, wristband; *Rüssel~* napkin), only two are left in actual use today; they, with a third one, all meaning 'handkerchief', can be arranged on a scale from light to blunt coarseness of expression: *Schneuztuch* nose wipe(r), nose clout; *Schneuzhadern* noserag, *AmE* also blower, blow rag; *Rotzhadern* snotrag. - **2.** *contp.* (*leichtes Mädchen*) loose(-living) woman: good-time girl, *NorBrE* flighty faggot.

Hadernmann [-ɔː-] *m* -(e)s/...männer *or* ...leute *colloq.* a man who travels about, buying and selling cheap things such as old clothes and old furniture: rag-and-bone man, ragman.

Hafen [-ɔː-] *m* -s/Häfen [< MHG *haven* 'large earthenware or cast-iron pot'] (cooking) pot; *irdener ~* earthenware *or* stoneware pot, crock ‖ *colloq. phr.* (1) a vile remark on a person who squints badly: *der schaut mit einmal in neun Häfen hinein* he looks nine (*or* forty) ways for (*or* to find) Sunday. - (2) a piece of tongue-in-cheek consolation for an old maid: *jeder ~ findet seinen Deckel - auch ein alter, wenn er seine Löcher nicht weist* *there is (bound to be) a lid for every pot - even for one with holes in it, if the holes aren't showing.

Haferl [-aː-] *n* -s/-(n) [*dim. of* Hafen↑] *colloq.* **1.** (sturdy little) pot, sometimes made of enamelled metal, but most often of earthenware or porcelain: mug; *trink dein ~ Tee aus* (or *fer-*

tig)! drink up your mug of tea ‖ as a second compound element: **Kaffee~** coffee cup; **Milch~** milk jug; → *Nachthaferl*. - **2.** *colloq.* an imaginary mug, one of many such fictitious objects for which unsuspecting and gullible mortals, esp. children, are sent for as a practical joke: *geh, hol mir ein ~ Igelsamen* go and get (*or* fetch) me a pint of pigeon's milk (*or* a bagful of bumblebee feathers, *or*, BrE *also*, a yard of pump-water). - **3.** *prov.* (1) a consolatory wisdom telling us that everyone gets a mate in the end: (*ein*) *jedes ~ hat* (or *kriegt*) *seinen Deckel* every Jack must have his Jill, every Johnny will get his Joan. - (2) a graceful comment, usu. made in the presence of the mother concerned, on beauty being hereditary: *schöne ~(n) geben schöne Scherben* *the comeliness of the parent is mirrored in the offspring. - (3) a rather unfair tease according to which a small person is claimed to be more easily angered than a tall one: *kleine ~(n) laufen* (or *gehen*) *leicht über* a little pot is soon hot. - (4) a reproachful taunt directed at one who expects his wishes to be fulfilled without delay: *du brauchst ja bloß sagen „~" - nachher ist die Wurst auch schon drin!* *all you've got to do is command, "Pot, be filled!", and in pops the sausage for you. - (5) a considered opinion that, in a contentious issue, two quarrelers, often a married couple, are likely to share the blame: *der eine hat das ~ zerbrochen, der andere das Schüsserl* *one has gone and broken the pot, and the other one the dish; 'tis six of one and half-a-dozen of the other.

Haferl...: ~fest *n* -(e)s/pl. rare: -e *hist. folklore* held until the 1970s at Ilzstadt, a northern suburb of Passau, along the banks of the River Ilz: "Potters' Parade", a popular one day festival in August, originally organized by the members of that guild. - **~gucker** *m* -s/pl. rare: - *hum.* an inquisitive male, most often a member of the family, who takes a quick and rather stealthy look at what is being prepared by the cook:

nosy lift-lid, (pot-and-pan) pokenose, (old) snoopie (among the saucepans), *AmE also* kitchen kibitzer. - ~**schuh** *m* -s/usu. pl.: -e [hardly, as has once been suggested, < E *half-shoe*, but rather implying a jocular comparison to a *Haferl*↑] a sturdy walking shoe with a fringed tongue: brogue [brɔʊg]. - ~**sprung** *m* -(e)s/...sprünge *skiing* a jump done in a crouching position which, with the skis parallel, yet shoulder-width apart, eases the impact of the touchdown through the springy give of the man's knees: "potty-squat" (jump).

Haftelmacher *m* -s/- [first el., *Haftel n* 'hook', part of a two-piece clothes fastening the manufacture of which once required special care and attention to detail] *obs.* except in the *colloq. phr.* both preserving the occupational name, 'hook-maker', and honouring the ticklish nature of the man's work: *aufpassen* or *achtgeben* (*müssen*) *wie ein* ~ (to have) to keep one's eyes peeled *or* skinned; *wir müssen jetzt aufpassen wie die* ~, *daß wir die Ausfahrtstafel nicht übersehen* we now must keep our eyes peeled we don't miss the exit sign.

Hakelstecken, less correctly also **Hack(e)lstecken** *m* -s/- [first el., *Hakel n* 'curved end of a [walking] stick', used to retrieve objects or to suspend objects from] largely *hist.* **1.** walking staff (*or* stick), the frequent companion of a countryman, useful also as a retrieving device and a defensive weapon. - **2.** packstaff, slung over one's shoulder when carrying a burden suspended from its crooked end.

Note: According to some etymologists, the English analogue of our *Hakelstecken* lives on in the popular simile *as plain as a pikestaff*, meaning 'anything obvious and easy to understand': the pikestaff, it is presumed, was originally the packstaff used by pedlars on which they carried their pack, and which was worn "plain" (or smooth) from continual use.

Halbe *f* -/-(n) *bev.* (*eine halbe Maß* [*Bier*]) half a litre (E approx.: a [sizeable] pint) of beer; *eine ~ um die andre trinken* to have one beer after another; *trinken wir noch eine ~?* shall we have another half?; *er* (dial. *der*) *sitzt stundenlang vor einer einzigen ~n* he can nurse his one pint a whole evening; *er* (dial. *der*) *hat schon einen* (dial. *an*) *Rausch, wenn er eine ~ Bier sieht* even the smell of beer fumes is enough to make him drunk; a rhymed warning by Eugen Roth:

Auf Pille nicht noch Salbe hoff, wer täglich dreizehn Halbe soff
No physic breaks the bond of fears of one who's grown too fond of beers.

KARL STIELER
A Halbe und a Maß

I kimm auf d' Post 'nein: - „Guat'n Ab'n,
A frische Halbe möcht i hab'n."
„Was?" sagt die Kellnerin und geht,
„A Halbe - schaamen S' Ihna net?
Da roas' i nit zum Faß deszwegen,
Z'erst warten S', bis S' a Ganze mögen."

Pint and Quart

My mark's the "Post" pub. "Luv', what cheer,
Gi' us a frothy pint of beer."
"What?", scowls the waitress dour of face.
"A pint, Ah tell ya 's a disgrace,
Mon. Tappin' that's not worth the trouble -
You bide until yer thirst's grown double."

Hallodri *m* -s/-(s) [< Gr *allótria* 'mischief', 'tomfoolery' < Gr *allótrios* 'extrinsic', 'not belonging to the body'] **1.** *contp.* a reckless, workshy, and morally depraved adult male: ne'er-do-well. - **2.** slightly reproachful, but usu. *hum.* (then often marked by downtoning attributes like *kleiner, na so ein,* etc.) for a trouble-making but usu. playful child: scamp, *BrE* scallywag, *AmE* scalawag.

halt *adv* [< MHG & OHG *halt* 'rather', an old comparative without ending, originally meaning 'more inclined' (since related to G *Halde* 'incline', 'slope')] *colloq.* an always unstressed sentence modifier that well fits the mental pattern of the unobtrusive, but also reticent and rather phlegmatic; it tends to beg questions, makes utterances less harsh and keen (and also less precise), conceding points to one's interlocutor and, in turn, wishing to have one's own peace and privacy respected (*eben, wohl, nun einmal*): just, simply; *ja mei, so ist es ~ (einmal)* ah well, that's the way it is; *wir müssen's ~ probieren* we'll just have a try; *ich bin ~ dumm und bleib's auch, was kannst (du) da machen?* I am a fool, and I'll stay one - there's nowt you can do about it; A: *warum magst du nicht?* B: *so ~!* A: why don't you want to? B: just because.

handsam *adj* [a classic case of "false friends": G *handsam* and E *handsome* are made up of identical structural elements - *Hand*: hand, *-sam*: -some ('like', 'same') - but in composition their meanings differ widely, the latter among others denoting a 'good-looking' man, a 'strong-looking' woman, and a 'large' reward] *colloq.* **1.** of a format, tool, etc. (*handlich*): easy to handle, handy, convenient. - **2.** of a human being or an animal (*gut zu haben*): easy to manage, manageable, docile, gentle.

Hartschier, rarely **Hatschier** *m* -(e)s/-e [< It *arciere* 'bowman (on horseback)'; akin to E *archer*] *mil. hist.* on duty at the Royal Household: soldier (*or* member) of the mounted bodyguard; *die ~e des Königs (von Bayern)* the King (of Bavaria)'s Guards *pl.*

Ha**usl** *m* -s/-(n) [< *Haus* '(public) house' + *-l*↓] *colloq.* (*Hausknecht, Hausmeister*) a boy or man, usu. big and muscular, who does practical work in an inn or hotel: houseman, *AmE also* houseboy, *BrE also* boots *pl.*

Hau**terer** *m* -s/- [see *-erer*] *colloq.*, often *contp.* skinny person: (one [who is] all bones *or* ribs, *contp.* rattlebones, skinnymalink; said of an emaciated labourer considered unfit to do any heavy work: *mit dem alten ~ ist nimmer viel los* that old bag of skin (and bone[s]) is past making the fur (*or* the sparks) fly.

Hạ**x** *m* gen. rare: -es/-(e)n *dial.* = *Hax(e)n*. - **H**ạ**xe** *f* -/-n, *dial.* **H**ạ**x(e)n** *f* -/- [? < Germ. **hanhsenawō* 'sinew to suspend a slaughtered animal from'; cp. OE *hōhsinu* 'hamstring'] **1.** *zo.* (*Hachse*) (a quadruped's) lower leg. - **2.** *cul.* as an item of food, used in compounds only, to specify the customer's wish: *Kalbs*⁓ knuckle of veal; *Schweins*⁓ knuckle of pork, trotter. - **H**ạ**x(e)n** *m* -(s)/- *dial.*, *anat.* (*Bein*) (human) leg; *mei ~ tuat ma weh* me leg hurts; (*ja) mei, hat die ~!* (oh) my, ain't she got some legs! ‖*fig. phr.* graphically describing the fact that someone makes every possible effort to be helpful: *sich die ~ ausreißen* to bend over backwards, to lay oneself out, to break (*AmE also* to bust) an arm *or* leg *or* a gut; *Dick Neuheisl (auszusprechen: Njuheisl), der Präsident des Freundeskreises Tempe-Regensburg, hat sich fast die ~ ausgerissen, um den „Domspatzen" den Aufenthalt in der Partnerstadt möglichst angenehm zu gestalten* Dick Neuheisl (pronounced [ˈnjuːhaɪzl]), the president of the Tempe-Regensburg Circle of Friends, just about bust an arm to make the "Cathedral Sparrows'" stay in their twin town as enjoyable as possible.

Hei**mgarten** *m* -s/pl. rare: ...gärten, with its popular *dial.* variants **H**oi**garte** *m* -n/pl. rare: - (Allgäu) and **H**oa**gart([e]n)** *m* -/pl. rare. - (Lower Bavaria) as well as **H**oa**gascht** *m* (s)/pl.

rare: - (Upper Bavaria) [faintly reminiscent of old peasant pride in troubled times: the man of the soil was as capable of, and jealously insistent on, staging festive occasions in his "home garden" as was the lord in his manor house or palace] *folklore* a friendly informal meeting in the evening of (usu. young) country folk, who engage in local chitchat, song and dance at one of the farms in the vicinity; as so often after the Second World War, the custom has been partly exploited for commercial ends: cosy get-together, social do (*AmE* to-do), *IrE* ceilidh ['keɪlɪ].

heimliche Hauptstadt *f* -n - *sobr.* "the unofficial Capital", i.e. Munich; the nickname has originated in the fact that Munich is not only a far larger cultural centre than Bonn, but also far more central, and that Munich, as the "city of one's dreams", is the fastest growing metropolis in Germany.

helfgott to a relative or friend, also **helfdirgott** *interj* to someone who sneezes (*Gesundheit!*): [God] bless you!

Helle *n* -n/-n *bev.* light (*or* pale) ale, *BrE also* lager; *ein (Glas) ~s, bitte!* one (glass of) light beer, please. ‖ a word on measures, and a gentle warning: *wen es nach Bier lüstet, der verlangt als übliche Menge „eine Halbe" (1/2 l) oder „ein kleines ~s" (1/4 l); bei dessen Bestellung von männlicher Seite aber zucken die Gesichtsmuskeln einer urbayerischen Kellnerin freilich wohl etwas verächtlich zusammen* whoever hankers after beer, the customary measure asked for is "a half" (i.e., half a litre, or 0.88 pint) or "a small light" (i.e., a quarter of a litre, or 0.44 pint); if the latter order comes from the lips of a male, though, the facial muscles of a proper Bavarian waitress may well give a twitch of faint disdain.

heraußen *adv* (*hier außen*) out here, outside (here); *das Wetter ist so schön, wir könnten eigentlich genausogut ~ auf der Terrasse essen* the weather is so nice we might as well have our meal out here on the terrace (*or*, on the patio).

herinnen *adv* ([*hier*] *drinnen*) in here, indoors; ~ *ist es gemütlicher als draußen*, dial. ~ *is*[*t's*] *grüabiger als wia draußn* it's cosier (*AmE* cozier) in here than outside (*or*, ... indoors than out).

Herzepopperl, Herzipopperl *n* -s/-n [second el., dim. of *Puppe*, in baby talk *Poppa* 'doll'] *apprec.* usu. preceded by *mei(n)* a doll or a small child one is very fond of: (my) ducky darling, lovey-dovey, popsy-wopsy.

Herz...: **~kasperl** [-ʃp-] *m* -s/-(n) *med. colloq.* the impersonation of a cardiac infarction (*Herzinfarkt*), which suddenly lays low its victims, much like volatile *Kasperl*↓ of pantomime fame who, when in the mood, strikes down his opponents with a slapstick: heart attack, coronary; *ihn hat der ~ geholt, er hat den ~ gekriegt* he's had a heart attack. - **~kasten** *m* -s *colloq.*, sometimes *contp.*, a term used by males and females alike — large female breasts: boobs, knockers, melons; *mei, die hat dir ein Trumm ~!* wow, what a pair of headlights she's got!, *BrE* also my, she's well out in front! - **~zeug** *n* -s *colloq.* a term used by males and females alike — large female breasts: boobs; *mit dem Hammel tanz ich nicht gern, der flackt sich so auf mein ~ nauf* I don't fancy dancing with that bum, he just about crushes my boobs.

Heu *n* -(e)s [< MHG *höu(we)* < OHG *houwi*, literally, 'what is (to be) hewed down'] **1.** *agr.* (1) hay, i.e. grass which has been cut and dried. - (2) in a narrower sense: the first crop of hay, usu. harvested in June (cp. *Grummet*). ‖ *phr.* (1) ~ *machen* = *heuen*. - (2) *colloq. ins ~ gehen* to go haymaking; *wir gehen heute ins ~* we're haymaking today. - **2.** *fig. phr.* graphically exemplifying the fact that two persons are of divergent mentalities: *sie* (colloq., *die*) *haben das ~ nicht im gleichen Stadel* they don't talk the same language, they don't see eye to eye, they're not on the same wavelength, *IrE* also they don't dig with the same foot ‖ if said by the speaker

making his own point clear: he [she] is not my cup of tea.
Heu... *agr.*: **⁓baum** *m* -(e)s/...bäume (*Wiesbaum*) a long pole to weigh down a cart-load [*Fuder*] of hay (cp. *Heuseil*): hayboom, hay-pole, binder. - **⁓boden** *m* -s/...böden hayloft.

heuen, *dial.* **haign**, **heugn** [< MHG *höuwen*] *agr. v/i* to make hay, *AmE also* to hay ‖ *prov.* a piece of advice to use one's chances while conditions are favourable: ~ *muß man, wenn die Sonne scheint* (or, in dialect, *wann's Heuwetter is*) make hay while the sun shines. - **Heuen** *n* -s = *Heumachen*.

Heu... *agr.*: **⁓ernte** *f* -/-n, *dial.* **Heuet** *m* -s/-e; *f* -/-e; **Heugert** *n* -s/-e **1.** hay harvest; *zweite* ~ aftermath, second crop of hay. - **2.** (*Erntezeit*) haymaking time *or* season. - **⁓geige** *f* -/-n **1.** a high wooden structure with parallel bars (resembling the strings on a violin), for drying grass or clover: hay rack. - **2.** *fig., colloq.* and often *iron.* a tall, lanky person, usu. female: beanpole, lamppost, long drink (of water), *BrE also* beanstalk, *AmE also* clothes pole, string bean. - **⁓hupfer** *m* -s/- *colloq.* **1.** *zo.* (*Heuhüpfer*) grasshopper. - **2.** *fig., hum.* or *iron.* a tall and slender young man: skinnymalink, Harry Longlegs *sg.* - **⁓machen** *n* -s haymaking; *die Bauersleute waren schon beim* ~ the farm people were already scything the hay crop down. - **⁓ochs** *m* -en/-en [actually, 'hay-eating ox'] low *colloq.* a stupid, strong fellow: bonehead, numskull; *er ist ein* ~, *wie er im Buch steht* he's all brawn and no brain(s). - **⁓raufe** *f* -/-n hayrack. - **⁓reuter** *m* -s/- (*Heureiter*) a tripod for drying hay and clover (cp. *Heugeige* 1): hay prop, rickstand. - **⁓schober** *m* -s/- a large pile of hay gathered, usu. outdoors, for storing (*Heumiete*): haystack, hayrick. - **⁓schreck** *m* -s/-en *zo., colloq.* (*Heuschrecke*) = *Heuhupfer* 1. - **⁓seil** *n* -(e)s/-e hay rope, tied front and aft, to keep the boom (*Heubaum*↑) in place on the cart-load of hay. - **⁓stadel** *m* -s/- a small log structure away out in the meadows, to store hay for winter use: hay-hut, hay chalet. - **⁓stock** *m* -s/...stöcke haymow. -

~wagen *m* -s/- haywaggon (*AmE* haywagon), *BrE* also haycart. - **~wetter** *n* -s good weather for making hay ‖ for its proverbial use, see under *heuen*.

Himmiherrgotzaggramentzefixallelujamilextamarschscheißglumpfaregtz *interj.* a string of uncouth dial. curses, run together for aural and visual effect, to be found on car stickers: = *goshalmightysakesalivegloryshovitshitpissandcorruption.

<blockquote>
Here is a light-hearted gem in verse by Karl Stieler (1842-1885) on how some speech mannerisms can become so deeply ingrained that we are not aware of them any more:

's Fluachn

Der Vata is ganz ausanand:
„Wia mei Bua fluacht, dös is a Schand!
Mei Wei fluacht nit, und i fluach nit.
Und grad der Bua, der gibt koan Fried!
Der Himmiherrgottsakra, der -
Wo hat jetzt der dös Fluachn her?"

Swearin'

Dad puckers up his worried face:
"My lad's foul tongue's sure a disgrace!
The wife don't swear, an' swear don't I;
It's just that lad won't give a try!
God damn it, bloody hell - now where
Did that young devil larn to swear?"
</blockquote>

Hinter...: **~glasmalerei** *f - folklore* & *art* **1.** under-glass painting, a rustic technique of decorating glass in which the back is painted or gilded so that the ornamental pattern can be seen from the front. → **2.** -/-n (*Hinterglasbild*) gilt glass, F verre églomisé, a product of that art. - **~huglharpfing**, **~mondschein** *n* -s/pl. rare: -e *hum.* an imaginary place-name or area suggestive of rural simplicities (see also under *Niederschnarchlfing*↓): *BrE* Much-Binding-in-the-Marsh, Loamshire, *AmE* Appleknockerton, Clodville, Clucktown, Gooseneck, Podunk, Pumpkin Hollow, Rabbit Ridge.

Hirn... *colloq.*: ~**batzerl**; more matter-of-factly, ~**batzl** *n* -s/-(n) [the gestural roundedness of one finger and the thumb forming a Q, and the follow-up catapult motion combine to suggest the heavy lumpiness of a small projectile, which is at the semantic basis of *Batzl*↑, the second element of the compound] *body language* a playful or reproachful flick aimed at the forehead of a (usu. young) person with one's bent forefinger or middle finger; the finger is tensed against the inner top joint of the thumb, and then released with some force (*Stirnknips*): finger flick, finger nudgie. - ~**brandig** *adj* = *hirnverbrannt*. - ~**kastl** *n* -s/-(n) [second el., dim. of *Kasten* 'chest'] sometimes *hum.* the human skull as housing man's intelligence: brain-box, *AmE also* old bean, think tank, upper story; *ja geht denn das gar net in dein ~ 'nein?* can't you ever get this into your thick skull? - ~**rissig** *adj* outrageously foolish: crack-brained; *ein ~er Vorschlag* a lunatic proposal; *der tut ja ganz ~ NorBrE* he's going on as if he were cut in the head. - ~**schmalz** *n* -es another concrete visualization of something impalpable - *Schmalz* 'lard', 'grease' (cp. *Irxenschmalz*↓, *Muskelschmalz*↓), in simple folk belief, obviously being a proper nourishment for brawn a n d brain (*praktische Intelligenz*): gumption, what it takes (to get along), *AmE also* milk in the coconut; *~ haben* to have a head on one's shoulders, to have (plenty of) stuff on the ball. - ~**verbrannt**, *dial.* ~**verbrennt** *adj* [literally, 'having one's brains destroyed by fire'] stupid: cockeyed, crazy; *ist das wieder eine von deinen ~en Ideen?* is this another one of those cockeyed (*AmE vulg. sl. also* half-assed) ideas of yours?

Hochzeitlader *m* -s/pl. rare: - *folklore* = *Hochzeitslader*↓.

Hochzeits... *folklore* [these compounds still testify to the presence, though now on the wane, of two quaint prenuptial customs in rural areas]: **~lader** *m* -s/pl. rare: - (*Hochzeitsbitter*) bride's messenger; *der ~, niederbayerisch „Prog(r)oder" genannt, geht mit geschmücktem Hut und Stock herum und bittet dabei mitunter an die zwölf Dutzend Gäste zur Festlichkeit* the bride's messenger, known as "proctor" in Lower Bavaria, festively adorned with hat and wedding staff, duly makes the round, at times bidding some twelve dozen guests to attend the celebration. - **~schmuser** *m* -s/pl. rare: - *colloq.* (*Heiratsvermittler*) marriage broker: matchmaker.

Hoftrauer *f* - [actually, court mourning, i.e. the conventional manifestation of sorrow for the death of a member of the ruling house, shown esp. by the wearing of black garments and of black mourning-bands, as well as the hanging of flags at half-mast] also simply **Trauer** *f* - *colloq.* in a *hum.* phrase to, or of, one who has a dirty edge to one or to all his fingernails: ~ *haben* (or *tragen*) to be in court mourning, to have a mourning-band; *du hast* (or *trägst*) ~*!* you're in mourning for the cat.

Holzkirchener Wallfahrt zum Bogenberg *f* -/no pl. *relig.* & *folklore* a two-day Whitsun procession from Holzkirchen, a village south-southeast of Vilshofen, across the Danube to Deggendorf, and then to its end destination, a renowned place of Marian worship, on the next day: "Holzkirchen Pilgrimage to Bogenberg Hill", a time-honoured annual custom, observed with almost uninterrupted regularity since 1492, according to which an enormous wooden candle (→ *Pfingstkerze*) is carried the whole way, and during the final ascent in an upright position by only one man; the tradition arose from a conflict with the then recently converted Protestant Counts of Ortenburg, against whom the devout Holzkirchen Catholics thus conspicuously asserted their old faith.

Hölzl *n* -s/-(n) [< *Holz* 'wood' (in both senses) + -l↓] *colloq.* **1.** (1) a very little stick, short and thin, often dry and broken off from a branch: tiny little bit (*or*, piece) of wood; *geh, wirf dem Käferl ein ~ ins Wasser, vielleicht kann er draufkrabbeln* go and throw the (poor) little beetle a bit of wood into the water for it to scramble up (to safety) on. - (2) *fig.* said of an examiner or interrogator: *j-m ein ~ werfen* to make a helpful suggestion to the person examined: (a) to give somebody a leg up, to lend somebody a hand; (b) to jog somebody's memory, to give somebody's memory a prod. - **2.** a small wood of trees or bushes, often found as a second place-name element, e.g. in *Kapuzinerhölzl* (e.g., in Munich's Nymphenburger Park): copse, coppice.

Hopfen, *dial.* **Hopf** *m* -s/no pl. *bot.* hops ‖ some current proverbial lore of the Hallertau, north-west of Landshut, the third-largest hop-growing area in the world: (1) the delicate plant, which is trained to climb along the slanting wires of trellises some 30 feet high, is often subject to mildew, blight, and other diseases, the prevention of which keeps farmers busy from early April until late August, when harvesting begins: *der ~ will täglich seinen Herrn sehen* *the hops want to see their master every day, *hop flowers want attendance danced upon them every day. - (2) besides, world market prices tend to fluctuate and may play havoc with man's "best laid schemes": *der Hopf ist ein Tropf* *hops are wayward crops.

Hopfen...: **~anbau** *m* -(e)s hop cultivation, hop growing; *wollten wir den ~ in England und in Bayern miteinander vergleichen, dann sollten wir Kent und die Hallertau ausgiebig durch-*

streifen if we were to make a comparative study of hop growing in England and in Bavaria, we should be well-advised to go on an extensive ramble through Kent, and the Hallertau, respectively. - ~**pflücker** *m* -s/- hop-picker, *BrE also* hopper. - ~ **schmuser** *m* -s/- *econ.*, *colloq.* (*Hopfenaufkäufer*) buyer-up of hops (usu. acting merely as the wholesale trader's assistant, who is engaged in the verbal preliminaries [hence, *Schmuser↓*] of the transaction). - ~**stange** *f* -/-n **1.** *bot.*, largely *hist.* a slender pole of spruce-wood, up to some 16 feet tall, for training a hop-seed along: hop-pole. - **2.** *colloq.*, often *hum.* or slightly *sarc.* tall, lanky person: bean-pole, beanstalk, lamppost; *das ist dir eine zaundürre ~!* there's a gangling lathlegs for you!, *NorBrE also* he [she]'s all legs and wings. ‖ → *zaundürr*. - ~**zupfen** *n* -s *agr.*, *colloq.* and *obsolescent* (since now often no longer done by hand) hop-picking: hopping. - ~**zupfer** *m* -s/-, ~**zupferin** *f* -/-nen *agr.*, *colloq.* and *obsolescent* hop-picker: hopper.

hoppala *interj* [< *hoppa*, the beginning of a famous jog-along knee song which makes the 'horseman' tumble down (or, as an English ditty of that genre has it, go 'bumpety-bump') + the echoic nursery suffix *-la*] in adult speech only **1.** a little gasp of surprise when stumbling, dropping something, or making a mistake; and used in lieu of an apology when accidentally brushing past or bumping into a person: whoops, oops(-a-daisy)! - **2.** a sympathetic catchphrase to a child that has knocked its head or falls over: boomps-a-daisy!

Hörndlbauer *m* -n/-n [first el., dim. of *Horn* 'horn', one of a pair, on the heads of cattle] *agr.*, *colloq.* (*Viehzüchter*) [opp. *Körndlbauer↓*]) cattle *or* beef farmer.

Hosentürl *n* -s/-(n) [second el., dim. of *Tür* 'door'] *colloq. hum.* (*Hosenschlitz*) fly (of [the] trousers): shop door ‖ *phr.* (1) in a warning to a male friend or relative, seeing that his trousers are unbuttoned: *du hast das ~ offen!*, *das ~ steht* [*dir*] *offen!* your shop door is open, your secret interests are in evidence, *AmE also* (depending on the number of fly buttons undone:) it's one [two, *etc.*] o'clock (at the waterworks), Johnny's out of jail. - (2) in a witticism given rise to by Prince Luitpold, the aged Regent of Bavaria, 1821-1912, who during a shooting party happened to reveal an awkward sartorial irregularity, which a junior hunting assistant tried to deal with in his own way: *Königliche Hoheit, halten zu Gnaden, wie wär's, wenn wir jetzt alle unser ~ zumachen?* Your Royal Highness, with your gracious permission, what about all of us now having a go at getting our shop doors shut?

hott *interj* [related to *hotzen* 'to run', 'to start moving' and to Czech *choditi* 'to walk'] a shout to a draught animal, usu. a horse, to turn right (cp. *wüst*): come out, gee back [dʒiː ˈbak], *ScotE* hop, gee (about) [dʒiː (əˈbuːt)].

hundig, hundselendig *adv* [ex the proverbial *Hundeleben*, or 'dog's life' (with its frequent vagrancy, and rejection by human beings), many such quadrupeds were condemned to lead in past centuries] *colloq.* said of, and more often even by, a person who is in a wretched state of health: miserable [miserably]; *seitdem ich mir den Husten geholt hab, geht's mir ganz ~* ever since I caught this cough, I've been feeling like death warmed up.

Hundling *m* -s/-e [in both G and E, the suffix *-ling* often adds a depreciative nuance to the person or quality denoted by the root - cp. Dichter*ling*, Schreiber*ling*, Weich*ling*, and author*ling*, squire*ling*, soft*ling*, respectively], less often **Hundlinger**

m -s/- *colloq.*, said in contempt, yet occasionally with an admixture of admiration for somebody who is clever in cheating ([*durchtriebener*] *Spitzbube*): tricky customer, slyboots *sg.*, AmE also slick *or* smooth article, con artist, sharp operator; *schau zu, wie du mit dem zurechtkommst, das ist ein ~!* be careful how you deal with him, he's a tricky customer (*or*, ... he's a sharp one).

hundselendig *adv* = *hundig.*

Hunds...: ~tapperer *m* -s/- [second el., < EarlyModHG *tappe* < MHG *tāpe* 'paw' + reduplicative noun suffix *-erer*↑; cp. E *to tap* 'to strike lightly', prob. an independent imit. formation similar to *flap, rap, slap*] *colloq.* a simple swimming stroke in which the legs are kicked while the arms make short quick movements up and down in the water like the front legs of a swimming dog: dog paddle, doggy paddle. - **~viech** *n* -(e)s/-er [second el., → *Viech*] low *colloq.* & *vulg.* — *contp.* for any dog whose specific behaviour, or mere presence, makes the speaker flare up in virulent abuse: *BrE* bloody (awful) dog, *AmE* goddamn bonecrusher (*or* fleabag).

Hupferer *m* -s/- [< *Hupfer* 'jump', one of the many words with a reduplicative ending (see *-erer*↑)] *colloq.* the act of bouncing up briefly, and often repeatedly: (kangaroo) jump ‖ *mot.* the typical bounce a motorcar is forced to make by the driver releasing the clutch too fast when stepping on the gas: *das Auto hat einen ~ gemacht* the car gave a jerk, *or* ... a (kangaroo) jump.

Hutzel... *colloq.*: **~brot** *n* -(e)s/-e *bak.* bread made, usu. for special occasions, from rye-meal and containing an assortment of dried fruit such as pears, apples, plums, raisins and figs: fruit bread, spiced currant bread; *ein ~* a fruit loaf. - **~weib** *n* -(e)s/-er (*altes Weiblein voller Runzeln*) wizened *or* wrinkled old woman.

☞ **I** ☜

Infaulẹnza *f* - [a nonce word based on *Influenza*, showing internal switch in the second syllable from *-flu-* to *-faul-*, to give the whole a meaningful twist. Similarly, in the first English equivalent the original basis is, of course, *undulant*, undulant or Malta fever being an 'infection with bacteria frequently causing abortions in animals and remittent fever in man'] *hum.* an imaginary illness lazy pupils are said to put on in order to escape unpleasant consequences: indolent fever, spring fever, (a dose of) lazyitis.

Ịrxen, Ịrxn, in the northern Upper Palatinate **Öißn** *f* -/- [the common, if unetymological, spellings of *Iaksn*, < MHG *üehse*] *dial.* (*Achsel*[*höhle*]) shoulder, armpit; *unter* (or *in*) *der* ~ under the armpit. - **~schmalz** *n* -es/no pl. *colloq.*, often *hum.* **1.** muscular energy, *colloq.* elbow grease, *AmE also* axle grease; *da brauchst schon ein ~ dazu!* it'll take (you) some elbow grease to do that!, *AmE also* that'll take some axle grease!; *die Burschen des Dorfes machen es sich zur Ehre, den Maibaum nach Urväterart, nur mit „~", unter Verzicht auf technisches Gerät, aufzustellen* following the tradition of their forefathers, the young men of the village consider it an act of honour to put up their maypole relying only on pure brawn and elbow grease, thus shirking the use of any technical tools. - **2.** *fig.* said of a dialect or slang that is marked by vitality and virile strength: pep, go; *das Bairische hat ein ~* (the) Bavarian (dialect) is full of vim and vigour.

J

Jackel..., **Jackl...**, also **Jaggl...** [< *Jakob*, a once popular Christian name in Bavaria, + dim. *-l*↓; English has *Jakob* and *James*, as well as colloq. *Jack* (which is also used for males baptized *John*) - *Jackel*, etc., is readily used in a metaphorical sense, too, and so is E *jack*, indeed for almost any mechanical figure, object, etc.]: **~hammer** *m* -s/...hämmer *tech.*, *colloq.* a large heavy hammer with a long handle, good for driving in posts, breaking stones, etc.: sledgehammer. - **~schutzen** *n* -s [second el., → *schutzen* 3] *folklore* an Upper Bavarian carnival custom on Maundy Thursday (*Unsinniger Donnerstag*) performed by four men manipulating the ends of a large linen sheet: "jack-tossing" (see next entry). - **~schutzer** *m* -s/usu. pl.: - *folklore* "jack-tosser": *nach einem alten Brauch, der sich in der Gegend von Garmisch seit etwa 1800 bewahrt, schutzen im Fasching die ~, vier weißgekleidete und mit schwarzen Zipfelkappen und Larven versehene Burschen, unter Absingen eines Verses eine Puppe vor den Bürgerhäusern; es gilt als Ehre, wenn vor einem Haus geschutzt wird* in the carnival season, after an old custom preserved in the Garmisch area since about 1800, the "jack-tossers", four men dressed in white and wearing black jelly-bag caps and masks, sing a song and fling up a doll in front of citizens' houses; it is deemed an honour for a house thus to be 'toss-toasted' to.

ja mei [jɔːˈmaɪ] [*mei*, the scant remains, altogether lacking in directedness, of a former appeal to Deity, < *mein Gott!*] *dial.*

interj expressing either indifference or good-natured resignation in the face of the complicated way the world goes (usu. to be verbalized more fully in what follows), but often also indicative of the speaker's reluctance to do something about it - which might benefit others, esp. his interlocutor: oh dear!; ~ ~, *da kann man nix machn!* oh dear, there's nowt [naʊt] to be done about it!

Jodel *m* -s/- & **Jödel** [< *jo*, an Alpine shout from hill to hill, drawing attention to the shouter, but also done for mere joie de vivre; thus *jodeln*, and *johlen* 'to bawl', once simply verbalized that distinctive loud cry] *mus.* = *Jodler* 1. - **ˀn** *vt/i mus.* to sing or warble with interchange of falsetto and the natural voice, in the manner of Alpine people: to yodel, to yodle, to jodel.

Jodler *m* -s/- *mus.* **1.** a melody or brief musical phrase inarticulately sung with interchange of the ordinary and falsetto voice (*Jodelruf*): yodel(l)ing song; *if brief*, yodel(l)ing cry. - **2.** one who yodels: yodel(l)er, yodler, jodler, yodelist. - **Jodlerin** *f* -/-nen *mus.* girl yodel(l)er; *sie ist in der Jugend eine großartige ~ gewesen* she was a fine one for yodel(l)ing in her youth.

Jugendstil *m* -s [lit., 'youth style'; first el., < the name of a weekly magazine, a mixture of art periodical and humorous journal, first brought out in 1896 by a Munich publisher who had assembled a group of young men about him] *art* a movement in decorative design which, running parallel with similar tendencies in England and France, soon became the great fashion at the turn of the century; the style is characterized chiefly by curvilinear motifs derived from natural forms: *BrE* Art Nouveau [ɑː(t)nuˈvəʊ], art nouveau; *F* le style Liberty.

Kaiser *f* -/- *colloq.* — short for **Kaisersemmel** *f* -/-n *bak.* (*Brötchen mit* [*fünf windradförmigen*] *Einschnitten*) a crisp white bread roll with windmill-shaped crust ridges, said to have been invented by Emperor Frederick III in 1487: "Emperor's roll", round (Vienna) roll; *fünf Kaiser bitte; die kosten im Sonderangebot ja eins zwanzig, gell?* five Emperor's, please; they're one twenty as a bargain offer, aren't they?

Kalbs...: ~**haxe** *f* -/-n, *dial.* ~**hax(e)n** *f* -/- [second el., → *Hax*] **1.** *husb.* calf's foot. - **2.** *cul.* knuckle of veal. - ~**schäuferl** *n* -s/-(n) [second el., dim. of *Schaufel* 'shovel' (ex the shape of the bone)] *cul.* shoulder of veal, boiled or grilled. - ~**vögerl** *n* -s/-(n) [second el., dim. of *Vogel* 'bird' (ex the vague resemblance of the meat dish, in its final shape, to the plump brown body of a little bird)] *cul.* a thin flat piece each of veal cutlet and bacon, with a layer of sliced carrots, onions, gherkins, etc., rolled up and held in place by a skewer or toothpick (*Kalbsroulade*): veal bird, *BrE* veal olive.

Kalfakter *m* -s/pl. rare: - [the corrupt form, first documented at Nördlingen in 1499, of L *calefactor* 'pupil who stokes the fire in the classroom'; the word later denoted a person doing other lowly duties, and derogatorily also one fawning on, or even spying for, his superior] *colloq.* a term of gentle, almost sympathetic criticism for someone who, through momentary oversight or awkwardness, did something wrong in a minor matter: silly-billy, clumsy-clot, clumsy so-and-so, *BrE sl.*

also pillock; *du bist ein ~, hast mir die falschen Brillen gebracht!* you *are* a one, bringing me the wrong pair of specs.

Karfreitagsratschen *f* -/- [last el., 'a simple mechanism that makes a repeated loud noise'] **1.** *R.C. relig.* "Good Friday clapper", a wooden rattle used by *Ratschenbuben*↓ on the last three days of Holy Week, when it is customary for the church bells to remain silent. - **2.** *contp.*, also **Regimentsratschen** *f* -/- a formidable gossip: great blabbermouth before the Lord; *if female, also* Dame Gossip in person.

Kasperl [-ʃp-] *m* -s/-n [dim. of *Kasper* or *Kaspar,* or *Jasper* (to give it the usual English form), the traditional Christian name of one of the Three Kings, *Caspar, Melchior, Balthasar* (cp. *C+M+B*), into whom medieval legend transformed the 'wise men' who came to Bethlehem to worship the infant Christ] **1.** *theat.* (1) the principal male character in a puppet show, known for his humorous fights with his wife and for other acts of clowning: Punch. - (2) a figure of mirth at funfairs and in carnival time: merry-andrew. - **2.** *colloq.* a male person whose silly behaviour makes him a laughing-stock: figure of fun, *AmE* oddball, wacko; *er ist halt einfach zum ~ geworden, keiner nimmt ihn mehr ernst* he's become just a figure of fun, and no one takes him seriously any more. - **3.** *colloq.*, said with indulgent humour — a child who, in the presence of adults, likes to engage in somewhat grotesque horseplay: (little) monkey; *jetzt kannst du aber schon langsam aufhören, du ~!* now that's about enough of your antics, you little monkey (*or, ...* you little show-off).

Kasperl [-ʃp-] ...: **~puppe** *f* -/-n *theat.* hand puppet. - **~theater** *n* -s/- **1.** *theat.* (1) puppet-theatre. - (2) puppet show, *BrE* Punch-and-Judy show. - **2.** *fig. contp.* a series of acts of inefficiency and empty pretence which those in authority, esp. politicians, make themselves guilty of in the eyes of the public: sustained farce of silly acting; *das ist ja ein ~, was uns* *die Großkopferten da vorspielen!* those bigwigs are just a bunch of clowns trying to pull the wool over our eyes.

Kathrein *f* -/no pl. the name of a female saint and martyr (d. 306) celebrated on November 25, a date marking the beginning of the "closed", or Advent, season which puts a stop to all official merrymaking until Christmas: St. Catherine [ˌsntˈkæθərɪn]; ~ *stellt den Tanz ein* *Catherine ends all dancin'.

Kessel... *gastr.*: ~**fleisch**, in Franconia known as **Wellfleisch** *n* -(e)s a delicacy after a pig has been butchered, in Franconia especially served on Shrove Tuesday: boiled pork, pork titbits (*AmE* tidbits), i.e. the snout, the kidney and other chitterlings (*AmE* chitlings), brought to the boil in a big pot, without any addition of salt, bay leaves, etc., and served with sauerkraut as well as potatoes peeled, salted, and boiled. - ~**suppe**, in Franconia known as **Griebelsuppe** *f* -/-n a dish on the menu on the same occasion as the above: chitterling (*AmE* chitling) soup, the fluid leftovers from *Kesselfleisch*↑, often served with fried bacon rind.

Kinderzeche *f* - *hist.* & *folklore* at Dinkelsbühl, a medieval city in Middle Franconia: "Children's Treat", a colourful festival celebrated every July in commemoration of the fact that a handful of children had rescued the city from destruction by the Swedes in 1632.

Kini *m* -(s)/- [as in ModE *king*, there is an umlauted, and later on unrounded, stem vowel, both words being < Germ. *kuningaz 'male sovereign ruler of a state'] *dial.* (*König*) king **1.** a popular reference to one of the Bavarian rulers of the Wittelsbach line, and with especial affection to King Ludwig II, also known as "Fairy King" (on the throne, 1864-1886). - **2.** in the games of skittles and bowling, the pin at the centre: kingpin.

Kirchweih *f* -/-en *relig.* = *Kirta(g)*↓. - ~**härtreiben** *n* & *folklore* at Burglengenfeld, and elsewhere, on the third Sunday in

October: "Kermis Bear Baiting", a popular entertainment staged by the traditional costumes society (*Volkstrachtenverein*) of the place. - ~**baum** *m* -(e)s/...bäume *folklore* in the Cham area, at Kemnath, Lupburg, and elsewhere: kermis pole, a symbol of harvest thanksgiving, decorated with firtwig wreaths and many gay ribbons, put up in a village square or in front of an inn. - ~**bursch** *m* -en/-en *folklore* "kermis attendant", one of a group of village lads officiating at a village fair; the duties include putting up the *Kirchweihbaum*↑ on the Saturday before the event. - ~**fest** *n* -(e)s/-e *relig*. = *Kirtag* 1. - ~**gans** *f* -/ ...gänse *gastr*. kermis goose, the mouth-watering centre of attention, especially if roasted nice and crisp, for any native kermis celebrant. - ~**krapfen** *m* -s/- *gastr*. at Waldkirchen, and elsewhere: kermis doughnut.

Kirta *m* -s/- Bavarian Forest *dial*., **Kirtag** *m* -(e)s/-e *colloq*. [< *Kirchtag* 'church anniversary'] **1**. *relig*. (*Kirchweihfest*) church dedication day, celebrated annually on the name day of the patron saint; also known as *der kleine ~*, to distinguish it from *Allerweltskirtag*↑. → **2**. *folklore* (*Jahrmarkt*) kermis, kermess, kirmess, an annual fair or festival held on the patron saint's name day, with games, merrymaking, etc.; formerly the feasting went on for some time, as is testified by this old rhyme: *A richtiga ~, der geht bis zum Irta, / und tuat a si schicka, geht's weita bis Migga* *Our kermis will last until Tuesday is past, / and if in a frenzy, we'll go on through Wednesday. ‖ *prov*. (1) a popular saying (found in many languages) that folly often results from the absence of a person in authority: *ist die Katz aus dem Haus, haben die Mäus' ~* when the cat's away the mice will play. - (2) an impatient warning that omnipresence is not an attribute of man: *man [ich] kann nicht auf zwei Kirtagen tanzen* you [I] can't be in two places at once (*or*, ... dance at two weddings in one day) ‖ *euphem*. *phr*. two instances in which the headword is a mere shield for something crude or awkward, the first implying the Goethean *Götzzitat* (corresponding to E "[he can] kiss my arse"), and the second referring to a woman's menstrual period: (1) *er kann mich in den ~ laden!* he can take me out on the town. - (2) *sie hat den ~* the curse has struck again, she's having friends to stay (*or*, visitors).

Kirwa *f* -/-s [< *Kirchweih*] Upper Palatinate *dial.* = *Kirta*.

Klapperl *n* -s/-(n) [< obsolete *Klapp*, an echoic noun suggesting a quick and repetitive movement, each time accompanied by a short explosive sound, + *-erl*↑] *colloq.* **1.** *tech.* a simple mechanism, with a hammer-like object, that makes a repeated loud noise: (1) (a child's [etc.]) rattle; *einem Buziwackerl macht ein ~ die süßeste Musik, und die Eltern klettern dabei die Wände hoch* for toddlekins a rattle is the sweetest music ever, enough to drive parents up the wall. - (2) *R.C.* (an altar boy's) clapper; *am Karfreitag bleiben alle Kirchenglocken stumm - sie sind, so heißt es, „nach Rom geflogen" -, und auf den Altarstufen treten hölzerne ~n an die Stelle des Ministrantengeläuts* on Good Friday, all church bells remain silent - they are said to have "flown to Rome" -, and on the altar steps wooden clappers take over from the servers' sets of little bells. - **2.** *hum.* or *iron.* a garrulous person's tongue: clack, clacker, clapper, gabber; *ihr ~ geht* (or, *das ~ geht ihr*) *in einem fort* her tongue goes clackety-clack; *hör dir nur an, wie im Saal unten die ~n gehen!* just listen to the mass of clacking tongues in the hall below. - **3.** *garm.*, usu. *pl.* a light open shoe for summer wear, with a thick flat bottom (thus making for inevitably loud progress): (1) if made of wood, and with a leather band to hold it on the foot: clog; (2) if completely made from one piece of wood: clog, sabot; (3) if made all of rubber, and held on by the toes and loose at the back: *BrE* flip-flop, *AmE* thong. - **4.** *tech.* (*kleines [Metall-]Blättchen*) a small flat thin part of metal or other material that either hangs down to cover an opening (e.g., a keyhole), or that falls open on an electrical impulse (e.g., from the room number of a hotel switchboard): flap.

Klause *f* -/-n [like E *close* and *clause*, a borrowing from the Romance, with the basic sense of 'enclosure'] **1.** *geol.* (*Engpaß, Felsschlucht*) narrow pass, defile (in mountains) - **2.** *hyd. eng., hist.* in the Bavarian Forest (*Wasserspeicher der Holztrift*) splash dam, retaining wall (to form an artificial lake); reservoir *or* spring lake, to be emptied "at one go" in spring, so that logs can be guided downstream.

Klettergarten *m* -s/...gärten *mount.* any Alpine peak or massif that is ideally suited for high-altitude climbing; or one of the limestone regions in northern Bavaria wherever jagged cliffs provide ample opportunities for budding mountaineers: climbers' paradise, rock playground.

Kletze *f* -/-n rare; = StandG for the next. - **Kletzen** *f* -/- *dial.* [< MHG *klœzen* 'to split' (the fruit is sliced before drying); cp. E *cleat* 'wedge'] *cul.* (*Dörrbirne*) dried pear.

Kletzen...: **~bene** *m* -s/-e(n) *contp.* a dull person (*Langweiler*), giving the appearance of being possessed of a dry and shrivelled mind: bore, *AmE also* droop goop, (cold) molasses *sg.* - **~brot** *n* -(e)s/-e *bak. & folklore* a type of bread containing dried fruit, esp. pears, plums, figs, apricots, and apples, and garnished with blanched almonds and raisins (*Früchtebrot*): fruit loaf; *an Weihnachten stellt man das ~ auf den Tisch, das Überbleibsel altheidnischer Festbrote* at Christmas fruit bread is served, which is a relic of pagan ceremonial breads. - **~kopf** *m* -s/-köpfe *dial., contp.* = *Kletzenbene*↑. - **~trocknen** *n* -s (the) drying (of) fruit; *auf dem Bauernhof gab es den Backofen, in dem das würzige Bauernbrot entstand, der aber auch zum ~ diente* on the farm, the bakehouse was the birthplace of the tasty coarse rye bread, but which also came in handy when drying all kinds of fruit.

klöpfeln *v/i* [< obs. *Klöpfel m* 'knocker', 'clapper', 'tongue (of a bell)'; the word form is due to vowel mutation (*ö* < *o*) and consonant shift (*pf* < *p*) in SouG speech; cp. E *clap* and *clapper*] *folklore* said of a group of youths, to produce the noises in accordance with the pre-Christmas custom here described: to go rapping from door to door. - **Klöpfelnächte** *f pl. folklore* "Rappers' Nights", the last three Thursday nights at Advent-time when masked lads noisily knock on doors and windows of their Alpine village; this is an ancient defence and assistance rite (now unfortunately often perverted for material gains), and draws attention to the season of change in the offing.

Knödel *m* -s/- [dim. of *Knoten* 'knot'] **1.** *cul.* (*Kloß*) dumpling, shaped by hand (cp. *Nockerl* 1), the mainstay or at least strongly supporting feature of many a substantial Bavarian dinner, whether sweet or meaty; samplings are, from A to Z: *Aprikosen~* apricot dumpling; *Erdäpfel~* potato dumpling; *Fleisch~* meatball, BrE also faggot; *halbseidene ~* dumpling made of boiled potatoes and potato flour; *Leber~* liver dumpling; *Nieren~* tiny dumpling filled with minced kidney; *Semmel~* bread dumpling; *Servietten~* large bread dumpling tied in a napkin and boiled in saltwater; *Tiroler ~* bread dumpling with bits of bacon, ham, or smoked sausage, chopped herbs and the odd caraway seed; *Zwetschgen~* plum dumpling. - **2.** *fig.*, in *colloq. phr.* (1) in slight mockery, to a young boy who is not strong enough yet to perform a certain physical task: *da(zu) mußt du noch mehr ~ essen!* you've got to eat dumplings (*AmE* ... eat your carrots) for strength! - (2) reproachfully, to one who speaks little or nothing: *hast du einen ~ im Mund* (or, coarsely dialectal, ... *im Mäul*)? has the cat got your tongue?, AmE also d' you have a bone in your throat? - (3) lump in one's throat, i.e. a feeling of pressure caused by emotion: *es ist mir kein Wort rausgekommen, ich* *hab einen ~ im Hals gehabt, und Tränen in den Augen* I couldn't get out a word, I had a lump in my throat, and there were tears in my eyes. - **3.** *colloq.*, slightly *contp.* silly person (*Dümmling*): silly (billy *or* goose); *du bist ein ~, das hättest du ihm doch gleich sagen können!* you were a silly, you could have told him right away.

Konnersreuth [also stressed on the second syllable when the word is in end position] *n* -s *place-name* [a village in the extreme north of the Upper Palatinate, some three miles from the pilgrimage church of Kappel, one of whose natives, Therese Neumann, between the late 1920s and the 1960s, held the attention of the faithful, of medical doctors, and of sensation-mongers at large: she regularly produced the marks of the Crucified on Fridays, and continued without any intake of food from 1927 until her death in 1962] *phr.* **1.** *die Stigmatisierte von ~* "the Stigmatised of Konnersreuth", the once common epithet of Therese Neumann, on whose body supernatural stigmata first appeared in 1926, when she was 26. - **2.** a popular couplet in those decades, indicative of the morbid fascination involved, but nowadays almost defunct or sense-depleted to the point of simply expressing the light-hearted joy spelt out in the first line: *Schaut's nur hi, is des a Freud: / Alle fahrn nach ~!* "Just you look and take delight, / Folks all flock to Konnersreuth!"

The autograph of the Stigmatised, bearing a pious dedication (trans., "God be with you!") on the back of a holy picture.

Körndl... [dim. of *Korn* 'grain']: **~bauer** *m* -n/-n *agr.*, *colloq.* (*Getreidebauer* [opp. *Hörndlbauer*↑] grain (-growing) farmer, cereal grower, *BrE also* corn (-growing) farmer. - **~fresser** *m* -s/- *diet.*, *hum.* or *contp.* vegetarian: cereal freak.

Kornkammer *f* -/-n *agr.* **1.** *archit. hist. BrE* corn store, *AmE* grain store (e.g. the one in Old Nuremberg, built by Hans Behaim on the moat of the second fortress wall). → **2.** *fig.* a region that produces much grain: granary, breadbasket ‖ a sobriquet for one of the rich, loess-covered tracts of land, in particular (1) the Dungau, or Gäuboden↑, which occupies the angle between the lower Isar and the Danube, in the Alpine foreland, and (2) the Ochsenfurt Country, S of the River Main, known as *die ~ Bayerns* [*Frankens ~*] Bavaria's [Franconia's] Granary, The Breadbasket (*or* Corn-bin) of Bavaria [Franconia], respectively.

Kötztinger Pfingstritt *m* - -(e)s/pl. rare: - -e *relig.* & *folklore* at and around Kötzting, in northern Lower Bavaria, on Whit Monday: "Riding the Bounds of Kötzting at Whitsuntide", a festive horseback procession to Steinbühl hill chapel, in the Zeller Valley, which at one stage involves the ceremonial blessing of both horses and nearby fields; a quaint legend has it that, in 1312, a priest was able to administer the last rites to a dying farmer at Steinbühl only because a group of young Kötzting horsemen volunteered to ride beside the holy man, and indeed valiantly defended him against an attack by evil brigands.

krachledern *adj* [< the creaky sound given off by old leather trousers, resonantly stiff for long wear, when slapped by their proud wearer; note also the - by now obsolete - word *lederkrachen*, which describes the sound made when the crackling, i.e. the hard brown skin of cooked pork (a delicacy highly prized by Bavarian gourmets!) is broken] *colloq.* **1.** with reference to long or short nether garments, much favoured in Upper Bavaria: made of tough leather. → **2.** *fig.* (said to be) typifying the wearer of such regional garment, but also his way of life and his diction - (1) unsophisticated (*urwüchsig*): homespun; *unser Gebirgstrachtenverein hat* *etwas dagegen, wenn man uns als ~e Gaudiburschen abtut* our society for the continued use of traditional Alpine costume refuses to be passed off as a bunch of peppy thigh-slappers; *die deftige, ~e Seite der bayerischen Liebe* the crude pungency of love among Bavarians. - (2) uncouth (*ungehobelt*): unpolished; *es fällt einem Nichtbayern manchmal schwer, die ~e Ausdrucksweise der Einheimischen zu schlucken* a Bavarian's unpolished way of putting things is sometimes hard for an outsider to swallow. - **Krachlederne** -n/-n *colloq.* **1.** *f* (*Lederhose*↓) leather shorts (*AmE* also pants). - **2.** *m* (1) (*Lederhosenträger*) leather-trousered man, *BrE* chap in leather shorts, *AmE* guy in leather pants; → (2) (*grobschlächtiger Mensch* [*vom Land*]) uncouth (country) yokel, local yokel.

Krachmandel 1. *f* -/-n [second el., < *Mandel* 'the kernel of the fruit of the almond (-tree), *Amygdalus Prunus*, which grows in warm temperate regions'] *cul.*, usu. *pl.* (*Knackmandel*) a kind of sweet often sold at fun fairs and on Christmas markets, named after its crackly sugar coating: blanched-almond caramel(s). - **2.** *n* -s/-(n), often spelt **Krachmandl** [second el., dim. of *Mann* 'man'; but even in the latter spelling meant to be a punning echo of *Krachmandel* 1] *colloq.* noisy, blustering male: *AmE* bigmouth, *BrE* rumbustious loudmouth.

Krammets... [the modern combining form of OHG *kranawitu* 'juniper (tree)', literally 'crane wood', so called because eagerly frequented because of its berries by the crane, but also by the fieldfare (with its equally revelatory name in German)]: **~beere** *f* -/-n *bot.* (*Wacholderbeere*) juniper berry. - **~vogel** *m* -s/...vögel *ornith.* (*Wacholderdrossel*) fieldfare, *BrE also* fellfare.

Krampf *m* -(e)s/- [actually, 'cramp', the sudden contraction of a muscle, which makes movement difficult] *dial.*, usu. said in disdain: **1.** something that should not be taken seriously: stuff and nonsense; *was die Leut da erzähln* (or *verzähln*), *ist ja ein ~* (or, *san ja ~*) it's all stuff and nonsense what the people are saying. - **2.** an unnecessary delay caused by a person's whim; *kimm scho(n), jetzt mach koane ~!* don't make any fuss (*or*, pull yourself together) now, get going.

krampfeln *vt/i* [< *krampfen* (now rare) 'to tighten the muscles - here, of one's hand - over an object, as if from a sudden cramp' + *-eln*↑] *colloq.* to filch (usu. something of small value): to swipe, *BrE also* to pinch; *da hat mir (doch) so ein Depp den Spitzer (ge)krampfelt!* (why,) some jerk's gone and swiped my pencil sharpener.

Krampfhenne *f* -/-n, usu. *dial.* **Krampfhenna** *f* -/- *contp.* a fashionable, wealthy, or society woman who talks a lot in a pretentious manner: *esp. AmE* (highfalutin) cackle-broad.

Kranewitter *m* -s/pl. rare: - *bev.* (*Wacholderschnaps*) **1.** spirit made from juniper berries. - **2.** *loosely* gin.

Kranzltag *m* -(e)s/pl. rare: -e *eccles. & folklore* in the Upper Palatinate: (*Fronleichnam*) "Wreath Day", so named from the head wreaths worn in procession by children and women on Corpus Christi Day (also known as *Prangertag*↓); further justification for the epithet comes from the fact that "weather wreaths" (*Wetterkranzln*) woven of thyme, mint, and other herbs are carried by altar boys throughout the ceremony, to be hung after consecration in the houses and stables as safeguards against lightning.

Kraut [< MHG, OHG *krūt* '(small) foliage plant'] **1.** *bot.* cabbage (*~ anbauen* to grow cabbage); *Blau~* (*Rotkohl*) red cabbage; *Sauer~* sauerkraut, sourcrout, sourkrout; *Weiß~* (*Weißkohl*) white cabbage; *ein kleines ~* (*Rübenkraut*) beet (*or* turnip) tops *pl.* (*or* greens *pl.*). - **2.** *colloq. phr.* (1) expressing a very low opinion of an idea, suggestion, effort, etc. which, if carried out, will hardly bring about an improvement of the lamentable status quo: *das macht das ~ auch nicht fett!*

that won't help matters any, that is much of a muchness. - (2) a more or less grim resolution to take deep offence, or indeed to have no more contact, social, business, or otherwise, with a person: *einmal hätte sie mit ihrer Gschaftlhuberei meinen Eltern bald das ~ ausgeschüttet* her fussiness just about made my parents reach a parting of the ways with her one day; *der hat mir das ~ ausgeschüttet!* his name is Mud with me!, *AmE also* he's on my ditch list (*or*, stinklist)! - (3) an exemplification, by humorous hyperbole, of frugal living: *besser eine Laus aufm ~ als (wie) gar kein Fleisch* better a bone in the faraway hills than nothing to gnaw on at all.

Krauterer *m* -s/- [see -erer↑] **1.** *agr.* & *com. hist.* cabbage gardener and retailer - the occupational name is variously preserved to this day, e.g. in *Krauterermarkt*, in the City of Regensburg. - **2.** *colloq.*, more or less *contp.*, and often couched in a specific phrase, *der alte* [*ein alter*] ~ the [a] decrepit old man: (old) cabbage, old codger, (old) crock, *AmE also* antique bozo; *vielleicht läßt aber das bei uns gebräuchliche Wort vom alten ~ auch eine Würdigung mitschwingen, daß nämlich im Volksglauben der Genuß von Gemüse hohes Alter verbürgt* it is possible, though, that our local term "old cabbage" also carries an appreciative connotation in that the eating of vegetables is popularly believed to vouch for a person's high old age.

Kraut...: **~acker** *m* -s/...äcker *agr.* field of cabbages, cabbage field. - **~häuptel** *n* -s/- *bot.* (*Krautkopf*) cabbage head. - **~roulade** *f* -/-n *cul.* stuffed cabbage leaf. - **~salat** *m* -(e)s/pl. rare: -e *cul.* dressed shredded cabbage, cabbage salad, coleslaw. - **~scheuche** *f* -/-n, *dial.* **~scheuch** *f* -/-n or **~scheuchn** *f* -/- **1.** *agr.* an object, usu. the figure of a man in old clothes, set up to frighten birds away from a cabbage crop: scarecrow, *AmE also* bird scarer (in a cabbage field). → **2.** *contp.* an ugly or

unpleasant woman, esp. one who is old: hag, harridan.
~stampfer *m* -s/- **1.** *agr.* a heavy tool for pounding white cabbage, duly sliced and salted, in a tub or barrel to make sauerkraut: cabbage pounder (*or* ram, *or* tamper). → **2.** usu. pl. *contp.* a woman's ungainly fat legs: tree trunks, stumps, pile drivers, keg-legs, elephant legs, *AmE also* ham hocks; *schau dir (nur) die ~ an, die die hat!* (just) look at her pair of (great big) elephant hooves! - **~wickerl** *n* -s/-(n) *cul.* (*Weißkohlroulade*) "cabbage roll", stuffed cabbage, i.e. minced (*AmE* chopped) meat and onions wrapped in savoy or white-cabbage leaves, gently browned and stewed.

Kren *m* -(e)s [< MHG *krēn(e)* < Czech *chřenu*] *bot.*, *NorBavG* (*Meerrettich*) horse-radish; *wir haben Frankfurter mit ~ gehabt* (or *gegessen*) we had frankfurters and horse-radish.

Kren...:~fleisch *n* -(e)s *cul.* fat boiled beef and (*or* with) horse-radish. - **~weiberl** *n* -s/- [second el., dim. of *Weib*, here 'itinerant saleswoman'] *colloq.* a female hawker of horse-radish: horse-radish girl.

Kreuzl *n* -s/-(n) [dim. of *Kreuz* 'cross'] *colloq.* **1.** any cruciform artifact: little cross. - **2.** *R.C.* the sign of religious reverence made with the right thumb on, or close to, one's forehead or over one's heart: cross; *hast du schön dein ~ gmacht?* did you nicely cross yourself? - **3.** a cruciform symbol made by hand, to mark against a passage in a written or printed text; *mach ein ~ am Rand, daß man weiß, wo der Fehler ist!* make a cross in the margin to show where the mistake is. - **4.** pl. *drei ~(n)* **a.** *hist.* an illiterate person's conventional substitute for his or her signature (a fact that also led to the title of one of Ludwig Anzengruber's peasant comedies, *Die Kreuzelschreiber*): three crosses; *selbst noch im vorigen Jahrhundert durfte ein Analphabet als Unterschrift drei ~(n) malen* even in the last century, an illiterate was allowed to put down three crosses for his signature. - **b.** *hum.* one's signature: *hum.* autograph, trademark, *AmE* also John Henry, John Hancock; *machn Sie mir da bittschön Ihre drei ~(n) hin?* would you please put your autograph (*AmE* John Hancock) on the dotted line?

Kriecherl *n* -s/-(n) [dim. of *Krieche* 'Prunus insititia'] *bot.* a small, purple or yellow subspecies of the domestic plum: bullace, damson. - **~baum** *m* -(e)s/...bäume *bot.* bullace tree. - **~strauch** *m* -(e)s/...sträucher *bot.* bullace shrub.

Kronfleisch *n* -(e)s *cul.* (*Rindfleisch vom Zwerchfell*) midriff of beef.

Kuhle...: **~muh**, **~muhle** *f* -/- [in child language, and previously of course in the speech patterns followed by adults when conversing with their little charges, allomorphic-variant duplications like this one (and *piggy-wiggy* [for 'pig'] in English) are quite common] *colloq.* a (pet) cow: moo-cow.

Kumpf *m* -(e)s/-e & Kümpfe [< MHG *kump, kumph* 'container', 'bowl'] **1.** *agr.* (*Behälter [für den Wetzstein]*) whetstone holder, of wood, cow's horn, or sheet metal, carried by reapers and mowers at their hips when scything ‖ *~gefäß*, or *Bombengefäß n* -es/-e *archaeol.* earthenware bowl, shaped like a hemisphere or three quarters of a sphere, dating from the Later Stone Age and found among the western groups of the Danubian Circle. - **2.** *hum.* or *contp.* a person's large, esp. hooked, nose: beak, proboscis, *AmE* also schnozz, schnozzola; *wer regelmäßig schnupft, so heißt es, kriegt einen richtigen ~* a regular taker of snuff, rumour has it, is bound to develop a king-size beak.

Kunkel *f* -/-n [< MHG *kunkel* < OHG *chuncla* < LateL *conucula*, cognate with *colus* 'the stick from which the thread is pulled in hand spinning'] *handicrafts* in Upper Bavaria (*Spinnrocken*): distaff.

Kunkel... in Upper Bavaria: **~abend** *m* -s/-e *hist.*, *folklore* "distaff night", an illicit nocturnal rendezvous and general get-together of unmarried persons, usu. held in the spinning room; forbidden in 1857 by decree of the regional government, since "frequently resulting in illegitimate births and a sharp rise in brawls and grievous bodily harm"; cp. *Heimgarten*. - **~lehen** *n* -s/- *hist.*, *jur.* a fief that passes to the female descendants upon the extinction of the male line: apronstring tenure (*or*, hold). - **~stube** *f* -/-n *hist.* (*Spinnstube*) spinning room.

Kürbe *f* -/-n, *dial.* **Kürben**, **Kürm** (through assimilation), **Kirm** (through unrounding) *f* -/- (*Flechtkorb*) (wickerwork) basket. - **Kürbenmacher**; *dial.* **Kirmzeiner**, **Kürbenzäuner** *m* -s/- [second el. < MHG & OHG *zein* „Schaft einer Sprosse, eines Zweiges von Pflanzen" (Schmeller); cp. E *tine* 'sharp projecting point, spec. of an antler'] largely *hist.* (*Korbflechter*) basketmaker.

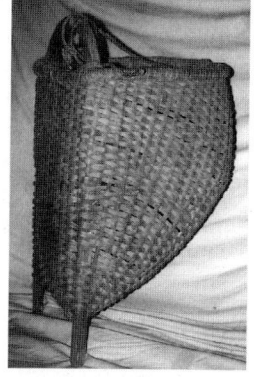

Kuttelfleck *m* -(e)s/-e *cul.* **1.** the rubbery stomach wall of a cow, sheep, or pig: tripe. - **2.** the intestines of a pig: chitterlings *pl.*, chitlings *pl.* - **Kuttlerei** *f* -/-en *com.* to be found on the Viktualienmarkt in Munich, and elsewhere: tripe shop *or* stand; shop *or* stall selling chitterlings.

☞ **L.** ☜

-l [-l̩] a syllabic <-l>, hence the notation with the subscript dot, which acts as a diminutive suffix to convey the idea of smallness, youth, or simply of familiarity, e.g. in *Bachl* 'brooklet', *Deandl*, *Dirndl* ScotE 'lassie', *Lampl* 'little lamb', 'lambkin', ScotE 'lambie', *Stierl* 'bullock' (where diminutive equivalents readily offer themselves for the purpose in English); in contrast with *-erl*↑, however, the diminution thus expressed is by no means always accompanied by feelings of warmth and tenderness, and sometimes even conveys a modicum of harshness and contempt, e.g. in *Feitl*↑ and *Mandl*↓.

lack *adj* [related to OE *vlac* 'tepid', Icel *lakr*, Sw *elak* 'bad', 'vile'] slightly *contp.* **1.** of beer: (*abgestanden, schal*) stale, flat; *eine Maß Bier, die länger herumsteht, schmeckt ~* a mug of beer left standing for some time tastes flat ‖ here is a Bavarian quatrain by Monika Pauderer, and its dialect translation in English - a froth-blower's grumble and the landlord's repartee:

„*Herr Wirt, des Bier, des is a Graus! Des is ganz lack und lau!*
Ham S' denn nix Kälters in Ihrm Haus?" „*Ja, leider scho' - mei Frau!*"
"Tha beer, ma lan'lord, 's a disgreeace, A' flat 'n' stale, nae life.
Ain't there nowt colder in yer pleeace?" "Och aye, sad truth - ma wife."

2. of an unmarried woman who is no longer young: old-maidish; *sie schmeckt ~* she's no spring chicken.

Lahmarsch *m* -(e)s/...ärsche [in this figure of speech, known as *pars pro toto* (or *synecdoche*), some part deputizes for the whole: a man without impetus is seemingly incapable of getting up from his comfortable sitting position] *vulg.*, always *contp.* a person who is intellectually, emotionally, or aesthetically boring, tedious, tiring, or colourless: *BrE* lame arse, *AmE* lame ass, drag, slack ass. - ~**ig** *adj vulg.*, always *contp.* boring (in all the above shades of meaning): *BrE* lame-arsed, *AmE* lame-assed, slack-assed.

La̱lle *m* -/- [an onomatopoeic noun, supported by *lallen*, the StandG verb form, to describe someone who speaks indistinctly since allowing his tongue to hang loose - which is exactly what the related E *to loll* must have once meant] *dial.* stupid person (*Trottel*): dolt, *AmE also* tommy noddy.

La̱nderer [-ɔ-] *m* -s/- [the repetitive suffix *-erer*↑ here may, but need not, hint at the superiority complex felt by some townspeople over their "country cousins"; opp. *Stadterer*↓] *colloq.* a country or small-town person: native. - ~**nummer** f -/-n *mot.*, *colloq.* a car registration number, shown on the front and back plate, whose particular set of letters (marked off from the rest of the letter-cum-figure combination by a dash) indicates that the vehicle received its licence from the administrative centre of a rural district: country number.

La̱ndler *m* -s/- [the *dial.* variant of *Ländler*, originally so named after *Landl*, a form of endearment for Upper Austria] **1.** *mus.* any of several rustic dances, most often in three-four time, to be performed by pairs of dancers in rows or circles: country waltz ‖ in Upper Bavaria and in the Tyrol, where the dance is often accompanied by the yodel: *Tiroler* ~ Tyrolienne. - **2.** *fig.*, in the *colloq. phr.* describing a severe tongue lashing: *j-m einen* ~ *blasen* (or, rarely, *machen*) to give s.o. (merry) hell, to make s.o. come out the little end of the horn, *BrE also* to give s.o. what for; *wenn sie* (colloq. *die*) *draufkommen, was du angerichtet hast, blasen sie* (colloq. *die*) *dir einen* ~ if they find out what a mess you've made of it, they'll give you merry hell (*or*, ... give you what for).

Laugen... *bak*.: ~**brezen** *f* -/- (hardly ever ~**breze** *f* -/-n or ~**brezel** *f* -/-n [see *Bretzel*]) "brine-treated pretzel", a shiny brown pretzel dipped in a solution of soda ash and sprinkled with fine salt before baking; *~ kann ich zum Bier nur wärmstens empfehlen, sie müssen allerdings knirschfrisch sein* I warmly recommend salt pretzels with beer, but only if they are crackle-fresh.

Leber... *gastr*.: ~**käs**, *dial*. ~**kas** [-kɑːs] *m* -es/pl. rare: -e, ~**käse** (the StandG form, which is very rare) *m* -s [first el., < *Laib* 'loaf' (because it is offered for sale in long cube-like loaves at butchers' and grocers' shops)] meat loaf; *der ~ besteht aus durchgedrehtem Rind- und Schweinefleisch, sogenanntem Brät* a meat loaf consists of finely ground beef and pork, or what is known as 'sausage meat' ‖ *fig.* in a piece of abusive speech imputing utter stupidity: *dem hat man ja das Hirn raus- und ein Stück warmen ~ hineinoperiert!* they must have gouged his brains out and filled the cavity with blubber (*or*, ... with fat [cheese, mush, sawdust])! - ~**knödel** *m* -s/- liver dumpling, made of minced (*AmE* ground) liver, bread and onions, cooked and served in soup; *~suppe f* -/-n liver-dumpling soup.

lebfrisch *adj* cheerful and active: sprightly, lively; *ein ~es Dirndl hat ein jeder gern* the world loves a sprightly lass.

Lederhose *f* -/-n an article of Bavarian men's wear: "lederhosen" **1.** if leaving the knees free (*Kurze*): leather shorts. - **2.** if reaching below the knees (*Bundhose*): *BrE also* leather breeches, *AmE also* knee pants.

Leich *f* -/-en [< *Leiche*, one of the many disyllabic nouns shorn of the final vowel in casual speech (cp. *Katz*, *Leut*)] *colloq*. **1.** (dead) body, corpse. - **2.** *dial. also* **Leicht** (*Begräbnis*) burial, funeral; (*Trauerzug*) funeral procession: (1) *auf die ~ gehen* to go to the funeral; *gehst du (mit) auf die* (*or*, *mit der*) *~?* will you be at the funeral?; *wieviel Leut sind bei der*

~ *gewesen?* how many folks were at the burial? ‖ with reference to Old Bavarian ceremonial obsequies, for which people have often taken their ghoulish delight since the Biedermeier Age: *eine schöne* ~ a lovely funeral; *er hat eine schöne* ~ *gehabt* he had a lavish funeral, *AmE also* ... a fine send-off. (2) *fig. & prov.*: *der Herr Geheimrat hat ein Gesicht gemacht, als wenn er mit einer* ~ *geht* *the Privy Councillor pulled a face as though he were one of the chief mourners at a funeral ‖ pleasing circumstances can work wonders to a strained atmosphere: *bei einer schönen* ~ *kann man sich sogar übers Sterben unterhalten* *a lavish funeral is as fine a setting as any to talk about dying ‖ a warning that difficulties tend to multiply, or a dryly humorous observation that somebody trying to swat flies, ants, etc. is duly faced with an even increasing number of the tribe on the scene: *eine bringst du um und hundert kommen auf die* ~ kill one fly [ant, etc.] and ten others come to the funeral.

Leichen...: **~auto** *n* -s/-s hearse, *AmE also* funeral car (*or* coach). - **~bitterin** *f* -/-nen wailer, professional mourner. - **~brett** *n* -(e)s/-er *folklore* = *Totenbrett*. - **~frau** *f* -/-en, **~schwester** *f* -/-n a woman who lays out the corpse: layer-out. - **~wärter** *m* -s/- (*Friedhofsverwalter*) sexton in charge of a cemetery, cemetery caretaker.

Leichtrunk *m* -(e)s/-e *folklore* (*Umtrunk nach einer Beerdigung*) funeral social (with drinks all round).

Leite *f* -/-n, *colloq.* **Leiten** *f* -/- *geog.* ([*Berg-*]*Hang, Abhang*) hillside, (mountain-)slope; *auch im Oberlauf der Donau wächst an mancher sonnigen* ~(*n*) *ein guter Tropfen* a delicious drop of wine is also grown on (*or*, to be had from) the sunny slopes along the upper reaches of the Danube.

Leonhard, sometimes in the variant form of **Lienhard**, *m* -s *R.C. & folklore* **Sankt** ~ St Leonard [ˌsntˈlenəd] of Noblac, in his lifetime (*d.* ca. 559) a courtier, and then a hermit in a forest near Limoges, Central France; his cult as a popular saint was widespread in the West during the Middle Ages, and his veneration as a tutelary saint for horses and cattle, esp. in the rural areas of Upper Bavaria, continues unabated to this day (cp. *Bauernherrgott*↑):

> *Sankt Leonhard ist für das Vieh der Patron,*
> *Den rufen die Bauern um Hilfe oft an.*
> *St Leonard will help should your cattle fall ill;
> To him often peasantfolk pray with a will.

Leonhạrdi [the pseudo-L genitive of *Leonhard*↑ (with *dies*, etc., to be supplied)] *R.C.*: *an* ~ on St Leonard's Day, November 6 (the date of the saint's feast) ‖ **~fahrt** *f* -/-en, **~ritt** *m* -(e)s/-e *R.C.* & *folklore* at Bad Tölz and elsewhere, on November 6, always a great event for the rural community: "St Leonard's Drive", "St Leonard's Ride", a festive procession through the streets of the market town or village, with the farmwomen in their decorative costumes sitting, closely serried on benches, in big horse-drawn carriages, and the menfolk astride their horses.

Lọla *f* - [a Spanish Christian name] *hist.* Lola, short for Lola Montez (Marie Gilbert), 1818-1861, an Irish dancer on the Munich stage in 1846, who soon became the mistress of King Louis I;* his spendthrift infatuation, combined with her political meddlesomeness and personal arrogance, caused widespread opposition, leading to the King's abdication, and exile for both, early in 1848. - **~ministerium** *n* -s *polit. hist.* "Lola Ministry", a nickname for the liberal cabinet of Prince Ludwig von

Öttingen-Wallerstein, which, in December 1847, was brought into power for a brief spell through Lola Montez's influence.

> *Note: Such disloyalty made King Frederick William IV of Prussia remonstrate, if ever so gently, with his relative's philanderings. But the womaniser was quick to counter with one of his barbed quatrains. The last line is a good example of the King's at times absurd syntax, and it also ranks as a masterpiece of veiled, and herefore all the more virulent, invective - the innuendo is, of course, sexual:
>
> | *Stammverwandter Hohenzoller,* | *Distant cousin Hohenzoller, |
> |---|---|
> | *Bist dem Wittelsbach ein Groller,* | Bearest Wittelsbach dark choler |
> | *Gönnst ihm nicht die Lola Montez,* | When he drinks from Lola's cup? |
> | *Selber habend nie gekonnt es.* | Why, you've never got it up. |

Lolette *f* - *hist.* Lolette, or Lolita, a form of endearment privately used by King Louis I for his paramour, Lola↑.

Lolus *m* - [pseudo-L, by analogy < *Lola*↑] *mus. hist.* Lolus, a nickname for Richard Wagner, the famous composer, 1813-1883, ironically represented as the male successor of Lola Montez because of the great influence exerted by him on King Ludwig II - another liaison between artist and sovereign leading to riches and exile for a royal protégé (1864-1872).

Lüftl... *art* & *folklore*: **~maler** *m* -s [< *Lüftl* 'windy place', the name of a locality, a homestead (cp. the E place-names *Windhill*, *Windle*, *Winscales*); hence a family name documented in the Oberammergau area as late as 1806] *hist.* "Lüftl Painter", the local name for Franz Seraph Zwinck, 1748-92, who, with consummate skill and industry, decorated house façades and interior walls with frescoes usually representing scenes from the Bible. → **2.** -s/- [by associative etymology, a re-interpretation in view of the fact that the work is done on a ladder in mid-*air*, or with effortless ease, *breathed* as it were on to the walls of houses rather than painted] *gen.* any exterior fresco artist in Upper Bavaria or in the adjoining parts of Austria: "painter in (the) air", "fresh-air painter", "airy painter", "aerial painter". - ~**malerei** *f* -/-en a distinctive and venerable trade plied in Southern Germany for centuries: decorative façade painting.

Luller *m* -s/- [< *lullen*, an imitative formation, in regional use meaning 'to suck'] **1.** a rubber teat for sucking, put in a baby's mouth to keep it quiet: *BrE* dummy (*NorBrE* & *IrE also* dumb-teat, soother), *AmE* pacifier. - **2.** the mouthpiece of a nursing bottle: *BrE* teat, *AmE* nipple.

Lüngerl *n* -s/-(n) [dim. of *Lunge* 'lung'] *gastr.* also [*das*] *Saure* ~ a typical mid-morning snack at an inn, and once a favourite entrée at traditional peasant weddings and funerals, hence also known as **Voressen**: calf's lungs *pl.* (*or* lights *pl.*) and heart, boiled in a stock of allspice, pot-herbs, one bay leaf, vinegar, and then cut into a light roux [ru:], and stock poured on, though boiling continues (to the addition of a little sugar and pepper and sour cream for seasoning); served with bread dumplings, the dish is a gourmet's delicacy, and often a full meal in its own right.

☞ **m** ☜

Magen *m* -s/- *or* Mägen - in a crudely *hum. phr.* expressing intense hunger: *mir hängt der ~ schon bis zu den Kniekehlen* (I'm so empty) I can feel my (*or* me) backbone touching my (*or* me) belly button, *NorBrE* my stomach thinks that my throat is cut, I'm hungered to the hole of the heart, *ScotE* ma belly's like to cut ma throat. - ~**tratzer** *m* -s/- [second el., < *tratzen*↓, here: 'to tease' *or*, alternatively, 'to whet s.o.'s appetite'] *colloq.* **1.** often *contp.* a ridiculously small amount of food or drink: smidgin, smidgen; *das ist alles? das ist ja grad ein ~!* is that everything? why, that wouldn't keep a sparrow alive. - ⁓**tratzerl** *n* -s/-(n) [a dim. of the former] *colloq.* **1.** *hum.* used in a friendly invitation to have a small amount of food or drink before a meal, just to increase the desire for the main affair: wee appetizer. - **2.** rare, slightly *contp.* = *Magentratzer*.

Maibaum *m* -(e)s/...bäume *folklore* maypole, a tall pole in an open place and symbol of reawakened life, richly decorated with wreaths and ribbons and emblems of the local trades; *Tanz um den ~* maypole dance. - ⁓**aufstellen** *n* -s setting up the maypole (usu. on the market-square). - ⁓**feier** *f* -/-n on May 1: May Day Celebration, with a procession and dances round the maypole. - ⁓**klettern**, *dial.* ⁓**krax(e)ln** *n* -s climbing the maypole, a competitive event among village youths on May Day. - ⁓**setzen** *n* -s = *~aufstellen*. - ⁓**stehlen** *n* -s robbing the maypole, one of the many expressions of village rivalry practised by youths one night in May; if successful, the trophy must be bought back with a heavy ransom of beer.

Mandl, less often **Manndl** *n* -s/-(n) [< *Mann* 'man' + *-l*↑, with intrusive *d* (as in *Hendl* 'chicken' < *Henne*) - structurally corresponding to the NorG dim. form *Männchen*] *colloq.* **1.** (1) slightly *iron.* or *contp.* — an adult male, slight, of middling or small size, often timid and not healthy-looking: (a) featherweight, half-pint, half portion, *AmE also* minus quantity, snip of a person; (b) if married: apology for a husband. - (2) without such pejorative connotations, for pure sex distinction (thus referring to human beings as well as to animals [opp.: *Weibl* 'female']): male; *es ist ein ~* it's a he ‖ *phr.* as an expression of utter bewilderment, excitement or disappointment: *jetzt weiß ich's nimmer - bin ich ein ~ oder ein Weibl?* I'm all in a dither now - am I on my head or on my heels? (*or*, ... - am I coming or going?) - **2.** *zo.* said of hares, rabbits, marmots, and dogs: sit-up position (with front legs raised, paws at an angle); *ein ~ machen* to sit at attention. - **3.** *agr.*, now somewhat obs. — a harvesting feature, observed immediately after cutting the grain (*auf dem Feld zum Trocknen aufgestellte Getreidegarben*): stook [-uː-], *NorBrE* also hattock, stack stowk [-ɔː-], [-əʊ-], i.e. several sheaves stood against each other like a pyramid, to facilitate further drying in the harvest field before removal to the farmstead; *acht bis zehn Garben gehen auf ein ~* eight or ten standers (= standing sheaves) make up a stook.

Manner... *dial.* [< the unumlauted plural form of *Mann*: Stand-G *Männer*]: **~leut** *pl.* men in general; male members of the family: menfolk *pl.*; *wenn es darauf ankommt, helfen ja doch alle ~ zusammen* when it matters, menfolk are sure to stick together; *was, heute allein? wo sind denn deine ~?* why, you're by yourself today? where are all your menfolk? - **~seite** *f* - [opp. *Weiberseite*] **1.** *eccles.* the right-hand section in a country church (when looking down the nave towards the altar), indicative of a seating arrangement according to the sexes, now no longer strictly adhered to: men's side, epistle-side. - **2.** *bak.* the bulgy side of a bread loaf: top crust.

Maria und Josef *interj* a R.C., usu. female, person's shout of unpleasant surprise or even horror (as if feeling the need, at that moment, to invoke divine assistance): Holy Mary and Jesus (*or*, ... and Joseph)!; *ja, ~, wie schaust denn du aus! Deine Kleider sind ja ganz verdreckt!* Holy Mary and Jesus, what a sight you are, with muck all over your clothes!

Maß [mɑs] *f* -/Masse (after numerical data: - [e.g. zwei Maß]; *dial.* pl. also: Massen) the customary term used when handling beer **1.** one litre (*BrE* = [somewhat less than] two pints, *or* one quart [cp. *Quartl↓*]) of beer; *eine ~ trinken* to have a large beer; *gehen wir eine ~ stemmen!* let's be off and tip a large beer! ‖ a conciliatory move, yet one with a selfish afterthought: *du hast schon ganz recht; und wer recht hat, der zahlt eine ~* you're quite right as it is; and the one who is right (*or*, whoever is right) has to buy me (*or*, treat me to) a beer. → *Daumen, Radlermaß*. - **2.** the customary nominal measure for Bavarian habitués when ordering their beer in a pub - in English-speaking countries, rather: pint (= 0.568 l); *keiner von den Spezln da möchte am Abend auf seine ~ verzichten* there's none of those lads here would like to miss their nightly pint. - **3.** = *Maßkrug↓*; *eine zünftige Kellnerin kommt mit fünf bis sechs ~ Bier in jeder Hand daher* a proper barmaid comes along swinging five or six steins of beer in each hand; *er hat einen tiefen Schluck aus seiner ~ gemacht* he took a deep draught from his mug (of beer); *die Fertigkeit, eine ganze ~ Bier ohne Absetzen auszutrinken* the skill of drinking (*or*, draining) an entire mug of beer without taking a pause for breath (*or*, without taking it from the lips).

Maßkrug *m* -(e)s/...krüge stoneware (*or* earthenware) mug, - if with a lid: *BrE* tankard, *AmE* stein -, commonly holding about a quart of beer ‖ *phr.*: *er hat den ~ genommen und auf einen Zug geleert* he took the mug and drained it at one gulp; *j-m einen ~ am Schädel zerschlagen* to break a beer mug over s.o.'s head; *er ist so klein, daß man ihn in einen ~ hineinstecken könnte* he's so small you could hold him in the palm of your hand (*or*, ... you could put him in your pocket) ‖ a *prov.* warning against Demon Drink (with *BavG* and *IrE*, as it were, "comparing notes"): *wo der ~ übergeht, (da) bleibt der Verstand stehen* thirst is a shameless disease.

Maßkrug...: ~**olympiade** *f* -/-n *hum.* a concealed pun on the following compound, which considers quaffing beer from heavy steins an Olympic discipline to be engaged in annually at the *Oktoberfest↓*: "Beer-mug Olympics"; *bei der ~ auf der Wies'n werden jeden Tag friedlich zehntausend Krüge um die Wette gestemmt* at the "Beeriad", under the shadow of the Bavaria, tens of thousands of frothing steins are being lifted in a merrily competitive spirit. - ~**stemmen** *n* -s *hum.* a pun on *Stemmen* 'weight lifting', an old type of sports or exercise of lifting specially shaped weights: "Beer-mug Lifting" **1.** a hilarious test of endurance among a convivial gathering of froth-blowers, according to which the one is declared champion who, arm outstretched, can hold a full stein of beer at eye level. - **2.** also ~**schutzen** *n* -s (cp. *schutzen*) *hum.*, sometimes *iron.* or *sarc.* drinking lots of beer, usu. in the company of friends: elbow-raising, elbow exercise, *AmE also* setting-up exercises; *wenn er daheim im Haushalt genausoviel Ausdauer hätt wie im Wirtshaus beim ~, dann wär er schon recht* there'd be no flies on him if he showed as much stamina at home in helping us with things as he does with his cronies bending his elbow at the beer table.

matsch [-ʌ-] *adj* [actually, a cardplayers' term (based on It *marcio* 'soft', 'lazy') for one who has not made a single trick in the game] *colloq.* exhausted: dead beat, done for, done in, *BrE also* fagged ‖ although used only as a predicative adjective in ordinary speech, *matsch* here twists a banterer's verbal kaleidoscope to offer a playful little quatrain:

Zwei Burschen krochen auf den Gletscher,
der eine matsch, der andre mätscher;
Two lads slogged up an ice-bound hill -
One, fagged; the other, faggeder still.

da ächzt' der Mätschere zum Matschen,
"Geh, tean ma wieder abehatschen!"
Then wheezed the faggeder of the twain,
"I say, let's slog downhill again!"

Mäuserl, due to dialectal unrounding of the diphthong also spelt **Meiserl** *n* -s [dim. of *Maus* 'mouse'; the prickly sensation felt by the sufferer is unpleasantly reminiscent of a tiny mouse scurrying along the person's forearm] *med.*, *colloq.* the tender part of the elbow, which when struck hurts very much (*Musikantenbein*): funny bone, crazy bone; *au! jetzt hab ich mir's ~ anghaut!* ouch, I just hit my funny bone.

mäuserlstad *pred. adj* [first el., dim. of *Maus*, '(sweet) little mouse'; second el., → *stad*] *colloq.* of persons (*mäuschenstill*) (as) quiet as a mouse; *die Klasse ist ~ gewesen* there was a dead silence (*or*, there wasn't a murmur) in the classroom, it was so quiet in the classroom (that) you could have heard a pin drop.

Meefischli *n* -/usu. pl.: - [first el., Lower Franconian dial. for *Main* [maɪn], the name of the local river (the word showing monophthongization [e:<aɪ] and loss of final consonant, as does elsewhere *nee* < *nein* 'no'); second el., a SW German dim. morpheme to describe the tiny size of the delicacy in question] *ichth.* & *cul.* "small fish of the Main (river)", one of the varieties of whitefish, esp. roach (*Rotauge*), bream (*Brachse*), gudgeon (*Gründling*), and chub (*Döbel*); fried whole in deep fat till crisp, and served with a slice of lemon, a dollop of potato salad or a croissant; *die ~ sollten nicht länger sein als der kleine Finger des heiligen Kilian auf der Alten Brücke von Würzburg* "Main river crispies" should not exceed the length of the little finger [on the statue] of St Kilian [heading a baroque procession of figures] on the Old Bridge of Würzburg.

Meter *m* -s/- **1.** *math.* an exact unit for measuring length (= 39.37 inches): *BrE* metre, *AmE* meter. - **2.** *colloq.* a rule-of-thumb way of indicating a distance, one that can usu. be grasped at a glance: yard, *or* yards; *seine Schätzung war fei ˟weit daneben* his estimate was yards out, mind (you). ‖

folklore here is a toast, favoured by convivial beer tipplers, in which the length mentioned is but incidental to the bizarre variety of motions the speaker goes to before downing his own mugful of "anti-rust throat oil":

Oan Meter auffi,	*It's one yard upwards,
oan Meter abi;	and one yard down;
oan Meter viri,	now push it forwards,
oan Meter zruck -	now pull it back -
Prost, daß d' Gurgel net varrost't!	Skoal [-ɔʊ-], and let the moisture roll!

A few dialect pointers:

auffi ['afɪ] < *aufhin*; *abi* ['ɔːbɪ] < *abhin*; *viri* ['fiːrɪ] < *vornhin*.

Mẹtte *f* -/-n, *dial*. **Mẹtten** and, by sineresis, **Mẹttn** *f* -/- [< L (*missa*) *matutinae* 'matins' *sg*. or 'early morning (mass)', so named because it was once celebrated at that time of day] **1.** *R.C.* midnight mass (*or* vespers *sg*.), esp. the one following Christmas Eve. - **2.** *R.C.* & *folklore*, also *Pumpermette(n)* a church service held in Holy Week, initiated by churchgoers who made clanging noises and beat drums (cp. *pumpern*↓) to voice their bitterness against the betrayal by Judas Iscariot. - **3.** *fig.*, often *dial*. obstreperous noise: hullabaloo; *macht's koa so a ~!* stop making such a racket (*or*, ... kicking up such a row [raʊ])!

Mẹtzelsuppe *f* -/-n [first el., < *metzeln* < MedL *macellare* 'to slaughter (an animal)'] *cul*. (*aus dem Wurstsud zubereitete Suppe*) sausage broth; *~ aus Blutwurstsud* BrE black-pudding broth, AmE blood sausage broth.

Mẹtzger...: **~gang** *m* -(e)s/... gänge [in former times, a butcher's visit from farm to farm in search of animals for slaughter often proved unsuccessful] *fig. colloq.* a practically useless enterprise: fool's errand, wild-goose chase. - **~handwerk** *n* -(e)s butchery trade (*or* business). - **~meister** *m* -s/- master butcher. - **~sprung** *m* -(e)s *hist. folklore* a picturesque and quaint custom of old Munich preserved to this day, now taking place every three years on the Monday before Shrove

"METZGERSPRUNG", MUNICH (1841).

Tuesday (*Faschingsmontag*): "Butchers' Leap", an initiation rite of butcher-apprentices (clothed in fur caps and garments, and covered from shoulder to heel with hundreds of dangling calves' tails) who, amid cheers from the mass of onlookers, plunge into the centre of the Marienplatz Fish Fountain in order to be freed from their indentures, to be washed free of the bad manners acquired during their apprenticeships, and to be made full-grown butchers.

Millionendorf *n* -(e)s *hum. sobr.* "village of a million people", a felicitous coinage for Munich: although a big and pulsating metropolis, the capital of Bavaria has yet, what with its beer gardens, a famous vegetable and fruit market for a pleasant morning's shopping chat, the typical *Weißwurst*↓ meal before noon, and the row of cosy pubs to go out to in the evening, preserved a good many features of a lifestyle that remains imperturbably rural.

Montur *f* -/-en [< F *monture* 'equipment'] *colloq.* **1.** *garm.* ([*Arbeits-* or *Dienst*] *Kleidung*) (work or service) clothes:

togs; (*er*) *schaut doch sehr flott aus in der Uniform, gell? ja, das ist eben „der Zauber der ~"!* (he's) looking very spruce in his military suit, isn't he? well, that's "the glamour of the uniform". - **2.** *agr.* (*Erdäpfelschale*) potato skin; *Erdäpfel in der ~* (*Pellkartoffeln*) potatoes (boiled) in their jackets: taters (*or* taties) in the mould.

Moos *n* -es/Möser, in place-names *Erdinger ~, Dachauer ~, Donau~* (to mention the three biggest ones in Bavaria) [< OHG *mōs* (1) 'moss', (2) 'moor'] *geog.* a wide area of waste ground overlaid with peat, and usu. more or less wet (*Moor, Sumpf*): moor (e.g. in England, the Yorkshire moors; in Scotland, the Moor of Rannoch), moorland, marshland; *das ~ entwässern* [*urbar machen*] to drain [to cultivate] the marshland.

Mords... an initial morpheme in nominal compounds, meaning '(unusually) great', in the senses 'big', 'grand' or 'grave', *colloq.*: **~gaudi** *f* - [see *Gaudi* 1] hilarious fun; *bei unsrem Klassentreffen gestern abend hat's eine ~ gegeben* we had a whale of a time at our class reunion last night. - **~radi** *m* -(s)/-(s) **1.** *bot.* a white vegetable, *Raphanus sativus*, if of the uncommon size of a turnip (cp. *Radi* 1): giant *or* king-size radish. - **2.** *fig.* a sharp reprimand (cp. *Radi* 3): good dressing-down, proper telling-off; *die Lehrerin hat uns einen ~ gehalten, weil wir wieder zu spät gekommen sind* the teacher gave us a sound tongue-lashing for being late again. - **~schädelweh** *n* -s *med.* violent headache: splitting *or* blazing headache.

Münchner Kindl *n* -s [second word, dim. of *Kind* 'child'] *colloq.* "Little Child (*or*, Kid) of Munich" **1.** *her.* the armorial device chosen by the Municipality of the Bavarian capital - a child clad in an ecclesiastical garment roughly resembling a monk's habit, his arms raised as in blessing; the figure recalls the first settlement in the area of Benedictines from the Tegernsee, who became powerful under Reinald of Schäftlarn, a dwarf monk, about the year 1100, but it may also symbolize the *Christkindl*↑, in this version probably holding in his hands a Bible and the keys of St Peter. - **2.** *hum.* a native of Munich, often an attractive female: Munich lassie [lad]; *mit Ingeborg Hallstein war ein ~ zur Primadonna geworden* Ingeborg Hallstein, the First Lady of the Munich Opera, was a local lassie who has made good.

Muskelschmalz *n* -es [a standardizing approximation to dialectal *Irxenschmalz*↑] *hum. colloq.* = *Irxenschmalz*; *da mußt du schon mit beiden Händen zupacken, und wie! - ohne das nötige ~ geht da nichts* you've got to grab things with both your hands, and how! - nothing doing without a good bit of elbow grease.

☞ **n** ☜

Nacht... *colloq.*: **~haferl** *n* -s/-(n) (*Nachttopf*) = *Potschamberl*↓. - **~licht** *n* -(e)s/-er **1.** (*Nachtmensch*) a person who likes to stay awake most of the night to read, work, etc.: night bird, (night) owl, stay-up. - **2.** (*Nachtschwärmer*) a person who spends the night in enjoyment: bird of the night, night lifer, *BrE also* stop-out, *AmE also* stay(er)-out(er), sundodger; *er* *ist ein ~* he makes a night of it, *AmE* also he's a dirty stay-out.

neinschauen *v/i* [*nein-* (< *hinein*) and *naus-* (< *hinaus*) on the one hand, and *rein-* (< *herein*) and *raus-* (< *heraus*), or *aussa-* (< *ausher*), on the other, are antonymic dialect shortenings of directional adverbs and particles: the first two imply motion away from, the next three motion towards, the speaker] *colloq. dial.* to look in (from the outside) ‖ *phr.* (1) a tippler's suggestion on passing a beerhouse: *schauen wir nein, und trinken wir eine Halbe!* let's pop in and have a pint! - (2) a fatalist's semi-proverbial note of resignation on being negatively impressed by a look at himself in the mirror or on a photograph: *was neinschaut, schaut raus* (or *aussa*)! *as you look in, so you look out; *ScotE* ye canna tak oot what ye dinna pit in.

Nesthockerl *n* -s/pl. rare: -(n) [second el., < *hocken* 'to squat, i.e. to sit with the knees bent and the legs drawn fully up under the body', + dim. *-erl*] *colloq.* the youngest of a group; actually, the last of the fledglings in a bird's nest to learn to fly (*Nesthäkchen*): baby of the family; *ja der Hansi ist unser ~, er geht noch in den Kindergarten* Johnny is the baby of our family, he still goes to kindergarten.

Neue Welt *f* -n -/no pl. [a phrase echoing the older appellation, in use in many languages since about 1600, for 'the continent of America'] *forestry & agr.* "New World", the area south of the Dreisessel massif, including the villages of Neureichenau, Breitenberg, and Sonnen, a vast expanse of primeval forest until Prince-Bishop Wenceslas von Thun began moving would-be settlers there during the seventeenth century; to this day, the offsprings of those "*Nui*" *Welt* pioneers speak a quaint old dialect of their own, e.g. with a triple vowel heard in words like *reout* 'red' and *Breout* 'bread'.

Niederschnarchlfing *n* -s/pl. rare: -e *hum.* one of the many imaginary place-names suggestive of rural simplicities (cp. *Hinterhuglharpfing*↑): Lower Back Scratch; here is an example of what its mentality is said to be capable of:

> *Einmal ist aus dem Straubinger Gefängnis ein Häftling ausgebrochen. An die Polizeidienststellen gingen drei Fahndungsfotos, auf denen der Kopf des Flüchtlings von vorn, von links und von rechts zu sehen war. Bald darauf läutete beim Gefängnisdirektor das Telefon: „Hier Polizeistation Niederschnarchlfing. Ich hab meine besten Leut angesetzt, und ich kann stolz melden, mir ham alle drei gfangt!"*

One day it happened that a prisoner escaped from the penitentiary of Straubing. Three "wanted" posters were sent out to all the police stations in the area, showing the fugitive's head from the front and right and left profiles. Soon thereafter, the prison warden received a telephone call: "This is the chief of police in Lower Back Scratch calling. I put my best men on the case, and I'm proud to say that we've caught all three of them!"

Noagerl ['nɔagɑl] *n* -s/-(n) [< *neig-*, the stem of *neigen* 'to incline', 'to tilt' (since the glass or mug in question is tilted for closer inspection, to see how much liquid is really left at the bottom) + dim. suffix *-erl*↑] *dial.*, often slightly *contp.* or *iron.* dregs, esp. of beer: backwash, tail-end; *was, auf das ~ kommt's dir an?* what, you can't even polish off that little bit?; *vielen Dank, aber das ~ kannst du dir behalten!* thanks a lot, but you can keep your backwash! ‖ here is the word as a compound element, to embellish a little story (the whole, incidentally, also being applicable to a human beer addict, exactly in the sense described above under *Bierdimpfl* 2): *ein zahmer Hirsch im Wirtsgarten war ein richtiger Säufer; ganz zu Recht hieß er der „~-Sepp", weil er mit seinem Geweih die* *leeren Bierkrüge umstieß und den Rest auf der Tischplatte aufleckte* one tame stag in the beer garden was a real boozer - he fully earned the nickname of "Backwash Billy" by always tipping over the empty beer mugs with his antlers and then licking up the dregs from the tabletops.

Nocken *f* -/- [?< *Nock m* 'hummock', indeed 'any unspecified mass of something solid'] *contp.* a stupid and unenterprising person (the word tending, because of its grammatical gender, to be a little more often applied to a female): dope, *AmE* also dummy, dingbat, *BrE* also (great) lump; *das ist dir fei eine fade ~!* there's a lump on a log for you (I [can] tell ye)!

Nockerl *n* -s/-(n) [dim. of It *gnocco* ['njɔkɔ] 'dumpling (shaped by hand [G *Knödel*↑])'; but cp. also Schmeller's conjecture given under *Nocken*↑] - **1.** (1) *cul.* a (necessarily) irregular-shaped lump of dough, made with eggs, that - like its mates - is dropped from a spoon or cut slantwise from a board into boiling water (*Mehlklößchen* [*aus Eierteig*]): small dumpling ‖ in word combinations: (a) *Grießnockerlsuppe* semolina-dumpling soup; (b) *Salzburger ~ pl.* a frothy delicacy, actually indigenous to the City of Salzburg, Austria, but appreciated also in neighbouring Bavaria, either as a dessert or as a main dish: sweet soufflé omelette (*sg.*) Salzburg style. - (2) *fig. colloq.* in a sententious phrase conveying the futility of over-abundance in worldly riches (according to which a person who enjoys all the luxuries of life may be inclined to spend his excess money on a hobby, give to charity, etc.): *goldene ~(n) kann man nicht essen!* *you cannot eat golden dumplings; how can you use any more money than what you've already got? - **2.** *colloq.* an epithet bestowed with gently raised eyebrows or in amused humour on a young woman for an act of gaucherie or unprovoked touchiness (*Gänschen*): silly billy *or* goose; *so ein ~, das hab ich ja gar nicht gemeint!* what a silly (goose), I didn't mean that at all.

Nord...: **~gau** *m* -(e)s *hist.* "Northern Territory" of Bavaria, actually the Hohenstaufen territory inherited by the Wittelsbachs in 1268 and, under the family treaty of Pavia, 1329, made into a separate principality, which was later known as *Oberpfalz↓*; *die Güter, Waldsassen (Nürnberg, Eger),* etc. *auf dem* ~ the possessions, Waldsassen (Nuremberg, Eger), *etc.* in the Northern Territory. - **~lichter** *n* usu. *pl.* [a pun on the meteoric phenomenon of the aurora borealis] *hist.,* sometimes *iron.* "Northern Lights", a collective name for the scholars (Liebig, Sybel, Thiersch, etc.), poets (Bodenstedt, Geibel, Heyse, etc.) and other luminaries called to Munich from Northern Germany by King Maximilian II in the 1850s. - **~wald** *m* -(e)s *geog.* & *hist.* "North Forest" (an English sense parallel would be *Northolt*), from the Old Romans' point of view a ready coinage for what is now the *Bayerische Wald*; its almost impenetrable density, as well as the presence of the Danube, formed a natural barrier against the Germanic tribes, rendering the continuation of the *Limes* beyond Kelheim unnecessary.

Obatzte [ˈoːbatstə] *m* -n/-n; as a term of reference more often used with the indefinite article, *a Obatzta* [aˈoːbatstə] (sometimes spelt with the standard ending, *Obatzter*) [< StandG *Angebatzter*, p.p. of *anbatzen* 'to add to with a short flick of the wrist'] *dial., gastr.* "cheese clump", cheese mix, a prepared spread made from the combination of gervais and camembert cheeses, butter, egg yolk, pepper and other spices, as well as half an onion, finely chopped; for better spreading, a smidgin of beer can be helpful; *zu unserem ~n gehören Salzstangen oder ein deftiges Vollkornbrot* the perfect partners for our "cheese clump" are salted breadsticks or a few slices of heavy coarse-grained bread.

Oberpfalz *f* - *polit. geog.* Upper Palatinate, one of the seven districts (*Regierungsbezirke*) into which Bavaria is divided for administrative purposes (location in Bavaria, NE; capital, Regensburg); the Upper Palatinate and Lower Bavaria combined into one government district between 1932 and 1948.

Ochsen... *cul.*: **~augen** *n pl.* [since reminiscent of the animal's round big eyes] ([*zwei*] *Spiegeleier*) "ox eyes", i.e. (two) fried eggs, *AmE sl.* Adam and Eve, bride and groom ‖ a waiter's instruction to the chef: *zwei ~!* two eggs sunny-side up! - **~gurgel** *f* -/-n [aptly called thus because of the striking resemblance of the pastry's inside shape to the gristly unevennesses of an ox gullet] *bak.* at Daiminger's, Burglengenfeld, Upper Palatinate: "ox gullet", a cylindrical short-crust pastry (G *Mürbteig*; 500 grams of flour, 250 grams of butter, 3 eggs) some four inches long, fried in hot lard and rolled in sugar.

Odel or **Odl** ['oː-], rarely **Adel** ['ɔː-] *m* -s [cognate with dialE *addle*, *yeddle* 'cow's urine or other liquid filth', and StandE *addled egg* 'rotten egg'] *agr. dial.* (*Jauche*) liquid manure, *BrE dial.* cowpiss, muck-water; **~grube** *f* -/-n cesspit, cesspool, *BrE dial.* yeddle-hole, mucky pond.

Ohrenhöhler *m* -s/- [< from the supposition that it enters people's ear-holes] *ent.* (*Ohrwurm*) earwig: *BrE dial.* lugwig, twitch(y)-bell, (s)kutchy-bell, forky-tail.

o leck [by rigorous curtailment, to make the phrase socially acceptable, < *leck mich am Arsch* 'kiss my arse'] *interj* a polite curse, or an expletive expressing mild surprise or disappointment: dang it!, *AmE also* (oh) fudge!

Oktoberfest *n* -(e)s/-e *folklore* October Feast, October Fair, October Festival - **1.** on the Theresienwiese, Munich: an enormous fair, and the time of much merrymaking complete with a costume procession, horse races, side-shows, beer tents, open barbecues for roasting venison, oxen and chicken, observed every autumn for a fortnight beginning at the end of September; it originated with a popular celebration arranged by King Maximilian I for the wedding on October 12, 1819, of his son, the future King Ludwig I, to Princess Therese of Saxe-Hildburghausen. → **2.** any of the 170 or so beer festivals celebrated on the Munich model in Europe and elsewhere, especially in the United States, some such festival cities being Vienna, Paris, London, Toronto, Montreal, Melbourne, Sydney, Brisbane and Adelaide.

Österreicherliesl *f* -/no pl. [the combining form in *-er* connotes good-neighbourly feelings, which are neatly balanced by the diminutive ending of the second element, a personalized name for the sun; a mere *Österreich-* would have remained coldly factual, 'coming from Austria'] *hum.* in East Bavaria, esp. in the border country immediately north of the Danube: "Auzzie Liz", an epithet for the sun when rising above the hills of the Untere Wald ‖ an appreciative comment on a sunshiny morning: *die ~ meint's heute gut mit uns* *"Auzzie Liz" means (it) well with us today, "Auzzie Liz" is really doing us proud (*AmE* doing right by us) today.

P

packen v/t [short for StandG *anpacken*] *colloq.* to grip and try to carry through to the end with a will ‖ *phr.* a proposition to tackle some definite set of manual work, usu. requiring muscular strength, or to engage in one of sundry outdoor pastimes, from the adventure of scaling up the house wall to the window of one's sweetheart (*fensterln*↑) to a strenuous mountain climb - the natural medium is broad dialect, of course: *pack ma's!* let's go to it!, let's get going!

Panade *f* -/-n [< F or Sp, equivalent to *pan-* 'bread' (< L *pānis*) + *-ade* here indicating a food mixture of which the first element is the chief ingredient] *cul.* a thick paste made with breadcrumbs, butter and yolk: panada. - **Panadelsuppe**, **Panadlsuppe** *f* -/-n [in this compound, the <-l-> is not a diminutive suffix (cp. *-l*), but merely a convenient binding element] *cul.* a thickish soup with slices of white bread dipped in egg and lightly fried (*Suppe mit Weißbroteinlage*): panada soup.

Papp *m* -(e)s/pl. rare: -e *colloq.* **1.** a thin mixture of flour and water, used for sticking paper together or onto other surfaces (*Kleister*): (starch-flour) paste. - **2.** frozen snow clinging to the sole of one's boots ([*Schnee-*]*Klumpen*): lump(s) of snow.

pappen vt/i *colloq.* **1.** v/t ([*auf-*]*kleben*) to stick, to paste; *wieviel pappt man denn auf einen Brief nach Neuseeland?* what's the postage you slap (*or* smack) on a letter to New Zealand? - **2.** v/i (*fest* [*und klumpig*] *haften*) of snow under one's boots, etc.: to lump, to form lumps, to become lumpy;

der Schnee pappt so fest, ich geh wie auf einem Kothurn the snow's so lumpy on the soles I seem to be walking on stilts.

Pascherwinkel *m* -s/- *econ. hist. & geog., colloq.* a telltale nickname for the wild and lonely area of Lackenhäuser, at the foot of the Dreisessel mountain, on the border of Bavaria, Bohemia and Austria: "smugglers' stomping ground", a favourite corner of transit, around the turn of the last century, for illicit traffickers in cattle and merchandise such as saccharine (→ *Sacharinheilige*), sugar, salt, tobacco, footwear, textiles, and Swiss watches.

Patrona Bavariae *f* - *relig.* the honorific title in Latin of Holy Mary, the mother of Christ: Our Lady the patron saint of Bavaria; *Zehntausende Bayern strömen anfangs Mai zum Fest der ~ ~ nach Altötting* in early May, Bavarians by the tens of thousands flock to Altötting for the feast of their lady patron saint.

Patrozinium *n* -s *relig.* **1.** patron ['peɪ-] saint's patronage ['pæ-] of a church; *diese Kirche steht unter dem ~ des heiligen Martin; ihm zu Ehren gibt es am zweiten Sonntag im November einen Martinsritt, auch nimmt dann der Pfarrer eine Pferdesegnung vor* the church is under the patronage of St [snt] Martin; in his honour a procession on horseback is held on the second Sunday of November, and the horses are being blessed by the parish priest. - **2.** or *Patroziniumsfest n* -(e)s; *wann feiert ihr hier das ~?* when is the feast day of the patron saint of your local church here?

Pfandschaab *n* -(e)s/-e [second el. < StandG *Schaub* 'sheaf'] *dial. & folklore* on the borders of meadows and pastures in the Straubing area, a whisk of straw tied to a handle, a non-verbal symbol of the "No Trespassing!" message (*Verbotszeichen für Durchgang*): no-entry post.

Pfannenkuchen, Pfannkuchen *m* -s/-, *dial.* **Pfannakuacha** *m* -/- [first el., < OHG *pfanna* 'pan'; the *-en* of the combining form *Pfannen-* is an old genitive ending] **1.** *cul.* pancake, *AmE* also crepe ‖ *phr.* a provocative query, uttered as a friendly banter or in slight annoyance, when somebody always leaves doors open: *habt ihr einen ~* (or, *einen [Stroh-]Sack) daheim (vor der Tür)?* are there no doors in your house?, why can't you put the wood in the hole?, were you born in a barn *or* in fields (*or, ScotE, ...* brocht up in a cairt-shed)? - **2.** pl. only, *vulg.* pendant breasts (*lappiger Hängebusen*): droopers, super droopers.

Pfannenkuchen..., often also *dial.* **Pfannakuacha...**: **~gesicht** *n* -(e)s/pl. rare: -er *colloq.*, used slightingly, a large, expressionless face: deadpan (expression), frozen face, poker face. - **~suppe** *f* -/-n *cul.* clear beef broth garnished with fine strips of pancake.

Pfeiferl *n* -s/-(n) [dim. of *Pfeife* 1. 'whistle', and 2. '(water) pipe', 'spout'] *colloq.* **1.** (tin) whistle. - **2.** *euphem.* a child's penis: peenie, whistle; cp. *Zipferl* 2. - **~wasser** *n* -s/pl. rare: - [a refined speaker's variant for what others would bluntly refer to as *Soachwasser* 'piss water'] *hum.* or mildly *contp.* any non-alcoholic drink, esp. carbonated water (naturally held in contempt by 'a real man' [*ein gestandenes Mannsbild*], who in Bavaria doubtless plumps for beer): gargle, gullet wash, mouthwash, wish-wash.

pfeilgrad *adv* [< *pfeilgerade* '(as) straight as an arrow'] *colloq.* used in the sense of *pfeilgeschwind* '(as) swift as an arrow (*or*, as lightning)', and from there to other semantic widenings, all generally connoting emphasis and specificity: **1.** directly, right away, without a second thought; *er hat gefragt, was ich gemacht hab, und ich hab's ihm ~ gesagt* he asked what I did, and I told him off the cuff (*or*, without blinking an eye). - **2.** really (and truly); *mir fällt jetzt ~ nicht ein, wie das Buch heißt* I cannot for the life of me remember the title of the book. - **3.** the very [+ noun]; *heut bin ich* *doch ~ dem Menschen über den Weg gelaufen, den ich nie hab treffen wollen* I came across the very person today I never wanted to meet.

Pfingst...: **~geißel**, *dial.* **~goißl** *f* -/-n *folklore* as a relic from pagan times, the agent of obstreperous noise-making in order to chase away the evil spirits of Winter: "Whitsun whip", a lengthy piece of rope attached to a short handle that is alternately jerked to the left and to the right, always allowing the rope to stretch out fully in order to produce a sharp crack; a special sense of rhythmic timing is required when a group performs this spirited act (*Tuschen*). - **~kerze** *f*-/no pl. *relig. & folklore* on Whit Sunday, the centrepiece of a Marian procession to Bogenberg Hill (→ *Holzkirchener Wallfahrt*): "Whitsun candle", a 43-foot-long ornamental pole encased in wax, weighing some 110 pounds; these unusual dimensions, purporting to give ocular proof of the serious devotion of those taking part in the pilgrimage, demand an inordinate feat of strength from the lads, each one taking turns in carrying the candle in an upright position to its destination on high. - **~lümmel** *m* -s/pl. rare: - **1.** *folklore* a seasonal village prank: "Whitsun lout", a straw doll in ragged trousers and jacket, placed in front of a window or on the rooftop of the house where a particularly quarrelsome girl (elsewhere, where the servant girl presumed to be the laziest in the community) is resident. → **2.** *hum.* one who gets up last on Whit Sunday morning: *Whitsun slug-a-bed. - **~ochs** *m* -en/pl. rare: -en [actually, the finest bull of the herd, festively bedecked with a wreath and streamers when the cattle are taken uphill to their summer pasture] *hum.* or *contp.* a young fop who takes too much interest in his outward appearance: (jack-a-)dandy; *BrE* Beau Brummel, *AmE* drugstore cowboy; *er war aufgeputzt wie ein ~ BrE* he was all done up to the nines, *contp. also* he was dressed up like a dog's dinner, *AmE* he was dressed like a fashion plate, he was all duded up. - **~ritt** *m* -(e)s/pl. rare: -e *relig. & folklore* → *Kötztinger Pfingstritt*. - **~schwanz** *m* -es/no pl. = *Pfingstlümmel*. - **~tuschen**, or **Hexen-Austuschen** *n* -s/no pl. *hist. folklore* in the evening of Whit Sunday: "whipping the witches", a prolonged hullabaloo of whip-cracking staged by peasant lads in the Kötzting area in order to banish the witches who, though invisible, are in those hours believed to be riding about thick and fast on their broomsticks.

Pfinsta, less often **Pfinstag** *m* -(s)/- [*Pfins-*, more lucidly spelt *Pfints-* or *Pfinz-*, to show the result of the OHG Consonant Shift, < Gr *pénte* 'five'; hence, *Pfinsta* 'the fifth day' of the week, counting from Sunday] *rural dial.* (*Donnerstag*) Thursday; cp. *Antlaßpfinsta*↑.

Plache *f* -/-n ([*Wagen-*]*Plane*) canvas, tarpaulin.

plattert *adj* [suffix -*ert* forms adjectives from noun or verb stems; its meaning describes a quality or property, and as in this case there is often a pejorative connotation] *dial.*, slightly *contp.* bald (*glatzköpfig*): *sarc.* barefooted on top of the head, sunny side up. - **Platterte** *m* -n/-n [the adjectival noun derived from the former] *dial.*, slightly *contp.* bald-headed man: *colloq.* baldy, *sarc.* bald coot, cue ball ‖ *joc.* a facetious piece of "remedial" advice for one seized by sudden hiccups or a fit of sneezing: *denk an drei ~ und halt die Luft an!* *just (try to) think of three baldies and hold your breath!

Plempel *m* -s/- [< *plampen* (of a liquid) 'to swash heavily from side to side'] slightly *contp.* stale beer: slipslap, slipslop, slops, dishwater, bilgewater.

Postkastl *n* -s/-(n) [dim. of *Postkasten*] *colloq.* a box in a post office, street, etc., in which letters can be posted: letterbox, postbox, *AmE also* mailbox, mail drop, *BrE also* pillar box; *wo ist denn da bittschön das nächste ~?* where is the nearest letterbox, please?

Potschamberl *n* -s/-(n) [dim. of F *pot de chambre*] *colloq.*, often *hum.* chamber pot (*Nachttopf*): chamber (of commerce), piddle potty, *BrE also* geography (under the bed); *ich weiß in der Nacht vielleicht nicht genau, wo man bei euch hingeht, wenn man hinausmuß, so wäre mir in meinem Kammerl ein ~ schon ganz recht unterm Bett, bittschön* at night, when I feel like wandering (you know where), I might perhaps have my problems with the geography of your house; so I wouldn't mind having a little geography under the bed, please.

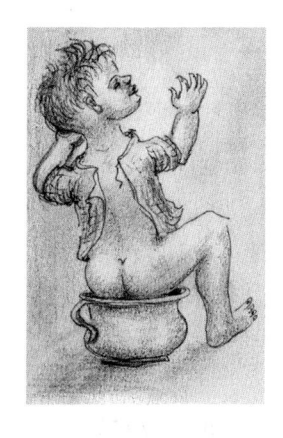

Prangertag *m* -(e)s/pl. rare: -e [< *prangen* 'to be festively garbed' - said with reference to Mother Nature, then in the prime of the spring season, but especially to the prettily dressed young girls attending the religious ceremony described here, to the houses gaily decorated with branches and sprigs of light-green birch wherever the procession passes and, not least, to the impressive pageant of *Prangstangen*↓] "Glory Day" **1.** *eccles.* & *folklore* (*Fronleichnam*) Corpus Christi Day, celebrated with great splendour by R.C. communities, the central feature being the Corpus Christi Day procession, during which wreaths and garlands, brass bands, bell-ringing and gun-salutes are much in evidence. - **2.** *fig.*, often *joc.* a day to show one's festive garb, for any reason whatever: *sich wie zum ~ herausputzen* to dress in one's best clothes: *colloq.* to titivate oneself, to put on one's best bib and tucker (*AmE also*, ... best duds); *ja, ist denn heute ~, daß ihr euch so schön herausgeputzt habt?* why (*or*, I say), what kind of red-letter day are we having today that you are so spruced up (*or*, decked out) for? - **Prangstange** *f* -/-n *eccles.* & *folklore* (*Prozessionsstange*) "glory pole", one of the ornate poles carried in church processions.

Preiß, the *dial.* pronunciation and spelling of **Preuß** *m* -en/-en *colloq.*, often with a negative bias: (so-and-so) Prussian; *er ist ein* ~ he's a Prussian (, mind you; *or*, what [else] do you expect?); *diese ~en* (well,) those Prussians; *dial.*: *da siecht ma halt wieder de ~n* Prussians will be Prussians, that's like them all over ‖ a semi-malicious little invitation to fellow-Bavarians: *Heidaufdnachtwernpreissnabgschlacht / werpreissnfleischmogsoikummadedog!* *Folks, tonight is butchering night / if you love Prussian meat drop in for a treat!

Preßsack *m* -(e)s/pl. rare: ...säcke *gastr.* (*Schwartenmagen*) *BrE* jelly brawn, *AmE* headcheese, head souse, hog maw, i.e. meat from the head (and feet) of pigs, pressed into a cheese-like mass after suitable seasoning and boiling; the word is often qualified by the attributes *schwarzer* or *weißer*, according to whether blood, liver, kidneys, and other entrails (causing the dark red colour) have been added or not.

Prinzregent *m* -en/-en *hist.* a title reserved for a member of the royal family who, if the monarch is incapacitated for carrying on his duties, takes over without being crowned king; this happened to be the case with Prince Luitpold of Bavaria, 1821-1912, who deputized from 1886 on the throne of Bavaria for his nephews, Kings Ludwig II and Otto, since both were declared insane and unfit to rule (note the English parallel of 1811, when the eldest son of King George III had to step in, to be crowned King George IV only after his father's death in 1820): Regent. - **~entorte** *f* -/-n [< Prince Luitpold's fondness of that delicacy] *bak.* "Regent cake", a rich chocolate cake, with alternate layers of sponge mixture and chocolate cream, and a coating of chocolate.

pumpern *v/i colloq.* (*stark klopfen*) to thump, to hammer; *sein Herz hat vor Aufregung gepumpert* his heart was thumping (away) (*or*, hammering [away]) with excitement ‖ venting one's anger in blasphemous dialect speech: *Kruzifix noch einmal, wer pumpert denn da ans Hoftor wia net gscheit?* who the devil is pounding on (*or*, against) the (yard) gate like mad (*or*, like a madman)?

Putzer *m* -s/- [actually, 'cleanser', an agent noun to denote the substance, or in this case the action, that is supposed to or does bring about an improvement in the status quo] *colloq.* reprimand: dressing-down, going-over, *AmE also* bawling-out; *einen ~ bekommen* to be scolded: to be on the carpet, *AmE also* to get it ([good and] hot); *die Fratzen haben einen ordentlichen ~ gekriegt, weil sie so spät nach Haus gekommen sind* the naughty children got a good dressing-down (*or*, a real going-over *or*, a real telling-off) for coming home late.

Quartl *n* -s/-(n) [< L *quart(us)* 'fourth' + SouG dim. suffix *-l*↑] a liquid measure, the fourth of a litre or *Maß*↑ (= 0.44 UK pints, or 1.76 UK gills): "quarter"; *drei ~(n) hist.* three quarters of a litre (= 1.32 UK pints), a set mark on the liquid-measure scale once popular with that section of Bavarian froth-blowers that had to, or simply wanted to, economize - tendering their one-litre family mug and placing an order of "three quarters", hoping, often quite rightly so, that the landlord would comply by filling her up to the brim; → *Dreiquartlprivatier* 1.

☞ R ☜

Radi *m* -(s)/- [a truncated SouG dialect variant (cp. *drah di'!* < *dreh dich!*) of *Rettich*; both forms, and E *radish*, are ultimately derived from L *radix* 'root'] *colloq.* **1.** *cul.* ([*Weichser*] *Rettich*) in the Regensburg area: giant radish, the size and colour of a turnip ‖ an historical reflection and eulogy, adapted from tongue-in-cheek Otto Julius Bierbaum (1910):

> *Ratisbona, der keltische Name (den die Römer übernahmen), ist korrumpiert; es muß Radisbona heißen, und das bedeutet die Stadt der guten ~. Doch der Regensburger ~ ist sanfter vom Geschmack als andere. Es ist ein lyrischer ~, gar ein Produkt römischer Gartenkünstler, die seine Rauheit gemildert haben, weil es galt, den armen, zu den Hyperboreern verschlagenen Legionären aus dem sonnigen Süden die fehlende Feige wenigstens radisisch spüren zu lassen.*

Ratisbona, the Celtic name (duly adopted by the Romans), is a corrupted form; it should be Radisbona, meaning The City of Good Radishes. As it is, the Regensburg radish is gentler in taste than others. It is a lyrical kind of radish, perhaps even a produce from Roman horticulturalists, who took the edge off its pungency - after all, it was the poor legionaries, cast out among the Hyperboreans, and having to go without the soft figs of the sunny South, who were to at least get an idea of what a radisical fruit tasted like.

‖ *hum. phr.* (1) a formulaic description of what a Regensburg radish is, or should be, like: *er ist weiß wie ein Osterlamm, saftig wie eine Schweinshaxn, rund wie eine Weißwurst oder spitz wie ein Domturm* it is white like an Easter lamb, succulent like a pig's knuckle, round like a white sausage or pointed like a cathedral spire. - (2) a cheerful prediction of dexterity from fingers to feet: *wer gut ~ schneidet, kann gut tanzen* *a dandy radish-slicer makes a dandy hoofer (*or* leg-shaker). → **2.** ~-~ *interj* the boisterous rallying call and shout of jubilation used by the Lusticania, one of the Regensburg carnival societies: *Radish ain't baddish; *lautstarkes ~-~-Rufen kündigte den Einzug des Hofstaates an, mit dem Hofnarren an der Spitze, der munter einen Riesenradi hin- und herschwenkte* loud shoutings of "Raddish ain't baddish!" heralded the entrance of the princely court, led by the court jester, who gaily waved a giant radish about.

Radieserl *n* -s/-(n) [a dim. (→ -*erl*) of *Radies* < Du *radijs*, F *radis* < It *radice* < L *radix* (gen. *radicis*) 'root'] *bot.* (*Radieschen*) (red) radish; *ein Bund ~* a bunch of radishes ‖*colloq.* said in grim humour of somebody lying dead and buried: *die ~(n) von unten anschauen* (or *wachsen sehen*) to push up (*BrE* the) daisies, to turn one's toes up to the daisies.

Radi... *colloq.*: **~frau** *f* -/-en (*Rettichverkäuferin*) in front of the Regensburg Cathedral, or elsewhere: (streetside) radish vendor, radish-girl, *BrE also* radish-wife. - **~kopperer** *m* -s/- low *colloq.* radish burp, a noisy belch caused by the gourmet's sizeable intake of radish and beer; *einen ~ lassen* to give (*or* let out) a radish burp. - **~schneider** *m* -s/- *tech.* radish-slicer, a special blade attached to a metal spindle which, when revolved, transforms the radish into a long, accordion-like spiral. - **~weib** *n* -(e)s/-er in brusque speech, for *Radifrau*↑: radish-woman. - **~weiberl** *n* -s/-(n) **1.** in affective speech, for *Radifrau*↑: dear ([*or* sweet] old) radish-lady; **2.** *hum.* in Carnivaltime, as part of the Lusticania pageant, one of the court girls who is flashily dressed as a radish vendor: snazzy radish trouper.

Radl *n* -s/-(n) [dim. of *Rad* 'wheel'] *colloq.* **1.** little wheel; *hum.* or *sarc. phr.* aimed at a person thought to be slightly mad: *der hat ein ~ zuviel (im Kopf)!* he has a screw loose, he's a bit off (*or* weak) in the upper stor[e]y, *BrE also* he's touched in his upper works, he's one loaf short of a picnic, lights are on but there's no one in, *AmE also* he's minus some buttons, he's a bit short of a full deck. - **2.** [short for *Fahrrad*] bicycle: bike, *BrE also* pushbike, *AmE also* wheel; *bring dein ~ weg und laß es* (or *dir's*) *reparieren* take your bike and have (*or* get) it repaired. - **3.** a thin round piece cut from certain items of food, roughly cylindrical in shape, e.g. from a length of sausage, a carrot, a beetroot, or a cucumber: slice; *drei ~ Wurst langen (ganz) sicher* three slices of sausage will do nicely.

Radler *n* -s/- [with the gender transferred from *Bier*], short for **Radlermaß** *f* -/...masse (after numerical data: - [e.g., zwei Radlermaß]; *dial.* pl. also: Radlermassen), or **Radlerhalbe** *f* -/-(n) *bev.* half beer and half lemonade, reputed to be splendidly refreshing and considerably less potent than beer neat - a drink for "knights of the wheel" (and other devotees of the mixture): (one litre of) *cyclists' special (*or*, ... *cyclists' delight), *BrE* shandy.

Randstein *m* -(e)s/-e *civ. eng.* (*Bordstein* [*e-s Gehsteigs*]) *BrE* kerb(stone), *AmE* curb(stone), edgestone; *er hat das Auto nicht nah genug am ~ geparkt* he didn't park the car close enough to the curb [kerb].

Rannen *f* -/- [< EarlyModHG *Randen* 'Beta vulgaris rubra L.'] *bot.* (*rote Rübe*) beetroot, *AmE also* beet.

rappel... [< *rappeln* *v/i* (in a by now obsolescent sense) 'to make loud and quickly repetitive noises'; cp. E *to rap* 'to hit with a series of quick blows'] *colloq.* a sense-depleted, and now merely emphatic compound element: **~dürr** *adj* said of human beings and quadrupeds (*klapperdürr*): (as) thin as a rake (*or, less often,* ... a rail). - **~trocken** *adj* said of wood, a piece of cake, etc. (*staubtrocken*): bone-dry. - **~voll** *adj* said of roads, theatres, etc. (*gedrängt voll*): chock-a-block (e.g., with cars), chock-full (e.g., of people), jam-packed.

raß *adj, dial.* (*beißend*) **1.** causing a burning sensation in one's mouth: sharp, pungent, hot-tasting; *der Kas [Radi] da is mir zu ~* this cheese [radish] tastes too hot for my liking. → **2.** said in awe, or with amused criticism, of a chronically ill-tempered woman: waspish; *mei, die hat aber ein rasses Mundwerk, das is fei ganz a Rasse!* my, that woman's got a rare sharp tongue, she has a vicious tongue in her head!

Ratisbonerl *n* -s/-(n) [a humorous dim. of *Ratisbon(a)*, E *Ratisbon*, the old name of Regensburg, a venerable Imperial city on the Danube, now the capital of the Upper Palatinate + *-erl*↑] *bak.* "Little Ratisbon roll", a small oval bread loaf made from rye and wholemeal flour, whose mixture also contains wheat germs, linseeds, sunflower seeds, as well as fragments of an assortment of dry fruits (such as walnuts, raisins, and tangerines).

Ratsch *m* -es/pl. rare: -e [< *ratschen* 1] *colloq.* **1.** (*gemütliche Unterhaltung* [*im vertrauten Kreise*]) a friendly informal conversation: chat; *komm doch auf einen gemütlichen ~ herüber, so was um neun - meine Leut sind dann alle aus dem Haus* do come over for a cosy chat, let's say about nine - my folks will all be gone by then. - **2.** rare — gossip: chatter stuff; *das ist alles nur ~, an dem ist nichts dran!* it's all tittle-tattle (*AmE* prittle-prattle), there's nothing in it.

Ratsche *f* -/-n, the rare StandG variant of the next; **Ratschen** *f* -/-, [see the verb↓] *colloq.* **1.** a baby's toy; or an apparatus, in juvenile hands, that makes a repeated loud noise, e.g. in order to communicate to others a liturgical message (→ *Rat-*

schenbub) or one's participating glee over the events in a football stadium: clapper, rattle. - **2.** often *contp.*; if female, also **Ratschenweib** *n* -(e)s/ -er (1) a talkative person: chatterbox; *das ist dir eine Ratschen, da kommt kein anderer zu Wort!* what a prattler that man [woman] is - no one else can get a word in! - (2) if indiscreetly loquacious: blabbermouth; *das alte Ratschenweib schnüffelt allerweil bei anderen herum - kein Wunder, daß es über so vieles Bescheid weiß* the old tattler's always poking her nose into other people's business - no wonder she's so well informed.

ratschen *vt/i* [< *ratsch*, an interjection formed through sound imitation of the long sharp tear when quickly made into cloth, paper, etc.] *colloq.* **1.** *v/t* also **herunterratschen** to perform s.th. quickly, often mechanically: to rattle off *or* through (a poem, a prayer [e.g. the clapper-boy jingle given at the end of the next entry]). - **2.** *v/i* (1) to use a baby rattle. - (2) to use a clapper; *die Buben freuen sich schon darauf, am Karfreitag durch den Ort ~ gehen zu können* the lads are already looking forward to the chance of jangling their clappers through the place on Good Friday. - **3.** *v/i* (1) to talk in a friendly informal manner: to chat, to chitchat, to have a chinwag, *AmE also* to chew the fat (*or* the rag), to shoot the bull (*or* the breeze); *er ratscht ganz gern, ist aber ein lieber Mensch* he's a friendly, chatty sort of person. - (2) to be an exaggerated talker: to wag the tongue; *es haben schon zu viele geratscht, als daß die Sache noch vertraulich bleiben könnte* too many tongues have been wagging for the matter to remain confidential any longer.

Ratschen...: **~bub** *m* -en/-en *R.C. relig.* one of a group of altar boys "rattling" the street scene with their *Karfreitagsratschen*↑ every daylight hour between Maundy Thursday and Easter Sunday: clapper boy; *da nach frommem Glauben die Kirchenglocken nach Rom geflogen sind, laden jetzt ~en die Gläubigen zum Gebet ein* since, according to pious belief, the church bells have flown to Rome, clapper boys now invite the faithful to pray - this is the first of two couplets chanted by them before resuming the jangling:

Wir ratschen, wir ratschen	*We clapperdeclap
den englischen Gruß,	Ave Mary all day,
den jeder Christgläubige	which every good Christian
beten jetzt muß.	is now bound to pray.

~weib *n* -(e)s/-er *contp.* = *Ratschen* 2.

Ratschkathl *f* -/-n [second el., a dim. variant of *Katharina* 'Catherine' > 'Cathy'] *hum.* or *contp.* = *Ratsch(e)* 2 (but restricted to females).

Ratz *m* -es/-e, *dial.* -(en)/-(e)n [this SouG variant (MHG *ratz(e)* < OHG *ratza*) looks like a late consonant-shifted form of MHG *ratte* < OHG *ratta, rato*, but is possibly to be explained as a pet-form, < *ratizo (cp. *Spatz*); in any case, the word is an old migrant from the Mediterranean, as is testified by It *ratto*, F *rat*, and Sp *rata*, all referring to a rodent of some of the larger species of the genus *Mus*] **1.** *zo.* (1) (*Ratte*) rat. - (2) (*Hamster*) hamster. - (3) *hunter's jargon*, also: *Mummel*~ (*Iltis*) polecat. - **2.** *phr.* in a *colloq.* simile describing deep and peaceful sleep: *er hat geschlafen wie ein ~* he slept like a top (*or*, like a log); *ich kann schlafen wie ein ~* I could sleep without rocking, I could sleep on a clothes line.

Regenbogenschüsserl *n* -s/-(n) *colloq.* "tiny rainbow dish" **1.** *archaeol.* one of many small and slightly convex gold coins, similar to a trouser-button in size, found on the sites of former Celtic settlements. - **2.** *folklore* a treasure left by an angel at the end of a rainbow, not unlike a crock (or pot) of gold found in the proverbial lore of Ireland, England, and New England.

Reherl ['rɛ:-əl] *n* -s/-(n) [actually, 'little roe' (with the dim. suffix *-erl*↑, the tertium quid being the fawn, i.e. light yellowish-brown, colour common to the young deer and to the mushroom] *myc.* (*Pfifferling*) chanterelle, egg-mushroom.

Reiber... [< *Reiber m* 'grater' (= a simple kitchen appliance with a metal surface full of sharp-edged holes)] *cul.*: **~datschi** *m* -(s)/-(s) (*Kartoffelpuffer*) potato pancake ([like the next item] made from grated raw potatoes). - **~knödel** *m* -s/- (*Kartoffelkloß*) potato dumpling.

Reißmathias or **Reißmatthias** *m* -s [a plain case of folk, or popular, etymology: what the doctor diagnoses as *Rheumatismus* means nothing to the unsophisticated patient; but his ear picks up (or so he fancies) the sounds of a well-known Christian name and, above all, the element *Reiß-en*, the very word for the sudden "screws" of pain he is subjected to at times - and a bond of understanding is established] *med.* rheumatism ['ru:-], *colloq.* rheumatics [ru:'mætɪks]: *involuntary, or deliberate, hum.* screwmatics.

resch *adj* [? through back formation < *röschen, reschen* 'to make crisp by heating'] **1.** *bak.* of rolls and bread (*knusprig*): crisp(y), crunchy. - **2.** *colloq.* said of a lively female, often a businesswoman or a waitress, down-to-earth and good at repartee: sharp and crusty.

Riegelhaube *f* -/-n [first el., < LateMHG *rigel* < OHG *riccula* < L *ricula*, the dim. of *rica* 'kerchief'] *folklore*, obsolete except in circles upholding the tradition of wearing regional costumes — a woman's little swallow-tailed headdress embroidered in gold or silver, and set with white lacy frills: decorative linen cap, Munich cap.

Rigi *m* -(s) [a massif between the Lakes of Lucerne and Zug, from which a world-renowned panoramic view can be had] *geog.* the Swiss mountain-name is used as a basis for sobriquets extolling similarly impressive prospects in Bavaria: **1.** *der bayerische* ~ 'The Bavarian Rigi', for Hohenpeissenberg, near Weilheim, south-west of Munich, Upper Bavaria, the northernmost outpost of the Alps, allowing the eye to sweep along the majestic glory of that mountain range. - **2.** *der* ~ *des Frankenlandes* 'The Rigi of Franconia', for Sodenberg, south-west of Bad Kissingen, with a crown of basalt rock, a conspicuous landmark above the Saale valley.

Ringlo *n* -s/-(s) [< *Reine Claude* 'Queen Claudia' (or 'Queen Gladys', to use an alternative said to be the Welsh form of the name), wife of King Francis I of France, *d*. 1524; two centuries later, Sir William Gage, a botanist, introduced the fruit to his native country - hence the English name] *bot.* (*Reneklode*) greengage, a soft juicy greenish-yellow kind of plum.

Ripperl *n* -s/-(n) [dim. of *Rippe* 'rib'] *cul.* ([*Kasseler*] *Rippenspeer*) cured, smoked pork spareribs.

Rohbau *m* -(e)s/-ten *archit.* shell construction of a house (which is finished "in the raw" only) - *colloq.* in the gibe heard when somebody fails to close the door (cp. *Pfannenkuchen* 1): *habt ihr einen* ~ *daheim?* are there no doors in your house?

Röhrl *n* -s/-(n) [dim. of *Rohr* 'pipe', 'tube'] *colloq.* (*Röhrchen*) **1.** *gen.* (thin, rather short) piece *or* length of pipe (*or* tube); *was soll ich mit dem* ~ *da anfangen - wegschmeißen?* what am I to do with this bit of pipe (*or* tube) - throw it away? - **2.** *med.* sterile (*or* test) tube, tubule ‖ a small tube used for the alcohol test: breathalyzer; *promilleverdächtige Fahrer ins* ~ *blasen lassen* to give drivers suspected of being under the influence (of drink) a breathalizer test.

Röhrlhose *f* -/-n, *dial.* ~n *f* -/- [see entry above] *colloq.* tight-fitting trousers with narrow legs: drainpipe trousers, *colloq.* drainpipes.

Rohrnudel *f* -/-n [not to be confused with *Dampfnudel*↑], in the Bavarian Forest also **Ofenknödel** *m* -s/- *bak.* a popular delicacy, arranged with a dozen or so of its "mates" in a pan and baked in the oven: (sweet) yeast dumpling, often filled with cherry or plum jam, plum purée, and other centres.

Rom *n* -s/no pl. *place-name* Rome, the spiritual and geographical world centre for all orthodox Christianity, who look or go there with reverent belief ‖ *phr.* in rhyme and proverbial lore, pious country folk have the word *Rom* glibly on their tongues, both in matters religious and trivial: **1.** said in humorous allusion to a woman's pregnancy: *sie ist nach ~ (ge)gangen* "she has gone to Rome" (*scil.* in order to pray for a safe delivery); or said with a ribald thought of the Holy Ghost's intercession in mind [cp. St Matthew 1:18, St Luke 1:15, 24, 31], *euphem.* she's in an "interesting" condition. - **2.** said in slight annoyance about the bluntness of a cutting tool: *auf dem Messer da kannst nach* (or *bis*) *~ reiten!* you could ride to Romford on a knife like that! (*BrE only*), that knife wouldn't cut butter! - → *Butterfaß, fliegen* 1.

Roßbollen *m* -s/- [second el., < *Bolle* (*f*) and *Bollen* (*m*) 'onion'] **1.** *vet. med.* (1) a general proof of sound equine digestion: (*Pferdekot*) (round) horse dung, horse dropping, *colloq.* horse apple; *er hat frische ~ aufgekehrt, um damit seine Rosen zu düngen* he swept up some newly dropped horse dung to manure his roses with. - (2) if such proof is found in the roadway: *colloq.* alley apple, road apple. - **2.** *fig. colloq.* a countryman's elaborate description of a downpour: *da hat's dir geschüttet, daß die ~ nur so gehupft sind* it was surely raining cats and dogs (*AmE also* ... bull frogs and heifer yearlings, *or* pitchforks with the tines on both ends).

Rübe *f* -/-n *agr.* one of several root vegetables: (1) *gelbe* ~ (*Möhre, Mohrrübe*) carrot. -(2) *rote* ~ (*Beete*) BrE beetroot, AmE beet; *roter ~nsalat* beetroot salad.

Rumfordsuppe *f* -/pl. rare: -n [*Rumford-* < Count Rumford, Sir Benjamin Thompson, 1753-1814, American by birth, soldier, philosopher, and statesman, a capable organizer and inventor in Bavarian services during the 1780s and 90s; because of his great merits, the then Elector of Bavaria made him a Count - Rumford (today's Concord) being for the honouree a well-remembered town in New Hampshire] *cul.*, largely *hist.* an eighteenth-century attempt at providing a nourishing and inexpensive diet: "Rumford soup", a mixture of peas, barley, and potatoes boiled together in water and stirred until uniform, with croutons of bread added at the last minute for the eater to have something to chew on; the soup was to become famous all over Europe and is still to be found in some cookery books.

runtergerissen *p.p.* [< (*he*)*runterreißen* 'to tear off', with regard either to a piece of cloth where, if ripped to equal shreds, one fragment differs very little from the other; or to a tear-off calendar, in which the individual sheets look speciously identical to the casual eye] *colloq.* only used in phrases that speak of a striking resemblance in appearance or disposition - **1.** generally, not necessarily restricted to one's next of kin: *j-m* ~ *gleichschauen* (or *gleichsehen*) to be the dead (*or* the spitting) image [actually, < the spit and image] of someone. - **2.** with reference to a parent and child: *der Bub schaut* (or *sieht*) *dem Vater* [*der Mutter*] ~ *gleich*, or, for short, ~ *der Vater* [*die Mutter*]! the lad is a chip off the old block, his father [his mother] will never be dead while the son is alive.

Rüscherl *n* -s/-(n) [< *Rüsche f* 'frilly ornament (in dressmaking)' + dim. *-erl*↑: the alcoholic part in the mixed drink here described is looked upon as a "frilling", or "lacing", that adds decorative distinction to the whole] *bev.* a small glass or drink of brandy (often, Asbach cognac) and Coca-Cola, two centilitres each, the total roughly being equal to one-third of a gill [dʒɪl], or one-twelfth of a pint [paɪnt] liquid measure: tot of laced coke.

Sach [-ɔ-] *n* -s [a dial. variant of StandG *Sache* f 'thing', 'object'] *colloq.*, often *apprec.* **1.** (1) (*Besitz*) possessions, property ‖ prov.: *willst dein ~ haben recht, mach dein'n eignen Knecht!* if you want a thing done well, do it yourself. - (2) (*Bauernhof*) farm(stead); *er hat a schöns ~* he can call a large farm his own. - **2.** *euphem.* ([*ansehnlicher*] *Busen*) (beautiful) bosom: *sie hat a schöns ~* she's got big brown eyes. - **3.** (*Aufgabe, Arbeit*) task, job; *er hat sein ~ können* he knew his stuff (*or*, his onions).

Sacharinheilige *m* -n/no pl. *R.C.* & *econ. hist.* the figure of John Nepomucen (*Johannes von Nepomuk*), a Bohemian martyr (*d.* 1393), carried in rogations across the border from Bischofsreut to Böhmisch-Röhren: "Saccharine Saint", a wooden effigy whose hollowed-out back served as a cache for smuggled Swiss saccharine, which was much in demand in Bohemia; Bavarian frontier guards (history tells us) had to present arms as soon as the procession came in sight, and the smugglers, well represented among the worshippers, must have chuckled at the ruse so successfully practised, indeed from the mid-1870s until the First World War.

sacklzement, or **Sacklzement** *interj* [literally, 'sack of cement' - a harmless-sounding (and indeed semantically vapid) corruption of and stand-in for *Sakrament* [-'ment] 'sacrament', a word within the sainted aura of the Church and hence taboo for other uses; in low colloquial and vulgar speech, however, *Sakrament!* brazenly holds its ground as an expletive, and so do *damn!* and *Jesus Christ!* as the English non-euphemistic equivalents here listed] said in considerable, yet controlled annoyance: dang it all!, oh fudge!

sakra *interj* [a euphemistic shortening of *Sakrament* (cp. the prec. entry); here and elsewhere, a solemn affirmation by the holy Host can lightly be turned into a blasphemy, flippantly thoughtless of origin though it may be] **1.** a mild imprecation: dang it! - **2.** a word of surprise, and possibly also of appreciation: well, I'm damned!, I'll be damned!

Saubär *m* -(e)n/-(e)n [second el. not related to *Bär* 'bear', but < OHG & MHG *ber* 'breeding boar'] **1.** *zo.* (*Eber*) boar, male swine. - **2.** low *colloq.* an emotional word used in critical condemnation: (1) a dirty fellow, often a child or young person, torn clothes sometimes offending the eye even further: scarecrow, *BrE also* mudlark, *AmE also* (nasty) bum. - (2) a man with a marked predelection for bawdiness: smuthound, *AmE also* muck spout, porn lover.

säumen *vt/i* [< VulgL *sauma* < Gr *ságma* 'packsaddle'; cp. OE *sēam* 'baggage of a packhorse'] *hist.* to carry (merchandise, esp. salt) on horseback. - **Säumer** *m* -s/- [cp. OE *sēamere* in the same sense] *transport hist.* salt driver, one of a group of men who moved salt by packhorse from the Inn-Danube area to Bohemia.

Schachtel [-ɔ-] *f* -/-n: **alte ~** [this metaphorical phrase harks back to centuries when minor family trinkets and keepsakes, e.g. a *Fatschenkind*↑, were saved by the female members of the household in chip, or splint, boxes (G *Spanschachteln*), to be taken out and admired at appropriate times; these boxes, often beautifully painted, were inalienable possessions, and grew old with their owners] *hum.*, but mostly *sarc.* an elderly woman, made the butt of a thoughtless or cruel remark simply because of her advanced age: old hag (*or* frump).

Schachterl ['-ʌ-] *n* -s/-(n) [dim. of *Schachtel f* 'box'] little box; *emot.*, esp. when expressing praise: *das ist (aber) ein süßes ~, das du da hast!* that's a sweet little box you've got there ‖ a *colloq. phr.* describing a disappointing and sometimes even critical state of disarray or bewilderment in one's personal life: *jetzt hab ich den* (or *an*) *Dreck im ~!* this is a real mess I've landed up in!

Schachterlteufel *m* -s/pl. rare: - **1.** a children's small toy box holding an amusing figure, often that of a devil, on a spring, which jumps up when the top is opened (*Kastenteufel*): jack-in-the-box, *AmE also* jack-in-a-box ‖ in *fig. colloq.* used of a person dancing and skipping about like a jointed figure, also known as jumping jack (*Hampelmann*): *ein schwarzer Sänger, dem das schweißnasse Hemd am Leibe klebte, sprang vor den Musikern wie ein ~ hin und her* a black singer, his sweaty shirt all stuck to his body, was up and down like a jack-in-the-box in front of the orchestra. → **2.** *colloq.*, often *hum.* a person with an explosive temper: spitfire, *AmE also* half brother [sister] to a shot of dynamite; *er* [*sie*] *geht auf wie ein ~* he [she] 's an easy (*or* quick) one to blow his [her] top (*or* stack).

Schäffler *m* -s/- [an agent noun, < *Schaff n* 'tub'] the name of a trade (*Faßbinder*): cooper, barrel-maker. - ~**tanz** *m* -es/pl. rare: ...tänze *folklore* "Coopers' Dance", a procession and dance of the Munich coopers, alternating with scenes of hoop-swinging, performed every seventh year in January, to commemorate the town's deliverance from the fearful Plague in 1517; towards the middle of the last century, a Munich journeyman-shoemaker carried the tradition to Nonnenhorn, in the Bavarian sector of Lake Constance, and more recently the custom has spread to some twenty other towns as far apart as Geisenfeld, Eichstätt, Landshut, and Garmisch-Partenkirchen.

Schafkopf *m* -(e)s [< *Kopf* 'head' + *schaffen* 'to work'] *cards* "brainwork", one of the oldest and most popular card games, not unlike poker or *Watten*↓; the 4 or occasionally 3 players can choose between *Fragespiel*, where two play against two, and *Solospiel*, where three play against one; the pack contains 32 cards and Queens and Jacks are trumps, as well as one of the four suits; money is bet on each hand. - ~**rennen** *n* -s/- 'Schafkopf' prize contest.

Schariwari *m* -s/-(s) = *Charivari*.

scheps, also **schebs** *pred. adj & adv* [< Yid. *schibes gehn* 'to get lost'] *colloq.* (*schief*) said of a household (etc.) object that is not exactly in the right position, and thus slightly annoys the eye of the fastidious by lying or hanging **1.** diagonal: cater-cornered, kitty-cornered; **2.** slanting: cockeyed, slantingdicular; and **3.** generally not straight: crooked, askew; *das Bild da ist* (or *hängt*) ~ that picture there is hung crooked, ... is hanging askew.

Scherzl *n* -s/-(n) [< MHG *scherze* 'cut-off piece' < MHG *scherten* 'to cut off' (related to E *shard* and dial. *sherd* 'fragment') + dim. -*l*↑] *comest.* (*Anschnitt oder Reststück e-s Brotlaibs*) end *or* heel (of a loaf of bread), crust (of bread).

schicken v/refl, colloq. (*sich beeilen*) to make haste: to hurry (up), to stir one's stumps; *ich muß mich jetzt ~* I must be stirring, I have to get a move on; *du darfst dich ~, wenn du den Bus noch erreichen willst* you'll have to be nippy if you want to catch the bus ‖ the imperative often denotes impatience at someone's slowness: *schick dich!* get a move on!, *AmE also* shake a leg!, *BrE also* look sharp!, look slippy!, look alive!, get cracking!, get weaving!; *schick dich, wir schaffen's sonst net hin!* go on - we shall never get there!; *bring mir was zu trinken, schick dich!* bring me a drink - and be quick about it!

Schiefer m -s/- [< MHG *schiver* 'fragment of wood or stone'] colloq. **1.** (*Holzsplitter*) splinter of wood, *NorBrE* spile, spelk; *ich hab mir, wie ich das Holz gesägt hab, einen ~ eingezogen* I got a splinter in (*NorBrE* I ran a spile [*or*, there's a spile run] into) my finger while I was sawing the wood. → **2.** *fig.* a social blunder (*Fauxpas*): gaffe, *BrE sl. also* clanger; *sich einen ~ einziehen* to do or say something foolish and socially uncomfortable: to drop a brick.

Schlacht... *cul.*: **~fest** n -(e)s/-e "butchering party", a village custom by which a farmer, on having slaughtered a pig, gives a dinner of fresh meat, fresh home-made sausages with sauerkraut etc. to neighbours and friends. - **~partie** *f* -/-n in Upper Franconia: = *Schlachtschüssel*. - **~platte** *f* -/-n "platter of fresh meat and sausages", a slightly more sophisticated variant of *Schlachtschüssel↓*, garnished with pickles, tomatoes, small onions, and asparagus shoots. - **~schüssel** *f* -/-n "bowl of fresh meat and sausages", a popular selection of boiled pork, liver sausage and black pudding, served with sauerkraut, dumplings or brown bread.

Schlawuzi m -/- [a blend of *Schlawiner* m 'rogue', 'good-for-nothing' and *Wuzi* m & n, a form of endearment for a pleasantly plump little child (cp. *Wuzerl* 3 [1])] *hum.* a child who plays tricks but is regarded with fondness: little rascal (*or* rogue, *or* savage); *wo hat denn mein ~ den Schirm (hin) versteckt?* where has that little mischief of mine (gone and) hidden the umbrella?

Schlegel *m* -s [< MHG *slegel* < OHG *slegil*, cognate with *schlagen* 'to beat (with a club)'] *cul. (Keule)* either of the back legs of a four-legged animal: haunch, leg; e.g. *Reh*~ leg *or* haunch of venison.

Schmai, rarely **Schmei** *m* -s/no pl. [a dialect abbreviation of *Schmalzler*↓, with an /l/ mouillé represented by the letter <i>, as in *Waidler* < *Waldler*] *dial.*=

Schmalzler *m* -s/no pl. [< *Schmalz* 'grease' + the compound suffix *-ler*, signifying occupational relationship with what is expressed in the first element] originally a *trade name*: "butter snuff", North Bavarian type of snuff, chiefly made from Brasilian-grown tobacco: its leaves are ground together with melted butter to keep the tobacco moist; assorted scented ingredients and a fine glass powder are also added, the latter to provide stimulation to the mucous membranes; *der Kenner schüttet ein bißchen ~ in die Mulde am Ansatz des gestreckten Daumens, knapp oberhalb des Handgelenks, und zieht es genußvoll in die Nase ein* the connoisseur taps out a little bit of snuff into the pocket formed at the base of the straightened-up thumb just above the wrist, and then inhales it through the nose with deep satisfaction. - **~dose** *f* -/-n, *dial.* **~dosen**, **~dosn** *f* -/- (*Schnupftabak*([s])*dose*) snuff-box. - **~glasl** *n* -s/-(n) *dial.* (*Schnupftabaksglas*) snuff-bottle, made of glass or earthenware, shaped like a small *Bocksbeutel* 'Franconian wine bottle' and closed with a wooden stopper; *in den gediegenen Brauereigasthöfen stellt der Wirt aus Kulanz ganz selbstverständlich ein ~ auf den Stammtisch* in the quaint old brewery-inns, the landlord makes a habit of placing a bottle of snuff on the regulars' table as a token of his appreciation. - **~tüachl** *n* -s/-(n) [second el., dim. of *Tuch*, here 'handkerchief'] *dial.* "snuff hankie", a large and gaily coloured handkerchief used for wiping away remnants of snuff after use.

Schmalznudeln *f pl. cul.* deep-fried pastry *sg.*

Schmankerl *n* -s/-(n) [? < *Geschmackerl* (an endearing dim. of *Geschmack*) 'what appeals to your taste'] *colloq.* **1.** *hist. cul.* (*angebrannte Kruste [am Geschirrand]*) crusty bit (of food, e.g. of porridge), once appreciated by the poor as an extra dainty. → **2.** *cul.* (*gastronomische Spezialität*) any of the many Bavarian dishes prepared as a culinary delicacy: gourmet offering - for samplings, see *Baunzerl*, *Dampfnudel*, *Geselchte*, *Kesselfleisch*, *Kirchweihgans*, *Kletzenbrot*, *Krautwickerl*, *Lüngerl*, *Obatzte*, *Preßsack*, *Radi*, *Ripperl*, *Schlachtschüssel*, *Schweinerne*, *Tellerfleisch*, *Wammerl*, etc. → **3.** *cul.* a small piece of particularly nice food (*Leckerbissen*): choice morsel, titbit (*AmE* tidbit). → **4.** *fig.* always *apprec.* (*Besonderheit*): (1) specialty, special feature, highlight (of a programme, etc.). - (2) special event. - (3) special treat.

Schmarre *f* -/-n [< early ModHG *schmerr* < MLowG *smarre* 'slash wound', 'cut'] *med.* (*Wundschorf*) scab, crust; *eine ~ bilden* to form a scab (*or* crust), to scab ‖ usu. in pl. and in dial. form, **Schmarrn** scabs (in one's face); *mit Schmarrn im Gesicht* scabby-faced.

Schmarrn, less often **Schmarren** *m* -s/- *dial.* [< *Schmarre*, see prec. entry] **1.** *cul.* a simple dish originally made in a pan from a mixture of flour, semolina or bread (curds or forest berries, sugar or cinnamon being later additions); today the dough consists of flour, milk, eggs, salt, and sugar, all fried in hot fat and duly chopped up into irregular lumps with a small iron shovel (*fett gebackene Mehlspeise*): (dessert of) hot, torn-up pancake, scrambled pancake ‖ the variety of gustatorial refinements, and hence of titular dubbings, is great - here is a threesome: (1) *Apfel*~ "apple scramble cake", featuring two or three mellow apples, peeled and cubed, in the mix, with everything poured into the pan, scrambled and baked. - (2) *Erdäpfel*~ "potato scramble cake", boiled potatoes grated and fried, optionally sprinkled with flour. - (3) *Kaiser*~ [first el., ? < *Kaser* 'Alpine woodcutters' hut'] "woodsmen's scramble cake", a rich creamy pancake broken into small pieces while being baked in butter, with sultanas or raisins added. - **2.** *colloq.*, often *contp.* (*Geringfügigkeit*) pittance; *sie kriegt, wo sie jetzt ist, einen ~ bezahlt* she gets paid a (mere) pittance in her present job; *ja, hör einmal, Spatzl, mußt du denn dei Naserl in jeden ~ neinstecken?* now listen, sweetie(-pie), do you have to be poking your nose into every abbreviated piece of nothing? - **3.** *colloq.*, often *contp.* (*wertloses Zeug*) something worthless; *das Essen ist ein ~* the food's not worth eating; *die Uhr ist einen (großen) ~ wert* the watch isn't worth a (damn) thing; *IrE* ... worth a cuckoo-spit; *ich bin zu alt für so einen neumodischen ~* I'm too old for such newfangled trash. - **4.** *colloq.*, often *contp.* ([*verbaler*] *Unsinn*) nonsense: hot air, rubbish, twaddle, *AmE* also hokum; *einen ~ zusammenreden* to be talking through one's hat; *red nicht so einen ~ daher! BrE* don't talk such rot!; *so ein ~!* get away with you, (and) don't be silly!; *das ist doch ein (ganz großer) ~!* oh, this is just (a load of) rubbish!; *Ehrenwort, ohne ~!* on my honour, cross my heart (and hope to die)!, honest Injun! - **5.** *colloq.* a rudely emphatic way of expressing negation: (1) *einen ~ macht er sich draus!* a fat lot he cares! - (2) *einen ~ hat sie ihm verziehen!* like hell she forgave him! - (3) *das geht dich einen ~ an!* this is none of your bloody (*AmE* goddamn) business! - (4) an energetic, yet at the same time rather mildly worded refusal to do something (, preceded by the rhetorical question, *ich [soll] das machen?*): *einen ~ werde ich das!* I will - on never-never day, *BrE also* I will - like billy-oh.

Schmarrngericht *n* -(e)s/-e *cul.* (any) dish of the scrambled-pancake variety.

schmatzen *v/i* [< MHG *smatzen*] *colloq.* (*plaudern*) to chat: to gab, *BrE also* to natter; *es war nett, mit euch, lieben Leutln, zu ~* it was nice having (had) a chat with you, dear people. - **Schmatzer** *m* -s/- *colloq.*, often slightly *contp.* (*einer, der viel daherredet*) a talkative person: chatterbox, *AmE also* gabber; *der Mann ist dir ein ~, da kommst du fei gar nicht zu Wort!* my, what a talker that man is - you can't get a word in edgeways. - **Schmatzerer** *m* -s *colloq.* an angry curt remark: taunt; *er hat die Tür noch einmal wutentbrannt aufgerissen und einen ~ hineingeworfen* he angrily yanked open the door once again, firing off a vicious parting shot.

Schmiedl *m* -s/- [dim. of *Schmied* '(black)smith', a common SouG proper name, originally distinguishing either the son from the father, or a younger (and therefore less prestigious) village blacksmith from one established in rank and authority; cp. the E appellatives *Smithson* and Smith *junior*] *colloq.* a generic name for somebody ranking beneath somebody else, somebody second (or indeed much further down) in command: *BrE* dogsbody, *AmE* crap clerk; *ich bin in dem Amt da nur der ~* I'm just the dogsbody in this office ‖ often couched in the phrase that it is advisable to seek guidance in one's problem with the person in authority rather than with the one who is less qualified or less informed: *geh lieber* (or *gleich*) *zum Schmied und nicht erst zum ~!* go straight to the top (*or*, deal direct with the top dog) rather than deal with a middleman; don't bother (*or* mess) with the pawns, go straight to (*or, as the case may be,* for) the king.

Schmuser *m* -s/- [< *Schmus* 'blether', 'empty talk' (< Yid. *schmuoss*, pl. of *schmuo* 'chatter') + agentive *-er*] *colloq.* a broker who does business in all kinds of rural transactions, e.g. the buying and selling of cattle, agricultural produce, and homesteads: go-between ‖ → *Hochzeits⋍*, *Hopfen⋍*.

schnackeln *v/i* [the base of the word is due to sound imitation] *colloq.* **1.** said of an action accompanied by what may be taken to be a slight explosion: to (go) pop. - **2.** said of what is heard when the latch in a spring-bolt lock falls into place: to snap to, to click (shut). - **3.** said of slight short sounds made by a human being with either of two organs: (1) to click one's tongue. - (2) to snap *or* click one's fingers; *sie hat nach der Musik geschnackelt* she clicked her fingers in time to the music. - **4.** said with reference to a metaphorical snap of sudden recognition or comprehension: to catch the drift, *BrE* to tumble to the racket; *es hat geschnackelt* came the dawn, *BrE also* the penny has dropped, he's twigged, he got the message; *es hat schon seine Zeit gebraucht, bevor es bei ihm geschnackelt hat, was eigentlich gemeint war* it was a long time before he got the hang of (*or*, before he tumbled to) what was really meant. - **5.** an appreciative comment, again using the 'snap' metaphor, on a mutually satisfactory boy-meet-girl situation: *es hat (bei* [*or, zwischen*] *denen) geschnackelt* they hit it off; *beim Hans und bei der Anna hat es gleich auf Anhieb geschnackelt* John and Anne clicked (with each other) as soon as they met.

schnackerlfidel *adj* [first el., < *schnackeln* 3; the basic idea conveyed by the compound is that a Bavarian in exuberant high spirits gives vent to his feelings by snapping his fingers and clicking his tongue] *colloq.* cheerfully energetic: bright and breezy, bright-eyed and bushy-tailed.

Schnadahüpfl, Schnaderhüpfe(r)l, Schnaderhüpfl *n* -s/-(n) [< *schnattern* 'to chatter' + *Hüpfl* 'hop'] *mus.* a characteristic feature of Alpine merrymakings (*neckender Vierzeiler*): "chatter ditty", a gay and teasing little song of four lines, with innumerable verses, each taken up, or improvised upon the preceding one, by a different person (see Appendix B, pp. 222f.):

Ja, Leutln, seids achtsam,	*Yer landlord's a' tired,
der Wirt braucht sei' Ruah:	Drink up, folks, an' pay:
bis zwölfi da habts wohl	By twelve you've been boozin'
fei gsuffa grad gnua!	Enough for the day!

Schnapsl *n* -s/-(n) [dim. of *Schnaps* 'hard liquor'] *colloq.* a small amount of a strong alcoholic drink (*Schnäpschen*): tot; *wie wär's mit einem ~?* how (*or*, what) about a little drink, *ScotE also* ... a wee dram (*or* drappie)?

schnaufen *v/i colloq.* (*atmen*) to breathe ‖ *phr.* (1) *da herinnen kann man ja kaum ~* (my,) one can hardly breathe in here. - (2) said of a person who breathes noisily, for instance after having run for a longish distance: *der hat geschnauft wie ein Bierdimpfl* he breathed (*or* puffed, *or* wheezed) like a grampus [cp. p. 219].

Schneid *f* -/-(e)n [< StandG *Schneide* (see below, sense 1)] *colloq.* **1.** cutting edge (of a tool); *das nennst du ein scharfes Messer? die ~ ist ja ganz stumpf!* you call this a sharp knife? why, its edge is all blunt (*or*, it wouldn't cut butter)! - **2.** *mount.* (*Grat, Bergkamm*) narrow ridge, usu. long and straight, maintaining the same height for some distance; *so ein Stucker sechzehn Gams sind gstanden oben auf der ~* there were some sixteen chamois standing up on the ridge. - **3.** (*Mut und Entschlußkraft*) courage and determination: dash, ginger, go, guts *pl.*, pluck, snap, spunk ‖ *phr.*: (1) *j-m die ~ abkaufen* to prove to someone that it is not good to be overly confident: *das wär doch gelacht, wenn ich dem nicht die ~*

abkaufen könnt it would be ridiculous if I couldn't take him down a peg or two (*or*, AmE ... make him come down out of his pink balloon). - (2) ~ *haben* to be plucky; *meine Lehrerin hat gemeint, ich würde in der Schule viel besser mitkommen, wenn ich mehr ~ hätte* my teacher said I would get along a lot better in school if I had more spunk. ‖ a young man's challenge to a fist fight, and his adversary's truculent response: A - *geh nur her, wenn du a ~ hast!* put them up, I dare you! B - *geh nur d u her, von dir laß ich mir die ~ noch lang net abkaufen!* y o u come and get it, I'm the last one to crawl before you! - (3) *es braucht schon einige ~, durch den Kamin da zum Gipfel zu kraxeln* it takes some guts to scramble through that chimney to the summit. - (4) an Alpinist's outlook on life, as proudly proclaimed in the quatrain of a chatter ditty:

> *An da Schneid hats ma nia gfehlt,*   *Well, I've never lacked ginger,
> *aba öfta am Geld;*   But I often lacked cash;
> *is ma liaba koan Geld*   What the dickens is cash
> *als koa Schneid auf da Welt!*   Without ginger and dash?

Schnellspanner *m* -s/- [the image is that of a marksman who is quick to bend his bow or cock his rifle (→ *spannen*)] *colloq.* one who is intellectually on the qui vive: *sie ist ein ~* she's quick (*or* fast) on the draw, she's quick in (AmE on) the uptake, she's on the ball, AmE also she's (as) bright as a new dollar.

Schnürl *n* -s/- [< *Schnur* 'string', 'twine' + -*l*↑: the verbal diminution here involves both the length and the thickness of the twine referred to or envisaged; however, as seen under 2, usage can be an overriding factor (which linguists might be well advised to meekly bow to)] *colloq.* (*Schnürchen*) (short) length of twine, (thin) piece of string. - **2.** *folklore* a few yards of rope obstructing a wedding procession (cp. *schnürln* 1↓). wedding rope, WelshE quinten.

schnürln *vi/t* [< *Schnürl*] *colloq.* **1.** *folklore* in a custom practised by a gang of young boys, both in Bavaria and in the British Isles, when "waylaying" a wedding car (or the whole procession) and demanding such largesse as is considered necessary: (1) *v/i* to "rope" a wedding party; *wir haben geschnürlt, wie wir Kinder waren* we were busy "roping" wedding cars when we were kids. - (2) *v/t* only in *das Brautpaar* ~ to "rope" the bride and (bride-) groom. - **2.** *meteor. v/i* chiefly in Upper Bavaria, said of a brief downpour (popularly associated with the province of Salzburg, Austria) (*Bindfaden regnen*) to come down in long stringy drops: *es schnürlt* it's lashing with rain, it's coming down in stair rods.

schoppen *vt/refl* [< MHG *schoppen*, an intensifying variant of the basis *schieben* 'to shove'] *colloq.* **1.** *v/t* (*vollstopfen*) (1) with regard to a person: to stuff, to cram (with food, etc.) - (2) with regard to a farmyard bird, esp. a goose: to force-feed. - **2.** *v/refl* said of an article of clothing, usu. a stocking, blouse, or shirt — to form unwanted folds (*kleine Wülste bilden*): to ruck up; *dein Strumpf hat sich über dem Rist geschoppt* your stocking has rucked up at the instep.

Schotten Deutschlands *m pl.* — *sobr.* a somewhat whimsical epithet for the Bavarians, which claims to be based on certain intrinsic similarities: Scots of Germany ‖ a London publication has this to say on the subject:

Es geht oft das Wort um, die Bayern seien die „Schotten Deutschlands". Ähnlichkeiten bestehen in der Tat. Beide Male handelt es sich um kraftstrotzende Völker, die jeweils nur zögerlich den Weg zu ihrer Nation gefunden haben; beide fühlen sich eng mit den Bergen verbunden, sind Realisten und Romantiker zugleich, und in beiden lebt noch ein Element Eigenstolz weiter, das sie nach Unabhängigkeit streben, ja sie völlig allein leben lassen möchte. Außerdem zeichnet die Schotten und Bayern ein großes Maß an Phantasie und ein bizarrer Humor aus, was andere mitunter dazu verleiten mag, sie als verschroben, mürrisch oder gar als flegelhaft abzutun.

It has often been said that the Bavarians are the "Scots of Germany". There are indeed some similarities. Both are hardy races which have only reluctantly joined the rest of their nations; both have strong emotional ties with the mountains; both are realists and romantics at the same time; and there is still an element of nationalist feeling in both people, a desire for independence and even isolation. Besides, Scots and Bavarians have a great deal of imagination and an eccentric sense of humour; and others may, therefore, at times incline towards seeing them as cranky, grumpy, or even boorish.

Schrat, Schratz, Schraz *m* -es/-e and -en/-en, **Schrazel, Schrazl** *m* -s/-(n) **1.** *folklore* (*Heinzelmännchen des Waldes*) woodland gnome. - **2.** *contp.* (*uneheliches Kind*) child born out of wedlock, *contp.* bastard.

Schrothkur [ˈʃroːtkʊə] *f* -/pl. rare: -en [first el. < Johann Schroth, 1798-1856, its inventor] *med.* "Schroth nature cure", a method followed at Oberstaufen (Allgäu), Wernberg (Upper Palatinate), and elsewhere, of submitting patients with alimentary complaints to a strict slimming diet; damp-towel-wrap-cum-vegetable-soup days alternate with dry-fruit days, which clears the body (votaries claim) of any dross and excess weight within three weeks.

Schuberl *n* -s/-(n) [< *Schub-*, a noun stem denoting 'something pushed into shape' + dim. suffix *-erl*↑] *bak.* "shovey" roll, a small crusty ryemeal loaf, oval in shape, and with a light lengthways dent down the middle.

schuhplatteln *v/i.* (pr. t. *ich schuhplattle, du schuhplattelst*, p.p. *geschuhplattelt*) *folklore* to do an Alpine clog dance. - **Schuhplattler** *m* -s/- *folklore* "foot-slapper", a native Alpine clog dance symbolizing the strutting of the black-cock in front of the demure grey-hen; unless waltzing with their female partners, the men slap soles of shoes and thighs alternately, turn somersaults or cartwheels between the slaps and do other gymnastics in time to the music while the girls waltz slowly round in a circle.

Schupfen *m* -s/-, sometimes also **Schupf** *f* -/-en [actually, 'something pushed (or, literally, shoved) onto another building', < *schupfen* an intensive verb to go with *schieben* 'to push'; cp. E dial. *shippon* 'cow barn', 'cattle shed'] *colloq.* **1.** a lightly built single-floored building, often wooden, used esp. for storing things (*Schuppen*): shed ‖ the specific use is often indicated by composition, e.g. *Garten~* 'garden shed', *Geräte~* 'tool shed', *Wagen~* 'coach-house', 'carport', though not necessarily so: *trag mir eine Ladung Holz aus dem ~ rein* get me an armful of wood from the shed. - **2.** a small, often roughly made building that rests against the side of a larger one (*Wetterdach*): lean-to, shelter, carport; *du könntst ja den Wagen auch in den ~ stellen* you might as well put the car under the lean-to (*or*, in the carport).

schutzen *v/t* [related to G *schießen* and E *to shoot*] *dial.* **1.** to swing s.o. backwards and forwards: *ich möcht ein bißl schaukeln; geh, schutz mich!* I'd like to play on the swings a bit; please get me going. - **2.** to move (a small child) up and down in one's arms or on one's knee in play: *die Mutter schutzt das Kinderl* mother is dandling her baby ‖ cp. *Maßkrugschutzen*. - **3.** to throw in the air, to toss (up); cp. *Jackelschutzen*.

schwäbeln *v/i* [< the umlauted stem form of *Schwab(en)* + *-eln*↑] *colloq.* to speak with a Swabian accent.

Schwaige *f* -/-n, *dial.* **Schwoag** *f* -/-n [< MHG *sweige* < OHG *sweiga*] **1.** *hist.* (*Viehhof*) small cattle-raising farm in a remote pasture or woodland area, owned and centrally administered by a monastic order or leased to a tenant. - **2.** *obso-*

lescent a feature of rural economy in mountainous, southern Bavaria, now fast disappearing (*Alm, Alp*): mountain dairy, alp; (*Sennhütte*) (Alpine) dairy hut. - **3.** *econ.* on the mountainside, brought into use during the summer months (*Galtalm*): unattended pasture and cowshed for young cattle, inspected by a herdsman about once a week. - **schwaigen**, *dial.* **schwoagn** *v/i obsolescent* an activity of rural economy in mountainous southern Bavaria which, due to shortage of manpower, is fast disappearing, with dairy cattle now often kept in the valley below throughout the year (*eine Alm bewirtschaften, Käse bereiten*): to run an Alpine dairy (usu. from early June until mid-September), to be a cheesemaker at a mountain dairy. - **Schwaiger**, *dial.* **Schwoager** *m -s/- obsolescent* (*Senner*) (Alpine) dairyman; his place, in Upper Bavarian dairy farming, has now been taken by the *Stooz↓*, who continues to make cheese at a mountain dairy in small quantities, and who works under the direction of a valley-based *Schweizer*. - **Schwaigerin**, *dial.* **Schwoagerin** *f -/-nen obsolescent* (*Sennerin*) (Alpine) dairymaid. - **Schwaighof,** *dial.* **Schwoaghof** *m -(e)s/...höfe, dial.* ...höf mountain farm, farmstead above the zone of cereal production.

Schweinerne *n,* with *adj decl.:* -n *cul.* (*Schweinefleisch*) pork; a typical dish: ~*s mit Kraut* pork and sauerkraut (*or*, pickled cabbage) ‖ a proverbial warning that it is impossible to change the real character of a person, especially to make a gentleman or lady of one who is not: *man kann aus einem ~n kein Rindfleisch machen* you can't make a silk purse out of a sow's ear; what can you expect from a pig (*or*, a hog) but a grunt?; *IrE* it's only the Lord can make a racehorse out of a jackass; *AmE also* you can take the boy out of the country, but you can't take the country out of the boy.

Schweins...: ~**hachse** (standard spelling, very rare), ~**haxe** *f -/-n, dial.* ~**hax(e)n** *f -/- gastr.* pig's foot used as food (*Eisbein*):

pickled knuckle of pork, *BrE also* pickled pork trotter, *AmE also* pork knuckle. - ˜**karree** *n* -s/-s *gastr.* pig's rib used as food (*Schweinekotelett*): pork chop.

Schwelle *f* -/-n [actually, 'the basis of a thing'; E *sill* is an ablaut variation] *hyd. eng., hist.* = Klause 2.

Schwemme *f* -/-n [< *schwemmen* 'to cause to swim', the transitive derivative of *schwimmen* 'to swim'] **1.** *agr.* (*Pferdetränke*) horse-pond. - **2.** *bev.* at the Munich *Hofbräuhaus*, and elsewhere (originally, the entrance hall of beer cellars where barrels were rinsed [to rinse = G *ausschwemmen*]): downstairs beer hall, beer vault(s); *in der riesengroßen ˜ unten findet sich an langen Holztischen das Volk beim Biertrinken; viele haben dazu Schwarzbrot, Käs oder fetten Speck mit, sitzen so stundenlang und verplaudern die Zeit in seligem Dusel* downstairs in the huge hall set with long wooden tables you will find the general populace drinking beer; many take black bread, and cheese or fat bacon with them, chatting, and passing away the time in an agreeable coma. - **3.** *com.* at a department store, sometimes in its basement: thrift shop, bargain counter(s).

Schwertertanz *m* -es/...tänze *folklore* at Traunstein, Upper Bavaria: sword-dance, sword-dancing, a quaint old Germanic ritual performed by young men in medieval costumes on Easter Monday.

> Note: Such dances, in which swords are ceremonially flourished, or are laid on the ground and danced around, have also a long tradition throughout the English-speaking world.

Schwieger...: ˜**leute**, *dial.* ˜**leit** *pl. colloq.* one's relatives by marriage, esp. the father and mother of one's husband [wife]: in-laws; *sind das deine ˜?* are these your in-laws?

schwoabn; in its assimilated, truly dialectal form, **schwoam** [< StandG *schwaiben* < MHG *sweiben* < OHG *sweibōn* 'to wash off'; cognate with E *to sweep*] *v/t dial.* **1.** (*fortschwem-*

men) to wash away; *der Platzregn hat den ganzen Dreck von der Straßn gschwoabt* the downpour sluiced all the muck off the road. - **2.** (*spülen*) to rinse; *nach dem Waschn schwoabt man die Wäsch im reinen Wasser, damit die Seifenreste rausgehn* the laundry is being rinsed in fresh water in order to remove soap after washing.

Semmel *f* -/-n [< MHG *semel(e)* < OHG *semala* 'fine white flour' < L *simila* 'wheat flour'] *bak.* (*Brötchen*) (bread) roll, AmE also semmel; *geriebene* ~(*n*) = *Semmelbrösel* 2 ‖ *fig.*, *colloq.* said of merchandise that is much in demand (the thought here being of bread rolls crisply fresh from the oven, and therefore tasting particularly good [cp. F *se vendre comme des petits pains*]): *die Sachen gehen* (*weg*) *wie warme* ~*n* the things sell (*or* go) like hot cakes.

Semmel...: ~**brösel** *n* -s/- **1.** *bak.* roll crumb; *da liegt noch ein* ~ *auf dem Boden, klaub's bitte auf!* there's another (roll) crumb on the floor, pick it up please. - **2.** *cul. usu. pl.* (*Paniermehl*) stale bread rolls, grated for use in dumplings, for coating meat, fish, celery, slices of vegetable, etc. before frying: breadcrumbs; ~ *reiben* to grate (*or* grind) stale (bread) rolls. - ~**knödel** *m* -s/- *cul.* a light and soft ball of boiled dough made from dried rolls (soaked in milk), onions and parsley (duly chopped and braised), eggs, and salt, usu. served with a hearty roast: (white-)bread dumpling. - ~**teig** *m* -(e)s/pl. rare: -e *bak.* dough for rolls. - ~**wecken** *m* -s/- *bak.* an oval-shaped loaf made from wheat flour: white-bread oval (loaf).

Siemandl, more correctly **Simandl** *n* -s/-(n) [< *Simon Handl*, of historical fame, at Krems-on-the-Danube, Lower Austria, whose wife was the domineering personality in the home; he established the *Simandl-Bruderschaft*, a fraternity of fellow-sufferers under the yoke of matrimony (a quaintly impressive statue, in the lower Landstrasse of Krems City, graphically shows Hubby Simandl pleading on bended knees before the imperious ruler of the roost); the spelling *Siemandl* is unetymological, it makes capital of the elements *sie* 'she', or *Sie*, the respectful use even until recent times of the third person plural when addressing a spouse or a senior relative, and *Mandl*↑, 'apology for a husband' - the second alternative sketching the possible introduction to a curtain lecture witheringly delivered to the husband returning late, say, from a drinking spree with his companions] *colloq.*, a term often used with a merry or a pitiful smile for one who is the butt of his wife's nagging (*Pantoffelheld*): henpecked husband, *BrE also* henpeck, *AmE* milquetoast; *er ist ein* ~ he is henpecked, he is completely under his wife's thumb.

Singerl *n* -s/-(n) [a dim. qualifying the stem form of *singen* 'to sing', specifically 'to cheep' or *AmE* 'to peep', i.e. to sound the quickly repetitive weak high noise made by young birds in reply to the mother bird's call] *colloq.* **1.** often *apprec.* small farmyard chicken (*Küchlein*): chick(abiddy), *AmE also* baby chick, peep; *schau dir nur die süßen* ~ *an, wie die immer fleißig hinter der Mutter hertrippeln!* just look at those darling chicks anxiously scurrying after their mother! -**2.** [ex a little chicken's early confusion and unpurposiveness] in *iron.* phrases aimed at s.o. giving the speaker a vacant or uncomprehending stare: *schau mich nicht an wie ein* ~ (or, ... *wie ein Kalbl, wenn's blitzt)!* don't look at me as if I was talking double-dutch!

Soachwasser *n* -s/pl. rare: - low *colloq. & contp.* = *Pfeiferlwasser*.

sodala *interj.* [< a contentedly retrospective phrase, *so da* 'so there (then, things stand)' + the echoic suffix *-la* (like *hoppala*[↑], *huschala*, etc.) borrowed from cosy nursery talk] a quiet little note of satisfaction when bringing, or having brought, a minor matter to a successful close - **1.** said to oneself: that's it! ['ðætsɪt] - **2.** meant to encourage an aged or ailing person, when helping him or her to stand up, sit down, or change to a more comfortable position: oops-a-daisy; *bist (du) soweit, Omi? auf geht's ... ~!* are you ready, Granny? come on then - oops-a-daisy!

solala, a shortening of **sosolala** *comp. adv* [a repetitive creation, the balancing act of a wordsmith (and of his untold imitators) performed, one is tempted to believe, on the initials of StandG *so leidlich*; however, such seesaw pattern has its analogues elsewhere, e.g. in It *così così*] *colloq.* **1.** a less than enthusiastic comment on how somebody fared in a competition: (only) so-so; *seine Zensuren in der Prüfung waren grad ~* his results in the exam were only so-so. - **2.** a rather disgruntled response to the query, *wie geht's dir [Ihnen]?* 'how are you?' — moderately well (*nicht gut, nicht schlecht*): fair-to-middling, just middling.

spannen *v/t colloq.* [< MHG *spannen*, in a figurative sense, 'to be in a state of tense expectancy (like an archer's bent bow)'] **1.** (to begin) to understand (*begreifen*): to catch on, *BrE also* to tumble (to); *spannst (du) es?* (did you) catch the drift?, *hum. in pseudo-French* twiggez-vous?; *es hat lang gebraucht, bis er gespannt hat, was ich wollen hab* it was a long time before he tumbled to what I meant. - **2.** to guess that something wrong or dishonest is happening: to smell a rat; *mir scheint, der spannt was* I think he smells a rat.

Spatz *m* -en/-en [a form of endearment from MHG *spare* < OHG *sparo* 'sparrow', patterned on *Fritz, Heinz* (for *Friedrich, Heinrich*) and other such affective variants of Christian names, and rhyming with *Schatz*, a warmly familiar way of addressing people one loves or is friends with] *colloq.* **1.** *ornith.* (*Sperling*) sparrow, *BrE also* spadger, spag; a *prov.* advising us to accept something small than to reject it and hope to get more later on: *besser ein ~ in der Hand als eine*

Taube auf dem Dach a bird in (the) hand is worth two in the bush, *IrE also* a trout in the pot is better than a salmon in the sea, a wren in the hand is better than a crane to be caught. - **2.** sometimes also *contp.* a person who is small and weak, or poorly developed (*kleiner Kerl*): little imp, puny feller, *AmE also* wimp; *schau dir (nur) den ~(en) an; der tratzt in einem fort seine große Schwester* (just) look at that little imp, he's continually teasing his big sister. - **3.** *emot.* a pet name for a young person, often one's adolescent son or daughter: darling, dear, honey, *AmE also* (my) love, sweetheart; *wir müssen uns schicken, ~, sonst kommen wir zu spät!* we must hurry up, darling, or we'll be late.

Spatzen... used in uncomplimentary metaphors levelled at persons in contempt or good-humoured raillery: **~hirn** *n* -s: *ein ~ haben* (1) to be stupid or silly: to be bird-brained. - (2) to forget things easily: to have got a mind (*or* a memory) like a sieve. - **~wadel, ~wadl** *n* -s/usu. pl. -(n) spindly calf (*pl.* calves): *dem seine ~ sind eine Schau!* those spindle-shanks (*or* sparrow-legs) of his are a sight!

Spatzl [-ʌ-] *m & n* -s/-(n) [dim. < *Spatz* [-ɑ-] 'sparrow' + *-l*↑] *colloq.* **1.** *zo.*, sometimes *emot.* ([sweet] little *or* young) sparrow, *ScotE also* spuggy. - **2.** *emot.* a woman's form of endearment when addressing a male, usu. her son or husband: dear, pet, *AmE also* hon [-ʌ-]; *wie war's denn in der Arbeit heute, ~, alles in Ordnung?* did you have a good day at work, dear?; *~, wann du getrunken hast, fahrst (du) net!* you don't get behind the wheel, dearie, when you've been drinking. - **3.** usu. *pl.* [the unumlauted Bavarianized equivalent of the typically Swabian diminutive form in *-le*] *cul.* = *Spätzle*.

Spätzle *n* -/usu. pl.: - *cul.* a well-known Swabian food substance made at home from flour, eggs, water or milk, and intended for ready consumption: spaetzle(s), spätzle(s), Swabian noodle(s).

Spatzlhobler *m* -s/- [the compound, an agent noun, is based on the fact that *Spätzle*↑, unenthusiastically eaten by Bavarians, confirmed dumpling fans (who, at any rate, as dialect speakers, prefer the homey diminutive [cp. *Spatzl* 3↑]), receive their shape through the viscous batter being cut into shape by a to-and-fro motion resembling that by a *Hobel* 'plane'] *colloq. contp.* Swabian: "noodle cutter"; *diese knickrigen* ~ those noodle-cutting skinflints.

Spezi [short for (*der* or *das*) *Spezielle* '(the) special'; cp. It *lo speciale*] **1.** *m* -/- or, *dial.*, Spezen *colloq.* an intimate friend or companion: chum, pal, *AmE* also buddy; *ein alter* ~ *von mir* an old pal of mine. - **2.** *n* -/- *colloq.* > *stand., bev.* a mixed drink: half-and-half of Coca-Cola and lemonade; *bitte ein* ~*!* one lemon-and-coke (mix), please! - **~wirtschaft** *f* -/-en = *Spezlwirtschaft*↓.

Spezl *m* -s/-(n) [a variant of the former, with the diminutive suffix -*l*↑] *colloq.* **1.** an intimate friend or companion: chum, pal, mat (in cockney rhyming *sl.* > china [plate]), *AmE* also buddy; *die beiden sind schon von ihrer Bubenzeit an echte* ~ the two have been as thick as thieves ever since their boyhood days; *er sitzt jeden Abend mit seinen ~n im Wirtshaus* he spends every evening at the pub with the lads. - **2.** *iron.* or *sarc.* (influential) friend: crony; *er hat in allen Ministerien seine* ~ *sitzen* he has his "boys" in (*or*, his old-boy network spreads into) all the Ministries; *der Bürgermeister schanzt seinen ~n gewiß das eine oder andere zu* the mayor is sure to be doing a favour or two for his cronies. - **~wirtschaft** *f* -/-en *iron.* or *sarc.* favouritism, cronyism, *AmE* also logrolling; *daß der Sohn des Spezls den Posten gekriegt hat, war ein klarer Fall von* ~ giving that job to his friend's son was a clear case of cronyism; *diese* ~ *geht einmal zu weit!* this "old-boy network" has spread too far.

Springinkerl *m* -s/-(n) [second el., an ablaut variation of *Gan-*

kerl 'little devil'] *colloq.* a person, esp. a child, who moves his body around restlessly, so that he annoys people (*Zappelfritze, -philipp,* AusG also *Rutschepeter*): fidget, fidgeter ‖ falling into the cosy vernacular, a Bavarian and a North Briton might equally be tempted to coax: *sitz stad, Bua, sei net so a ~!* sit still, lad, (and) stop fidgetin'.

Spritzkanne *f* -/-n, **Spritzkrug** *m* -(e)s/...krüge (*Gießkanne*) watering can, AmE also watering pail, sprinkling can.

Spruchbeutel *m* -s/- *contp.* = **Sprüchmacher** *m* -s/- [first el., dial. form of *Sprüche* pl. 'idle talk'] *contp.* **1.** a person given to meaningless talk: = *Ratsche(n)* 2 (1); *was soll man denn so einem ~ überhaupt zuhören?* what's the point of listening to such a gurgling gargoyle? - **2.** a person given to rash promises: promise-monger; *der ~ redet dir fei das Blaue vom Himmel herunter!* that big-mouth just about promises you the moon (*or* the earth). - **3.** a person who brags a lot: boaster, BrE also romancer; *sie ist ein ~* she blows her own trumpet (*or* horn), AmE also she's her own cheerleader.

stad [ʃtɑːt], sometimes with the semi-phonetic spelling **staad** *adj* & *adv* [MHG *stæt(e)* 'continuous(ly)', 'constant(ly)'; related to ModHG *stet* (as in proverbial "*steter* Tropfen höhlt den Stein" 'constant dropping wears away the stone') and ModE *steady*] *colloq.* **1.** *adj* (*still, ruhig*) quiet: (1) *pred.* (a) (*sei*) *~!* be quiet!, hush! - merry drinkers favour the following singsong, which is accompanied by rhythmic swayings of their bodies and, for emphasis, their giddily lifting the table around which they are sitting:

Stad, stad, daß 's di' net draht!	*Slow, slow, steady on, whoa!
Gestern an Rausch, heut an Rausch,	Boozy last night, same thing tonight;
wer woaß, wia 's morgn ausschaut?	will we tomorrow be right?
Stad, stad, daß 's di' net draht!	Slow, slow, steady on, whoa!

‖ a verbal threat to cow a bawling child: *wennst net glei ~ bist, nacha friß i' di'!* if you don't dry up at once I'll put you on the chopping block! - (b) *um den berühmten Schauspieler ist es ~ geworden* there is hardly any more talk about (*or*, ... any more mention of) the famous actor. - (2) *attrib.* (a) said of a quiet, decent, and reflective sort of person, one whose philosophical bent the speaker is well aware of, but also said of a secretive, often introvert, individual: *ein ~(e)s Mannsbild* [*Weibsbild*], also in the form of an adj noun, *ein ~er* [*eine ~e*] a deep one. - (b) said of Advent, or of wintertime in general, when there is comparatively little open-air activity, and many hours are spent by the "fireside clime" with "weans and wife" (in preparation for Christmas, and in expectation of Spring, respectively): *die ~e Zeit* the off-season, the season of lull and leisure. - **2.** *adv* at a regular pace, quietly and unwaveringly, gently not hectically: *phr.* (1) *~ anfangen* to set to work without any hurry. - (2) *sich ~ halten* (a) (*nicht sprechen*) to keep quiet. - (b) (*sich nicht bewegen*) to keep still. - (c) *fig.* (*geduldig abwarten*) to lie low. - (3) *schön ~ machen!* go easy!, steady on!, don't rush things! - (4) *~ tun* to go easy (on the speed and intensity of work or any other activity, from climbing a rock face to downing quantities of alcohol). - (5) *schön ~ a so weitermachen!* carry on the good work, slow and steady carries the day!

Stadterer [ˈʃtɔːdərə] *m* -s/- [the repetitive suffix -*erer*↑ here may, but need not, hint at the mixture of complexes felt by some countrypeople with regard to their "cousins" living in big cities; opp. *Landerer*↑] *colloq.* townsman: townie, towner, city feller. - **~nummer** *f* -/-n *mot., colloq.* a car registration number, shown on the front and back plate, whose initial letter (separated by a dash from the rest of the letter-cum-figure combination) indicates that the vehicle received its licence from the authorities of a big city: city number.

Stamperl *n* -s/-(n) [an allomorph, with a <p> inserted as a result of articulatory interaction, of *Stammerl* 'little stem', 'anything small'] *colloq.* (*kleine Alkoholmenge*) shot, *AmE* jigger (of gin, whisk[e]y, etc.); *wie wär's mit einem ~?* how about a little drop?, what about a little pick-me-up? - **~glas** *n* -es/...gläser (*Schnapsgläschen*) shot-glass, *AmE* jigger.

Standl *n* -s/-n [dim. of (*Verkaufs-*)*Stand* 'stand', i.e. a small, often outdoor shop or place for showing things] *colloq.* a table or small open-fronted shop in a public place (*Verkaufsbude, Kiosk*): market stall.

Standl... *colloq.*: **~betreiber** *m* -s/- = *Standlmann.* - **~frau** *f* -/-en (*Marktfrau*) market woman, (woman) stallholder; *mit einem „Kauft ('s) schönes Tannengrün!" lockt die ~ in der Vorweihnachtszeit* "Get yourselves a lovely bunch of fir sprigs!" runs the marketwoman's spiel in the Advent season. - **~mann** *m* -(e)s/...männer ([*Markt-*]*Verkäufer*) marketman, (male) stallholder.

Stanitzel, Stanitzl, now rarely **Starnitz(e)l**, but by transposition of the *r* also **Stranitzel** *n* -s/- [dim. of ? < R *straniza* 'book page, rolled conically and used for holding small objects'; or, on the strength of *Skarnitzel* (a secondary form, now obsolete), possibly a blend of Trieste dial. *scartozo* (It *cartoccio*) 'cylindrical cardboard bag to hold a powder charge' + Slovak *kornout* 'triangular paper bag'] *colloq.* often used by fruit vendors (*spitze* [*Papier-*]*Tüte*): pointed paper bag, paper cone.

-stauf *n* a place-name element, as in *Donau~* and *Regen~*, indicative of a distinctive orographical feature, usu. an isolated hill, close by; its cognates are OE *stēap* and ModE *steep*.

Stefanitag, earlier **Stephanitag** *m* -(e)s/pl. rare: -e [first el., gen. of Gr-L *Stephanus* 'Stephen', the first Christian martyr of the original community of Jerusalem, d. A.D. 33; *Stefan*, or *Stephan*, was once a common baptismal name in Bavaria, where the saint is still venerated as a patron of cattle (along with *St. Leonhard* 'St Leonard' and *St. Wendelin* 'St Wendolinus')] *R.C.* December 26 (*Stephanstag*): St Stephen's Day, *BrE* Boxing Day [on which Christmas gifts, or *boxes*, are, or rather were, given to employees, postmen, etc.]

Stellwagen *m* -s/- [first el., short for *Gestell*, 'frame and wheels of a cart' (cp. StandG *Stellmacher* 'cartwright')] nineteenth-century *transport hist.* a long-bodied lumbering vehicle drawn by two horses, put on for direct long-distance passenger service, with people huddled together under a big hood: horse omnibus; *wer in München um die Mitte des vorigen Jahrhunderts zu den Passionsspielen nach Oberammergau wollte, nahm oft vom Sendlinger Tor den ~ dorthin; es wurde eine lange Polterfahrt, sie dauerte gut einen Tag und eine Nacht* around the mid-nineteenth century, those living in Munich and wishing to attend the Passion Plays of Oberammergau often took the horse omnibus from outside the Sendlinger Gate; it was a continual jolt, fully lasting a day and a night.

Stiegengeländermischung *f* -/-en, nearly always presented in its Old Bavarian dialect pronunciation, [ʃtɪəgn-glandə-mɪʃʊŋ] *hum.* or *contp.* a nondescript little mongrel dog, visible proof of a low-predigree canine love affair; the fated place of encounter - who knows? - could have been by some banisters to which the mother-to-be happened to be tied by its owner: "stairwell breed", cur, tyke, *AmE* mutt, Heinz 57 variety.

Stiegenhaus *n* -es/...häuser *archit.* **1.** the space, going up through all the floors of a building, where the stairs are (*Treppenschacht*): stairwell. - **2.** a set of stairs with its supports and side parts for holding on to (*Treppenhaus*): staircase, stairway; *im ~* on the stairs.

Stiftlkopf *m* -(e)s/pl. rare: ...köpfe [first el., dim. of *Stift* 'pin', 'wire brad'] *colloq.* a very closely cut style of hair: crew cut.

Stock *m* -s/Stöcke **1.** *forestry* stump (of a tree); *holst du einen ~ vom Wald, dann wirst du dreimal warm - beim Ausgraben* *aus der Erde, beim Zerkleinern zu Haus, beim Verbrennen im Ofen* getting the stump of a forest tree home makes you nice and hot three times - digging it up out there, chopping it up at home, and burning it up in your stove. - **2.** *curl.* short for **Eis**ˣ (wooden) curling stone. - **3.** *contp.* a stupid awkward ungraceful person: lump, clod; *du bist mir so ein ~!* what a bump on a log you are!

stock... [this is a purely emphatic element, semantically based on the sense of *Stock* 1↑] *colloq.* **~katholisch** *adj* ultra-Catholic: out-and-out Catholic; *sie sind ~* they are rigid Catholics. - **~narrisch** *adj* very angry: hopping mad. - **~sauer** *adj* thoroughly disgusted: pissed off.

Stock...: **~wurst** *f* -/...würste [< *gestockt* 'curdled' (with reference to the blood of a slaughtered animal)] *comest.* BrE black pudding, AmE blood pudding *or* sausage, esp. one with few pieces of fat in it. - **~zahn** *m* -(e)s/...zähne [here again the sense is that such a tooth is as firmly rooted in the gums as is the stump of a tree in its native soil] *med.* (*Backenzahn*) molar (tooth), back tooth, cheek tooth, grinder; *colloq.*: *auf den hinteren Stockzähnen lachen* to give a hearty guffaw: to give a belly-laugh (*or* horse-laugh), to laugh oneself to pieces, ScotE also to laugh one's socks off ‖ here is a light-hearted spoonerism by Eugen Roth, to show how cheek by jowl lie pleasure and pain in human life:

> *Wer kann mit frohem Herzen schmausen,*
> *wenn tief im Stockzahn Schmerzen hausen?*
> *Can you in gourmet dainties duly revel
> If one vile molar's an unruly devil?

Stooz *m* -es/-e Upper Bavarian *dial.* Alpine dairyman.

> Note: With hill-based dairy farming on the decline, the *Stooz* does not command the position once held by the *Schwalger*↑. He is responsible to the *Schweizer*, milks the small herd of cows kept on the pasture-land among the mountains, and makes cheese, which is duly fetched by tractor to the valley below.

Straußol<u>eu</u>m *n* -s [a blend of *Strauß*, the name of a distinguished Bavarian and German politician and statesman, 1915-88, and *Mausoleum* 'a shrine to Mausolos, king of Caria in Asia Minor until 353 B.C.', the palatial splendour of which was once looked upon as one of the seven wonders of the world (for native speakers of English, the Taj Mahal [ˌtɑːdʒməhɑːl], a magnificent white marble mausoleum, still to be seen at Agra, India, carries very similar, and even stronger, associations] said in due respect, though often with a *hum.* banter: "Taj Mahal to Francis Joseph Strauss", the sumptuous New Bavarian Chancellery (*Neue Bayerische Staatskanzlei*), seat of the Bavarian government since 1993 in the former Court Gardens of the Wittelsbach kings in Munich, of whose construction the then prime minister was highly deserved in the eighties.

Str<u>ei</u>chhölzl *n* -s/-(n) [dim. of *Streichholz*, with the same meaning] *colloq.* match; if a singleton, esp. one that has been used: matchstick ‖ a *hum.* or bantering remark to someone very sleepy, and apparently in need of a mechanical aid to prop open his eyelids: *jetzt brauchst du fei gwiß* (or, *ich borg dir fei gern*) *ein Paar ~!* now look, use toothpicks to hold open the eyes (*or*, I'll be glad to lend you a couple of matchsticks)!

str<u>eu</u>en, *dial.* **str<u>aa</u>n** [ʃtrɑːn] *vt/i* to strew, to scatter (e.g., ashes on frozen footpaths, in order to make them less slippery) ‖ *folklore* a custom widely practised by juvenile mischief-makers, to expose a former love relationship to public ridicule: *einem verlassenen Mädchen wird am Vorabend der Hochzeit des ungetreuen Burschen mit einer anderen heimlich gestreut* (dial. *gstraat*): *Häcksel oder Kalkmilch zeichnen eine auffallende Spur von ihrer Wohnung zu der des Treulosen* a jilted girl, on the eve of her former boy-friend's wedding day, gets the "hush-hush road-line treatment": chaff or lime is used to draw a conspicuous trail along the roadway from her house to that of her faithless ex.

Süffling *m* -s/-e [the stem syllable is an umlaut variant of *Suff* 'booze', with suffixal *-ling* adding, in both E and G, a note of contempt] *colloq.*, sometimes *contp.* = Bierdimpfl 1.

☞ T ☜

Tafelspitz *m* -es/-e *cul.* actually, an Austrian delicacy: boiled fillet of beef, prime boiled beef; *(der)* ~ *schmeckt mit Kren am besten* fillet of beef tastes best with horse-radish.

Tag...: **~blattl** *n* -s/-(n) [second el., dim. of *Blatt* 'sheet', '(news)paper'] *colloq.* **1.** said with a note of disdain of a daily (newspaper): daily blab, *AmE also* scandal sheet, *BrE also* tabloid; *wo ist denn das ~ wieder hin?* dang it (all), where's that blab sheet (ended up) again? - **2.** *contp.* gossiper, chiefly female: gabblemonger, tattlebox, *AmE also* mumble-news; *die alte Kathl ist das ~ von ganz Waxlaber* Old Cath is the gossipmonger of all Waxlaber. - **~läuten** *n* -s *relig.* reserved for special occasions in the ecclesiastical year of a rural R.C. parish, e.g. on the feast of the local patron saint *(Patrozinium↑)* or at Easter: "Ringing-in The Day", a concerted chiming of church bells, alternately of the large one and then of all the small ones, often divided into three periods of ten minutes each. - **~werk** *n* **1.** -s day's work (of ploughing, or of any other activity); *wir haben heute schon unser ~ getan, lassen wir's gut sein* we've done our share of work for today, let's call it a day. → **2.** -s/- [actually, a field that could be ploughed in one day; cp. the English field-name *Day(s) Work*, examples of which have been found with numerals as high as *Twelve*] *husb.* tagwerk, an area measure of 3.33 square metres, = 100 *Dezimal*↑; *drei ~ sind ein Hektar* three tagwerks equal one hectare.

Ta**uben...**, *dial.* **D**au**m...**: **~kobel** *m* -s/- *zo.* = *Taubenschlag.* - **~markt** *m* -(e)s /...märkte *com.* pigeon market, at Wasserburg on the River Inn, the largest of its kind in Europe, to be held on St Blaise's Day, February 3, since St Blaise is the patron saint of wild animals. - **~schlag** *m* -(e)s/...schläge *zo.* pigeon house, dovecot(e) ‖ *fig.* uses in *hum.* banter: (1) describing a place full of noisy movement or activity: *da geht's ja* (or *fei*) *zu wie in einem ~* it's like a railway station (*specifically also* [BrE] ... like Waterloo Station; [AmE] ... like Grand Central Station) here. - (2) a cheerfully indiscreet observation about a male's trouser-fly (*Hosentürl*↑): *dem sein ~ ist offen* (or *auf*)*!* his shop-door is open!, *NorBrE also* the cage is open, but the beast's asleep!

tau**gsam** *adj, obs.* capable; *sie ist ~ für eine gute Hausfrau* she has the makings of a good housewife.

Teller *m* -s/- plate ‖ in the *colloq.* phrase humorously, or patronizingly, warning a greedy eater not to scrape the bottom of his plate for the last remnants of soup, etc. (the English equivalent being based on the use of rustic crockery): *iß den ~ nicht mit!, daß du den ~ nicht aufißt!* leave the pattern on the plate! - **~fleisch** *n* -(e)s *gastr.* a popular mid-morning snack, served on a wooden plate: boiled foreribs of beef, boiled and sliced, to be eaten with bread rolls, some horse-radish and chives, one gherkin (or a few slices of beetroot), and washed down with a pint of beer.

Tobel *m* -s/- *geol.* a deep narrow valley, sometimes wooded, with steep sides usu. made by a stream which run, or once ran, through it (*enge* [*Wald-*]*Schlucht*): gorge, ravine, *AmE also* flume, gulch; *der Frühling findet spät im Jahr in den ~*

hinein [*herein*] spring is late in finding its way (*or*, making its entrance) [down here] into the gorge.

Tod *m* -(e)s death - there are some marked parallels in colloquial lore: (1) *der ~ sucht sich seine Ursach* death doesn't come without a cause. - (2) *für den ~ ist kein Kraut gewachsen* there's neither herb nor cure for death. - (3) *contp.* said of a notoriously slow person: *der ist gut um den ~ schicken* he'd be a good messenger to send for death. - **~austragen** *n* -s *folklore* at Lichtenfels-on-Main, Upper Franconia, on the eve of the fifth Sunday in Lent: "Bearing out the Corpse", a juvenile procession through the town - after parading a straw doll on a pole and chanting "*Hallo potz Maus, / den Toten tragen wir naus*" ('Folks, hear us shout: the corpse we're bearing out'), the dummy is at last made a bonfire of in a meadow; next morning, the children go carolling again from door to door, and are rewarded with eggs and money.

Tor *n* -(e)s [cognate with E *door*] *tourist trade* an often-used noun at the core of a cliché, drawing attention to the fact that a certain village or market town can serve as a good starting-point for excursions into a well-defined scenic countryside: *das ~ zu* the gateway to; *Deggendorf ist* (or, *gilt als*) *das ~ zum Bayerischen Wald* Deggendorf is "The Gateway to the Bavarian Forest".

> Note: A similar pride of place is given to Immenstadt and Treuchtlingen, in the Altmühl Valley and in the Allgäu Alps, respectively.

Toten...: **~brett** *n* -(e)s/-er *folklore* in the Bavarian Forest (*Leichen-* or *Gedenkbrett*): "death board", "memorial board", a bier to rest a recently deceased person on before the body is put into a coffin (cp. *Brett*); after the funeral the board is carved, sometimes painted, and erected with a fitting inscription either somewhere near the farmhouse, by the wayside or in the forest as a simple memorial; the custom is probably of pagan origin, intended to ward off the spirits of the departed, and was later assimilated by Christianity. - ~**frau** *f* -/-en, ~**weib** *n* -(e)s/-er = *Leichenfrau*. - ~**vogel** *m* -s/...vögel *superstition* "death bird", a telltale secondary name for the screech owl (*Käuzchen*) or little owlet (*Steinkauz*), whose strident notes at night are taken as a bad omen by the anxious, esp. if there is someone ill in the family. - ~**wache** *f* -/-n *folklore*, largely *hist.* a ritual observed at the home, or by the side, of a recently deceased person: deathwatch, vigil, *IrE* & *ScotE* wake, i.e. a gathering, on the night before the burial, to grieve over the loss sustained, sometimes accompanied by special food and drink; *die ~ halten* to keep the death-watch (*or* vigil), to watch over the dead. - ~**zehrung** *f* -/pl. rare: -en (*Leichenschmaus*) funeral banquet.

Tracht *f* -/-en [< *tragen* 'to wear (clothes)'] *folklore* the concept of tradition and regional identity as materialized in people's distinctive apparel: festive peasant dress, regional costume; *sie hatte die* (or *ihre*) *~ angelegt* she had dressed in her traditional costume; *auf Faschingsbällen tragen die*

meisten ~ at carnival dances people mostly wear the(ir festive) peasant dress.

Trachten... *folklore*: **~anzug** *m* -(e)s/...anzüge (a man's) regional suit. - **~fest** *n* -(e)s/-e a festive occasion where traditional costume is worn: costume festival. - **~gruppe** *f* -/-n group (dressed) in traditional costume; *~n aus Bayern* groups in (traditional) Bavarian costume. - **~jacke** *f* -/-n **1.** jacket worn as part of traditional costume. - **2.** traditionally styled jacket (made of thick woollen material). - **~kostüm** *n* -s/-e (a woman's) suit made of thick woollen material. - **~pflege** *f* - (the custom of) wearing the native costume. - **~verein** *m* -(e)s/-e society for the continued use of traditional costumes. -**~zug** *m* -(e)s/...züge parade (*or* pageant) of traditional costumes, folklore procession.

Trachtler *m* -s/- *folklore* **1.** man wearing the (proper) festive suit of the region. - **2.** member of a regional folklore society.

Tragl *n* -s/-(n) [< *Trage* 'carrier', 'container', 'case' + diminutive suffix -*l*↑] *colloq.* ([*Bier-* etc.]*Kasten*) crate; *Milch*~ milk crate (if there are no bottles or if the bottles are empty; otherwise: crate of milk [~ *Milch*]); *ich könnt noch zwei ~ Bier brauchen* I could do with two more crates of beer. - **traglweis** *adv colloq.* ([*bier-*] etc. *kastenweise*) by the crate, by the case; *wenn ihm danach ist, schwoabt er das Bier ~ nunter* whenever he's in the mood he downs (*colloq.* he swigs) his beer by the crate.

tratzen *v/t* [a MHG, and since about 1650 only BavG, variant of *trotzen* and *trutzen* 'to defy', 'to show no respect for'] *colloq.* to annoy on purpose: to tease; *hör auf und tratz den Hund nicht - der beißt dich noch einmal!* stop teasing the dog, it's going to bite you some day! ‖ → *Magentratzer* (1).

Trauer *f* - *colloq.* = *Hoftrauer*↑.

Treibauf *m* -s/-e [an exocentric agent noun, often also used as a proper name (like E *pickpocket, cutthroat, Shakespeare,* and F *Taillefer*), based on an imperative phrase, thus literally meaning 'Drive up!', in the sense of 'Make things stir!', 'Get things going!'] *colloq.*, chiefly *contp.* = *Auftreiber* 1.

Trottoir [-ˈwɑː(r)] *n* -s/-e or -s [< F *trottoir*, a substantivization of F *trotter* 'to trot', 'to trip (along)'; probably of Germanic origin] *colloq.* (*Gehsteig* [*neben der Fahrbahn*]) *BrE* pavement, footpath, *AmE* sidewalk; *geh, steig vom ~ runter!* step off the kerb, will you? - **~-Venus** *f* -/pl. rare: -se *hum.* a prostitute: Lady of the Scarlet Sisterhood, *BrE also* pavement pretty, *AmE also* sidewalk susie.

Trumm *n* -s/Trümmer, *dial.* before numerals sometimes - [< MHG & OHG *drum* 'endpiece', 'splinter'; E *thrum* 'piece', 'end'] *colloq.* **1.** (*großes*, often also *dickes Stück* [*von einem Ganzen*] a big portion or piece, e.g. of food: chunk; *jeder hat ein ~ Butterbrot gekriegt* each got *or* had a chunk *or* doorstep of bread-and-butter; *ein ~* [emphatically: *Mords-̽* or *Riesen-̽*] *Kalbsschnitzel so groß wie ein Abortdeckel* a [great] big veal cutlet the size of a manhole cover. - **2.** (*großer, unhandlicher Gegenstand*) an unwieldy piece, e.g. of furniture: hulking big thing; *ein ~ Holz* a big chunk of wood. - **3.** (*große, ungeschlachte Person*) hulk of a man [woman]; *er ist ein ~ (von einem) Mannsbild* he's a bull of a man, he's a man-mountain. - **4.** a *contp.* reference to a person, at the same time impugning a negative quality of his or hers, e.g., *so ein fades ~!* what a pepless pimple (lumberheels *sg*, wearybones *sg*, *AmE also* sad sack)!

Trutsch *f* -/-(e)n [< Christian name (*Ger-*)*Trud*(*e*), with devoicing of the final consonant, + *-sch*; like *Lutsch* < *Ludwig*] *contp.* **1.** a general term of abuse for a woman, often used in an aggressive phrase: dumb cow, glug, gump, lubber, scrubber; *diese* or *so eine ~!* what a fool [etc.]! - **2.** stupid girl or woman: Dumb Dora. - **~erl** *n* -s/-n [dim. of *Trutsch*↑] slightly *contp.* naive young girl: silly little goose.

U

Umgang *m* -(e)s/...gänge **1.** (1) a movement along a path that forms a complete circle round an area: circuit; *für den ~ um die alte Stadtbefestigung braucht man über eine Stunde* it takes one over an hour to make (*or* do) the circuit of the old city walls. - (2) *R.C.* a ceremonial moving along of the faithful (eventually describing a full circle, from and back to church), e.g. on Corpus Christi Day, or for blessing the fields of the parish: procession; *bayerische Berühmtheit an Fronleichnam besaß einst der große Münchner ~; an ihm nahmen noch der König, seine Minister und andere hohe Würdenträger wie ganz selbstverständlich teil* the great Munich procession on Corpus Christi Day was once a Bavarian solemnity, in which the King, his ministers and other high-ranking dignitaries made a point of taking part. - **2.** *archit.* the upper floor built out from all the four inner walls of a farmhouse (*Altane*): gallery. - **3.** sg. only *techn. colloq.* with reference to a worn-out screw thread: *die Mutter da hat den ewigen ~* this nut here is giving you the run-around, it's slipped its thread.

Umstands...: **~gewand** *n* -(e)s *med.* (*Umstandskleid*) maternity dress (*or* frock). - **~kramer** *m* -s/- *colloq.*, often slightly *contp.* someone who is too concerned about unimportant details (*Umstandskrämer*): fusspot, fussbudget.

Ur... 'original': **~bayer** *m* -n/pl. rare: -n, **~bayerin** *f* -/-nen *colloq.*, often *hum.* a person whose parents and grandparents come of Old Bavarian stock: solid (*or, hum.*, primeval) Bavarian; *die beiden sind Urbayern durch und durch, da ist kein Österreicher, aber auch kein Franke angestreift* the two are solidly Bavarian, through and through, with not a touch of the Austrian or indeed the Franconian brush added. - ~**viech** *n* -(e)s/-er [for the second el., see *Viech*] *colloq. hum.*, often used in appreciation — a person, usu. male, of much originality and liveliness, at the same time tending to reflect (or indeed clearly reflecting) the cultural likes and dislikes as well as the speech mannerisms, of the region where he was born (*kraftvoll humoriger Mensch*): one loaded with personality, knockout of a fellow, (real) card *or* character, prize exhibit, *AmE also* one hell of a guy, prize package; *der Hans ist ein ~, bei dem kommst (du) aus dem Lachen gar nicht mehr raus* Jack is quite a scream, he has you all in stitches (*or*, in fits of laughter); *er ist ein bayrisches ~* he's a robustly Bavarian natural.

☞ **V** ☜

Vergelt's Gott *R.C.* a common phr. expressing appreciation for kindness, alms, or help of any kind: **1.** *interj* God reward you!, God bless you!, thank you kindly! → **2.** *n* -/- heartfelt thanks, God's Blessings ‖ in post-funeral thank-you notices in newspapers: *ein ~ der hochwürdigen Geistlichkeit für die trostreichen Worte am Grabe* heartfelt thanks to, *or* God's Blessing on, the Reverend Clergy for their comforting words at the graveside.

Viech [fiːχ] *n* -(e)s/-er [< Goth *faíhu*, even then (since cattle and sheep were used in lieu of payment) in the metaphorical sense of 'property', 'money'; cp. ModE *fee* 'possession', 'ownership', 'payment for services'] *dial.* (*Vieh*) (*sg.* head of) cattle *pl.* ‖ *dial. hum.* said of an entertaining and amusing person, usu. male: ~ *mit zwoa Haxn* = *Urviech*.

Vogel...: **~scheuche** *f* -/-n, often *dial.* **~scheichn** *f* -/- **1.** *agr.* an object (usu. old clothes hung on sticks) in the shape of a person, which is put in a field where crops are growing in order to frighten birds away: scarecrow, *AmE also* bird scarer. → **2.** *contp.* often *alte* ~ a thin and very untidy-looking person, often a destitute old woman: scarecrow, *AmE also* old rag doll, hay bag. - **~suppe** *f* -/-n *cul.* a speciality of Middle Franconia: innards soup (made from the liver, kidney, lung, and heart of a pig).

Voralpenland *n* -(e)s *geog.* "Fore-Alps", a narrow strip of hilly country immediately in front of, and parallel to, the Eastern Alps; the term was coined by Albrecht Penck, a Bavarian geographer.

Voressen *n* -s/- *gastr.* → *Lüngerl*.

W

Waagscheitl, **Wagscheitl** *n* -s/- [literally, 'a piece of wood (meant to be held) in balance', + dim. -*l*↑] **1.** *agr.*, *colloq.* a crossbar, pivoted at the middle, to which the traces of a draught animal are fastened for pulling a cart or farm implement: *BrE* swingle-tree, swivel-tree, whipple-tree, *SouBrE* spreader; *AmE also* whiffletree. → **2.** *contp.* a drunkard staggering under the load of alcohol consumed: punch-drunk (*or* top-heavy) boozer; esp. in the dial. outcry of protest: *so a bsuffas* [< *besoffenes*] ~! what a booze hound loaded to the barrel!, look at that booze hound and his staggers!

Wachler *m* -s/- [literally, 'somebody or something that sways from side to side' < *wacheln*, a dialect variant of *wehen* 'to wave'] *folklore* a chamois brush (*Gamsbart*↑) of considerable length, jauntily waving about when worn by mountaineers at the back of their hats: top-quality gamsbart, choice (*or* prize) tuft of chamois hair.

Wadl *n* -s/-(n) *anat. colloq.* (*Wade*) calf ‖ said of an aggressive dog: *j-n ins* ~ (or, *in die* ~[n]) *beißen* to snap at s.o.'s leg (*or*, legs).

Wadl... *colloq.*: **~beißer** *m* -s/- **1.** a popular name, in farming communities, for (1) the stable fly (*Stomoxys calcitrans*): "cattle stinger", and (2) any breed of dog trained to snap at the ankles of cattle and other domestic animals in order to make them go faster or move in a certain direction: "cattle nipper". - **2.** *fig., hum.* or *contp.* a disciplinarian who makes people work very hard: pusher, slave driver, whip cracker; *er ist ein* ~ he puts the screws (*or*, the squeeze) on. - **~strumpf** *m* -(e)s/usu. pl.: ...strümpfe *folklore* tight-fitting calf coverings worn by men as part of their regional costume (*Wadenstrümpfe*): half hose.

Wald *m* -(e)/no pl. *geog. proper name* an endearingly possessive abbreviation of *Bayerische(r)* ~, therefore often in its dialect form **Woid** (with an /l/ mouillé represented by the letter <i> [cp. *Schmai*↑]), *colloq.*: "Forest"; *ich komm vom* ~, dial. *i bi(n) vom Woid dahoam* I come from (*or*, I'm a native of) The Forest, I'm Forest-born.

Waldbrand... 'forest fire', in compounds chiefly heard in the Upper Palatinate: **~austreter, ~bekämpfer** *m pl. hum.* or *iron.* large feet: beetle-crushers, clod-crushers, *AmE also* canal boats; a scurrilous quip speaks of such a person as "having six toes on each foot": *er ist zu seinem ersten Geld so gekommen, daß er mit seinen ~n im Forst herumgelatscht ist, wenn es draußen gebrannt hat* he got his start in life stamping out forest fires for a living.

Wald...: ~glas *n* -es/no pl. *com.* largely *hist.* "Forest glass", a typical product of the last few centuries when its colour, due to the impurities contained in quartz (a basic ingredient of glassmaking) was invariably green. - **~laterne** *f* -/no pl. *archit. hist.* "Forest Lantern", the aptly nicknamed manorial residence of Saldenburg Castle, north of Tittling, whose five-storeyed square structure towers high above the surrounding treetops; unique in Bavarian architectural history, the medieval relic, dating from 1368, now serves as a youth hostel.

Waldler (in its dialect spelling **Waidler**) *m* -s/-, **Waldlerin** *f* -/-nen [reference here is always to the Bavarian forest] *place-*

name derivative an inhabitant of, usu. one born and raised in the Bavarian Forest: Forest man [Forest woman] ‖ *Und was a echter ~ is, / der halt ebbs auf a frische Pris* *A Forest man that's worth his stuff / is bound to prize a pinch of snuff.

Walhạlla *f* - [< *Valhalla*, in Nordic mythology, the hall of immortality for the souls of heroes slain in battle] *archit.* six miles E of Regensburg, on a bluff overlooking the Danube: "Valhalla", Parthenon of German Honour, a national hall of fame containing some 200 marble busts and memorial plaques of distinguished personalities; it was inaugurated by King Ludwig I in 1842 but, as the illustration shows, had been given publicity by the British press several years before.

THE PENNY MAGAZINE
OF THE
Society for the Diffusion of Useful Knowledge.

274.]   PUBLISHED EVERY SATURDAY.   [JULY 9, 1836.

THE WALHALLA, OR HALL OF HEROES, IN BAVARIA.

Wammerl *n* -s/-(n) [dim. of *Wamme* < OHG *wamba* 'belly'; akin to ModE *womb*] *cul.* (*Schweinebauch*) pork belly, the fat meat from the pig's abdomen; lean bacon, occasionally smoked (*geräuchertes* ~), served steamed or roasted in chunky slices.

Wamperl *n* -s/-(n) [an allomorph of the prec. entry, with a <p> inserted through articulatory interaction] *colloq.* **1.** a person's (slightly) protruding stomach (*Bäuchlein*): little paunch, little pot, fat little belly. - **2.** *cul.* a small blood sausage: **BrE* mini black pudding. - **3.** *sports* = *Baucherer*, *Bauchplatscher*↑.

Watsche *f* -/-n StandG, rare, for *dial.* **Watschen, Watschn** *f* -/- [prob. an echoic word] low *colloq.* or *vulg.* **1.** (*Ohrfeige*) box on the ear, clip over the ears, slap in the face ‖*phr.* (1) *du fangst gleich eine (~)!* I'll land you one in a minute, you'll get a thick ear in no time, *Western AmE* I'll wat you one if you don't watch out. - (2) *j-m eine (saftige)* ~ *herunterhauen* to give one a (good) sock on the ear-hole, *IrE* to hit one a (great) clout in the lug, *Western AmE* to give one a (good) wat in the face. - **2.** *fig.* said in disappointment, at the sight of ill-matched architectural styles, colour patterns, etc.: *das gibt einem eine* ~ it's a smack in the eye. - **3.** *prov.*: *Gusto und Watschen sind verschieden* there's no accounting for tastes; tastes differ (*or*, every man to his own taste), said the farmer as he kissed his cow; *AmE also* one man's meat ball is another man's hamburger.

Watschen...: ~baum *m* -(e)s [jocularly, on the analogy of *Maibaum*, *Kirtabaum*, etc., and the ceremony of felling the tree in the end; on the "tree", which nominally deputizes for the blow-in-the-face-happy arm, hang choice fruits like "figs" (Ohr*feigen*) and "dates" (*Dachteln*), with the hand to take quick action as their potential dispenser] *fig.*, *colloq.* "ear-clout tree", an imaginary tree hung with "clips" and "clouts" that tend to come down rather suddenly on an incessant taunter, or other frivolous offender, once the victim's patience is exhausted: (1) *der ~ fällt um* "the ear-clout tree" falls, i.e. you *etc.* get a box on the ear (at last). - (2) a jocular warning to the unsuspecting, usu. a wanton child:

Rüttle nicht am Watschenbaum: *Do not shake the ear-clout tree:
Die Frucht, sie reift, du merkst es kaum!   The blow will fall, quite suddenly.

(3) a whimsical notice found in the public gardens of a Bavarian health resort:

> *Gemeinsinn hat dies Werk vollbracht*
> *Und freudig-stolz das Herz uns lacht:*
> *Zerstörern geben wir bekannt:*
> *Der Watschenbaum wächst hierzuland.*
>
>   *Through common efforts ne'er denied
>   The park here stands, our civic pride.
>   To roughs let this a warning be:
>   Our native growth's the "ear-slap tree".

~einfach *adj colloq.* very easy (*kinderleicht*): as easy as falling off a log, as easy as pie; *die Schulaufgabe war ~* the classroom test was a cinch. - **~gesicht** *n* -(e)/-er usu. *contp.* **1.** bloated *or* pudgy face. - **2.** face arousing antagonism; *der hat ein richtiges ~* that ugly face of his is just asking for a punch, he's got the sort of face you'd like to put your fist into. - **~schuhplattler** *m* -s/- *folklore* & *mus.* "box-your-ears" clog dance, a type of *Schuhplattler*↑ in which faked face-slapping symbolizes the mock rivalry between two male dancers for a beautiful girl.

watten *v/i* to play (the game of) "watten"; **Watten** *n* -s *cards.* "watten", a card-game between 2, 3 or 4 players with a tarot pack (hearts, bells, leaves and acorns) of 32 cards, from which each player is dealt five cards; elder hand names the denomination (*Schlag*) which for the time being is to outrank any other, and the opposing party does so for the suit (*Farbe*); besides, the king of hearts (*Max*), the seven of bells

(*Belle*), and the seven of acorns (*Biese*) are permanent trump cards (*Kritische*); a game is over if a player wins three tricks.

Wecken *m* -s/- [related to E *wedge* 'Keil'] **1.** *bak.* (*Brot in länglicher Form*) oval loaf (of bread). → **2.** *her., colloq.* one of the distinctive white or blue fields in the Bavarian coat of arms: diamond; *in so mancher Fehde zwischen dem Kaiser und dem Kurfürsten von Bayern behaupteten sich die weißblauen ~ auch gegen das Reichsbanner* in many a feud between the Emperor and the Bavarian Elector, the blue-and-white diamonds stood their ground even against the Imperial banner. - **Weckerl** *n* -s/-(n) [dim. of prec. entry] *bak.* (*kleines, längliches Gebäck*) oval-shaped roll, *BrE also* finger roll; cp. *Eiweckerl*.

Weihbrunn, *dial.* **Weichbrunn** *m* -(e)s/-en R.C. (*Weihwasserbecken*) holy-water font, stoup; (*Weihwasserkessel*) holy-water bowl; *einen ~ nehmen* to bless (*or* cross) oneself with holy water; *sie wollten alle die tote Großmutter noch einmal sehen und ihr ~ geben* they all wanted to see their dead grandma one more time and to sprinkle her with holy water.

weiß-blau, weißblau *adj* & *adv* blue-and-white **1.** denoting dynastic or regional colours, of or within Bavaria: *durch seine Vermählung mit Ludmilla von Bogen übernahm 1204 ein Wittelsbacher, Ludwig der Kelheimer, die ~en Rauten der in der Straubinger Gegend beheimateten Grafen von Bogen in sein Wappen; es ist seither neben dem pfälzischen Löwen das vornehmste Wahrzeichen aller Linien des verzweigten Fürstenhauses und des heutigen bayerischen Staates geworden und findet sich schließlich als wesentlicher Bestandteil vieler niederbayerischer Gemeinde- und Landkreiswappen* the blue-and-white diamond field of the Counts of Bogen, from the vicinity of Straubing, was taken over by a member of the Wittelsbach dynasty, Ludwig of Kelheim, when he married Ludmilla von Bogen in 1204; together with the

Palatine Lion, it has since become the noblest emblem of all the lines of this royal family with its many branches and of the modern State of Bavaria, as well as a prominent element in the coats of arms of a great number of Lower Bavarian communities and districts; *Bayern sind die Franken und Schwaben nur den gemeinsamen ~en Landesfarben nach; in ihrer Sprache sind sie es nicht und ihrem Charakter auch nicht* Franconians and Swabians may share the same blue-and-white flag with Bavarians, but their languages differ, and so do their characters; → **2.** *journ.* & *colloq.* denoting things Bavarian, esp. Bavarian realia, institutions, and characteristics: *innerhalb (außerhalb) der ~en Grenzpfähle* inside (outside) the pale of Bavaria; *fast 80000 Tonnen Käse überschreiten jährlich die ~e Grenze* nearly 80,000 tons of cheese roll out of Bavaria every year; *Freunde und Liebhaber unseres ~en Landes* friends and fans of this country of ours (with its blue-and-white); *das ~e Nationalgetränk* the national drink of the South, i.e. beer; *wenn sie hier in einem Biergarten sitzen, die frische Maß vor sich, daneben einen tränenden Radi und eine resche Brezn, dann sind sie alle - die Einheimischen, die Zugereisten und die Weitgereisten - sich darüber einig, daß der Himmel ~ und die Welt schön ist* when they sit in a beer garden, with a fresh mug of beer in front of them and alongside it a well-salted giant radish and a crunchy pretzel, then everyone - born here, moved here, or visiting from abroad - is united in the assurance that God's in his heaven and all's right below in Bavaria; *~e Engstirnigkeit* petty (Bavarian) chauvinism; *keine ~e Engstirnigkeit beeinträchtigt ihm die Sicht* his viewpoint isn't restricted by (the old) blue-and-white blinkers; *dieses alte Schwankbuch ist schön ~ garniert* this collection of merry old tales is nicely laced with Bavarian humour.

Weißkraut *n* -(e)s *bot.* (*Weißkohl*) white cabbage.

Weißwurst *f* -/...würste, *dial.* ...würscht *gastr.* a snack-time speciality "discovered" by a Munich apprentice butcher on February 22, 1857: white sausage, a fat white delicacy filled to bursting point with calves' brains, spleen and veal; if eaten in style, the gourmet's fingers and teeth do the squeezing ‖ *phr.* since its consistency does not last for many hours, it is well to follow the warning: *die ~ darf das Zwölfuhrläuten nicht mehr hören* (or *erleben*) a white sausage must have gone the way of all flesh before the clock strikes the hour of twelve.

Weißwurst... in *comps.*, mostly *hum.* or *contp.* in the sense of '(typically) Bavarian': **~äquator** *m* -s, **~grenze** *f* - *hum.* (*Mainlinie*) the River Main, considered by a staunch Bavarian to be the northern frontier of his beloved homeland, a visible divide to shield what is near and dear to him in his cultural "hemisphere": *Bavarian defence line. - **~metropole** *f* - *hum.* or slightly *contp.* = *Biermetropole*. - **~parlament** *n* -(e)s *contp.* a disrespectful nickname, with shades of Josef Filser (→ *Filser-Bairisch*), for the Bavarian Diet (*Bayerischer Landtag*): *local-yokel parliament. - **~perspektive** *f* - *colloq.* conventional mode (*or* angle) of seeing Bavaria and Bavarians; *Bayern aus der touristischen ~ betrachten* to take a picture-postcardy view of Bavaria. - **~pflanze** *f* -/-n *contp.* (*Kellnerin in einem* [*Münchener*] *Bierlokal*) a waitress in a [Munich] public house: *beer-hall [beer-garden] queen, *AmE* also beer-jerker. - **~tempel** *m* -s *art hist.*, *contp.* in Munich, erected between 1935 and 1936, in pseudo-Hellenic style (*Haus der* [*Deutschen*] *Kunst*): *Sausage Parthenon.

weitergehen *v/i* to go on - for its *colloq.* embedding in a sentence, see *zusammenrücken* 2 ‖ *phr.* a colloquial imperative, usu. in the form *geh weiter!* (less often, *gehn S' weiter!*) **1.** one of slight surprise, often used in a sarcastic way: you don't say (so)! - **2.** one of complete incredulity: (oh,) go on!, go along with you!, get along (*or* away) with you!, come on!; *für das brauchst du mindestens zwei Stunden? geh weiter, das schaff' ich in zwanzig Minuten!* it'll take you at least two hours to do this? oh, come on, I could do this in twenty minutes. - **3.** one of combining lingering disbelief with an act of encouragement or persuasion: come on!, *BrE also* come along!; *geh weiter, Herr Doktor, das werden Sie sich doch noch leisten können!* come on, doctor, you'll surely be able to afford that. - **4.** one of warning to keep to the truth: come off it!; *geh weiter, das hab ich nie gesagt!* now come off it, I never said that!

W<u>ei</u>tling *m* -s/-e, *dial.* **W<u>ei</u>ling** *m* -s/- [< MHG *witling* 'something that widens'] esp. in *agr.* — a deep round earthenware basin for milk etc., much more open at the top since once (before the days of the centrifuge) often used for cream to form in: large bowl.

W<u>ei</u>z *m* -es [< OHG *wizi* 'punishment'] *folklore* disembodied spirit, esp. a "poor soul" which, because of some misdeed committed while a human being or because of leaving this life as a result of torture or suicide, has to roam the earth and cannot find peace until somebody performs a particular deed, or uses a particular formula, to relieve the spectre of its wanderings. - **w<u>ei</u>zen** *v/i* said of a felonious person or one who has met a violent death (*geistern, umgehen, gespenstern*): to haunt a place; *es weizt* there is a ghost haunting the place, the place is haunted, the place has a ghost; *im Schloß weizt der Geist eines ermordeten Ahnherrn* the ghost of a murdered ancestor walks in (*or* haunts) the castle; *für im Leben begangene Untaten mußte man nach dem Tode ~: Hölle und Fegfeuer der Kirche waren dem einfachen Volk als Strafen zu ungewiß* one who had committed a crime in his lifetime was condemned to wander about as a ghost after death - the Church's hell and purgatory were too uncertain modes of punishment for the unsophisticated to accept.

Wellfleisch *n* -(e)s *gastr.* in Franconia = *Kesselfleisch*.

Weltkirta *m* -s/- *dial., folklore* short for *Allerweltskirtag*↑.

wer ko, der ko! [*ko* < *kann*: /a/ before a nasal early became a long closed /o:/, and the nasal was later dropped - another close parallel to English (cp. OE **gans* > [gɔ:s] > ModE *goose*)] *colloq. phr.* (used both in dialect texts and as a dialect implant in standard language) a self-confident answer cheerfully flung in the face of one who has just dared make a miserably envious remark about, or who has cast some doubts on, the speaker's manual skill or mental potential: those who can, do!; he who can, does!; *das positive Bild, das die Münchner zu Recht von ihrer Stadt haben, entspricht ganz ihrem Selbstverständnis, das da lautet: „ x̃ ~ ~ ~ " - und München „ko" eben* the positive view natives of Munich have of their city is entirely in tune with their view of themselves, which is that "Those who can, do!" - and Munich can and does, period; *du hast wohl geglaubt, daß ich den Schlüssel gar nimmer rauskrieg - da schaust aber jetzt, gell? ... ja, ~~~~* you thought I wouldn't be able to get the key out, didn't you? why, now, eat your words ... he who can does, see?

Wetterkranzl *n* -s/-(n) *eccles. & folklore* → *Kranzltag*.

Wiesel, Wiesl; sometimes, with affectionate overtones, **Wieserl** *n* -s/- *colloq.* **1.** [dim. forms of *Wiese* 'meadow' (cp. *-l*↑ and *-erl*↑) *agr.* a patch of grassland, beside a house or in a forest clearing: tiny bit of meadow ‖ → *gmaht*. - **2.** [the word for a nimble-footed rodent, 'weasel' (or for its diminutive form)] *zo.* only in the phrase *laufen* or *rennen wie ein* ~ to go fast: to go like a bat out of hell, to go like a (blue) streak, *AmE also* to go lickety-split; *er muß zwar schon in den Siebzigern sein, aber laufen kann er noch wie ein* ~ he must be seventy if he is a day, but he can still put a brisk foot forward.

Wolpertinger *m* -s/pl. rare: - [< *Wolperting*, an imaginary Bavarian place-name (containing the elements *Wald-brecht* 'famous in the forest' + *-er* 'inhabitant (of)'] *folklore hum.* a mysterious forest animal, with a highly prized fur, that allows itself to be caught only by candlelight in a bag patiently held open by the midnight stalker; the story is a hoax directed at gullible non-Bavarians, preferably 'Prussians', whom natives boast to have kept waiting in lure for hours while themselves enjoying the successful prank over rounds of beer at the local inn (→ *derblecken*): dodgie, fadger, bodger-fax, wadger-beasel, *ScotE* haggis, *AmE* catawampus, snark, hoofen-poofer, whiffen-poof, woofin-whiffle, *PaG* elpentrecher, elbedritch ‖ a spurious invitation to the unsuspecting: *j-n zum ~fangen schicken* to send s.o. on a wild-goose chase; *gemma* [< dial. *gehen wir*] *~ fangen!* let's go dodgie (*etc.*)-hunting!

wurst or **wurscht**, invariably pronounced [-ʃt] *adv* [the metaphor probably rose from the sense impression, ever recurring to millions of knife-wielding people every day, that it makes no difference whether they start cutting their sausage at one end or another] in the *colloq.* phrase cluster *das ist mir ~* [*gewesen*] I'm not [I wasn't] bothered; *das soll mir doch ~ sein, ob er kommt oder nicht!* as if I cared whether he comes or not!; *das ist mir völlig ~* (or, *~egal*) I couldn't care less.

wüst, wüstaha, wüst ụmi *interj* [a corruption of *winster* < MHG & OHG *winistar* '(turning) left'; ? related to *wenden* 'to turn' (cp. F *gauche* and *guenchir*)] **1.** a shout to a draught animal, usu. a horse, to turn left (cp. *hott*): come half, woa(f) come here, hauve way, *ScotE* heck. - **2.** embedded in a *phr.* graphically describing that a married couple, or some other partners, are locked in a life of spiteful opposition: *der eine sagt ~, der andere (sagt) hott* one says stop, the other go; one blows hot, the other blows cold; one zigs when the other zags.

wụzeln *vt/refl* [< a word stem that tries to imitate the motion and the sound made in the characteristic action] *colloq.* **1.** *v/t* (1) always with reference to something very small, soft, or little resistant to the touch, that invites a human being, often unwittingly, to roll it into a pellet (*drehen*) — to roll up and down between the fingers: to roll around; *ja weißt denn du nichts Beßres als deinen Rotz zu ~?* haven't you got anything better to do than roll around your snot? - (2) with reference to a cigarette or a cigar (*wickeln*): to roll, to make (by rolling); *ich wuzel mir jetzt eine* I'm going to wrap (myself) one up. - **2.** *v/refl* to twist one's way with some effort: *sich durch die Menge ~* to worm (*or* wriggle) one's way through the crowd.

Wụzerl *n* -s/-(n) [either an imitative parallel of *wuzeln*↑, or a dialect variant of *Butz(en)*↑, quite possibly a combination of the two, + *-erl*↑] *colloq.* **1.** any small light loose waste from wool, or human skin peeled off (e.g., after excessive exposure to the sun), which one sometimes tends to pick up and roll into a tiny ball before throwing it away: twiddlybit (of wool, peeled skin, etc.). - **2.** (*Fussel*) a feather-light adhesion, occasionally resembling an uncannily insubstantial roundness, of soft thin hair and dust particles that hover on or gently waft along the floor of an untidy room: *BrE* fluff, *AmE* fuzz, lint. - **3.** *hum.* (*Dickerchen*) a fat and round person; (1) if a child: humpty-dumpty; *die Kleine ist ein süßes ~, gell?* the little one's a sweet roly-poly, isn't she? - (2) if an adult: chubby chops; *das ~ könnte auch einmal ans Abspecken denken!* ('t) wouldn't be a bad idea if chubby chops were to go and shed a few pounds. - **4.** *physiol.* (*Nasenkrümel*) a piece of hardened mucus: bogey, *NorBrE* crow, *vulg.* blob (*or* piece) of snot.

w<u>u</u>zerl... *colloq.*: **~dick, ~fett** *adj* with reference to babies and little pigs, usu. connoting cheerful appreciation — nicely rounded: pleasantly plump; *seine ~en Handerln* his podgy (*or* pudgy) little hands. - **~viech** *n* -(e)s/-er [for the second el., see *Viech*] *dial.* an unidentified small creeping animal, vaguely associated with the beetle-cum-spider population: creepy-crawly.

☞ Z ☜

Zach<u>ä</u>us [tsɔˈχɛːʊs] *m* -/no pl. [actually, "a man ..., little of stature", according to the Bible (St Luke 19: 1-10, the gospel passage read on *Allerweltskirtag*↑), who had "climbed up into a sycomore tree" to have a good look at Jesus passing through Jericho on his way to Jerusalem; when Jesus came to the place, he looked up and told Zacchæus [zæˈkiːəs] to "make haste and come down", for the Lord wanted to honour the publican by "abiding" at his house for the night.] *colloq.* **1.** suspended from the steeple of a parish church, on the Saturday preceding the third Sunday in October: "kermis flag", so called because of the jocular folk legend that Zacchæus, when hastily making his descent at the Lord's bidding, had torn his undergarments, whose shreds thus duly fluttered on high in the breeze for everyone to see. - **2.** *phr.* with light-hearted reference to that church flag if it looks somewhat tattered from long use, but verbally harking back to the Bible figure proper: *der ~ ist so nötig, daß es ihm keine neue Hose leidet* *(good old) Zacchæus is so stingy he won't even shell out the money for a new pair of trousers.

Zahnspangler, by reviving an old umlaut variant also **Zahnspängler**, *m* -s/- *colloq.*, usu. *hum.* = *Fotzenspangler*↑.

Zamperl *m* -s/-(n) [dim. of It *zampa* '(dog's) paw' (possibly a blend of obsolescent *zanca* and *gamba* both meaning 'leg'), as well as definite overtones of G *zahm* 'tame': > **Zahmerl* > *Zamperl* '(any) harmless, and indeed often rather pitiable, creature', with an excrescent <p> on the analogy of *Stamperl*↑ and *Wamperl*↑] *colloq.* **1.** *hum.* or slightly *iron.* - a small dog: little yapper. - **2.** *sarc.* a small nondescript dog, often saddled with the onus of doubtful parentage: pooch, *AmE* mutt.

Zander *m* -s/- [? < Pol *sandacz*, R *sudák*] *ichth.* a predatory freshwater fish in the East and South of Germany, also known as **Schill** *m* -(e)s/-e (*Lucioperca sandra*): pike-perch, zander [ˈzændə]; a new delicacy now in East Anglia, where the fish is bred by the Great Ouse [uːz] River Authority.

zaundürr *adj colloq.* of a person who is very slim (*spindeldürr*): (as) thin *or* lean as a rake, (as) thin as a lath, skinny, spindly ‖ → *Hopfenstange* 2.

zeckerlfett *adj* [first el., dim. of *Zeck(e)* 'tick', i.e. a very small insect-like animal that can gorge itself to several times its original size] *colloq.* of a person, often *hum.* obese, esp. replete with food (and/or drink): full as a tick.

zefix; if given more weight, **zäfix** *interj.* [an abbreviated, and therefore de-emphasized, form of *Kruzifix* which, besides its factual meaning, 'crucifix', is a full-bodied curse, '(God) damn it (by the holy cross on which His Son had to die)!'; the English equivalents here offered are euphemisms for *Jesus* and *God*, respectively] a rather mild cry of annoyance: jeepers!, by golly!; *jedesmal wenn ich rausgeh - ~! -, fängt es zu schütten an* it starts pouring (*NorBrE also* teeming with rain) every blessed time I go out.

Zehnerl *n* -s/-(n) [dim. of *Zehner* 'any monetary unit of ten'] *colloq.* **1.** (*Zehnpfennigstück*) ten-pfennig piece, i.e. a coin worth one tenth of a German mark; *langen fünf ~(n) (für die Parkuhr), wenn du eine halbe Stunde parken willst?* will five ten-pfennig pieces (in the [parking] meter) last you for half an hour's parking?; *eine Dame sollte ein paar ~(n) und Fufzgerl(n)* (or *Fuchzgerl[n]*) *bei sich haben, wenn sie auf die Toilette geht* a lady should have a couple of ten- and fifty-pfennig pieces with her when she goes to the ladies' room. - **2.** (*Zehnpfennigbetrag*) sum of ten pfennigs, *loosely*: tenpence; *um ein ~ kriegt man nicht viel* you don't get much for (German) tenpence, tenpence won't buy you much of anything. - **3.** *fig.* in phrase *das ~ ist (bei mir* [etc.]) *gefallen* I've (*etc.*) caught the idea: the penny has dropped, the lightbulb has flashed (*or*, gone on).

zerreißen *v/t* [actually, 'to tear'] *colloq.*, usu. *iron.* or *contp.* (since often with a negative slant) *etwas ~* to succeed in doing something, to be an efficient worker: to be a born achiever, to pull off things; *o mei, der Hans zerreißt auch nix* oh my, Jack isn't one to pull off great things ‖ *phr.* embodied in a characteristic dialogue carried on between two lackadaisical fellows (with the first one asking in a languid tone) - A: *Was ~ wir denn heut noch?* B: *Des, was wir noch ~, ist vielleicht a nasse Zeitung!* A: Now, well, what are we going to knock off today? B: I suspect the manliest thing we can do is knock the skin off a rice pudding.

Zipferl *n* -s/-(n) [dim. of *Zipfel m* 'end', 'tip'] **1.** *colloq.* the small, tapering (or tied-up) endpiece of an article of food, esp. that of a length of sausage: end bit. - **2.** low or domestic *colloq.* a child's penis: tassel, *BrE also* winkle, *AmE also* wag; cp. *Pfeiferl* 2.

Zuagroaste *m & f* -n/-n [the popular South German variant of *Zugereiste* 'newcomer', actually the past participle noun of a defunct verb, *zureisen* 'to travel there'] *dial.* any person who, either recently or years ago, has moved into the community; one looked upon, sometimes indeed looked *down* upon, as a non-native (*Zuwanderer*[*in*]) - **1.** if from another town, or part, of Germany or from a German-speaking country (*Zuzügler*[*in*], colloq. *Neue*): newcomer, *colloq.* young-timer, Johnny [*if female*: Jeanie]-come-lately. - **2.** if from further abroad, esp. from the East (*Ausländer*[*in*]): immigrant, foreigner, *slightly contp.* one of those aliens; *jeder fünfte Münchner ist ein Ausländer; mit seinen „~n" aus aller Welt ist München unter den Spitzenreitern in der Republik* every fifth citizen of Munich comes from abroad; in this country, the town is among the front-runners as regards population influx from all over the world.

Zug... [< *ziehen*, here: 'to pull open and together, or to loosen and tighten, alternately']: **~beutel** *m* -s/- a small leather bag, with strings to tie, used for holding tobacco, money, etc.: pouch. - **~harmonie** *f* -/-n *mus. colloq.* concertina: (*Ziehharmonika*) pushbox, to-and-fromie, squiffer.

zündeln *v/i* [< Germ. **tund*- + the OHG iterative verb suffix

-ilōn 'to make it a habit of setting fire to some dry material from a spark'; cp. E *tinder* 'dry material that readily takes fire from a spark'] *colloq.* **1.** nearly always referring to a child, or children, impishly engaged in incendiarism: to play with fire (*or* with matches) ‖ a common folk belief, and a scary warning to potential culprits: *wer zündelt, bieselt in der Nacht ins Bett* he who plays with fire will wet the bed (*or*, will pee in bed). - **2.** said of one gripped by an uncontrollable, or criminal, desire to start fires: to be a firebug. -

Zündler *m* -s/- *colloq.* **1.** (1) child (*or, less often,* youngster) playing with fire. - (2) child having caused fire damage through the act of playing with live matchsticks: child incendiary. - **2.** arsonist: firebug, *AmE also* torch (man), torcher.

Zunftbaum *m* -(e)s/...bäume *folklore* erected in the centre of some villages as a permanent landmark of communal identity and pride: "guild pole", the trunk of a huge forest tree or a steel mast (in either case some thirty feet high), bearing at regular intervals, both left and right, some distinctive "guild emblems" (*Zunfttafeln*), the sometimes almost life-sized silhouettes of people or their occupational instruments (a man scything, a woman gathering sheaves of grain, a breweryman and his dray, etc.) which are typical of that village in its day-to-day activities.

zünftig *adj colloq.* **1.** (*prächtig*) fine, grand; to express satisfaction at being in a convivial group: ~ *ist's!* it's just grand!, it's really groovy!; *ein ~er Kerl* a jolly good fellow. - **2.** (*herzhaft*) genuine, proper; hearty; *zu einer ~en Brotzeit gehören Bauernbrot, Brezen, Salzstangerln oder Kümmelweckerln* a hearty snack includes black bread, pretzels, salt sticks, or crisp caraway-seed rolls.

zusammenrucken *v/i colloq.* **1.** usu. said of a convivial group of people seated on a bench or around a table, and trying to accommodate one or more comers: to move up closer, to huddle together; *der Bayer liebt volle Wirtshäuser, Bierzelte und Biergärten; am liebsten zwängt er sich, entschuldigend um Gunst buhlend, mit einem „Ruck ma a bisserl zamma, bittschön!" an einen bereits vollbesetzten Tisch* a Bavarian is fond of jam-packed inns, of brewery tents and beer gardens; and he just loves to edge in on a fully-seated bench with a coaxingly apologetic, "Let's move over (*or*, squeeze together) a wee bit, shall we?" - **2.** to start quarrelling: to have a set-to; *mir werden fei bald ~, mia zwoa, wann des so weitergeht!* we'll soon have it out, me and you, if things go on like that!

Zwergerl *n* -s/-(n), **Zwergl** *n* -s/-n [both are diminutive forms of *Zwerg* < MHG *twerc* 'dwarf'; the former is predominantly a term of endearment (and thus suited for baby talk), while the latter has lost most of its emotive strength; and both can also be caustic] *colloq.* **1.** (little) dwarf. - **2.** *hum.* or *contp.* short person: shorty, shortie.

Zwetschge *f* -/-n [a borrowing from the Romance dialects of southeastern France and northern Italy, VulgL **davascena* < L *damascena* '(plum) of Damascus'; related to E *damson*] *bot.* plum ‖ if dried (and gently boiled before eating), prune.

Zwetschgen...: ⁵**blau** *adj* (as) blue as a plum; *durch jahrelangen Alkoholgenuß war seine Nase ~ geworden* steady years of drinking had turned his nose a mottled red-and-blue. - **~datschi** *m* -(s)/-(s) *bak.* flat plum cake (made on a baking tray). - **~knödel** *m* -s/- *cul.* plum dumpling. - **~mus** *n* -es/-e *cul.* plum jam. - **~schnaps** *m* -es/...schnäpse, **~wasser** *n* -s/...wässer *bev.* plum brandy.

Zwickel *m* -s/- [an old word meaning 'gusset', and during the Second German Empire also, playfully, 'two-penny coin'; after its hundredfold revaluation since then, the word today may well be taken by some would-be etymologists to be a near-echo of *zw*ei Mar*kl*] *colloq.* two-German-mark coin:

two-mark bit; *kannst du mir einen ~ wechseln?* can you change me (*or*, give me change for) a two-mark piece?

Zwickerbusserl *n* -s/-(n) [first el., 'anybody or anything that pinches or nips' (here, the action of pinching is meant); for the second el., see *Busserl*↑] *colloq.*, always used in a cheerful mood — a playful pinch given by an elderly person to a youngster's cheek or cheeks, either with the thumb and forefinger or the forefinger and the middle finger, in a spirit of bonhomie: friendly little tweak; *der Direktor hat dem Buben ein ~ gegeben* the headmaster gave the boy a friendly little tweak.

Zwiderwurzn *f* -/- [the image is taken from a tree and its wickerwork of roots, each of which is twisting and turning as if in perpetual disagreement with all its fellows (< *zuwider* 'against'; < *Wurzen*, a weakly declined variant of *Wurz*, related to OE *wyrt* 'root', 'plant')] *dial. colloq.* a person with no sense of humor, who always complains and is never satisfied (*Griesgram*): grumbler, grouch, sourpuss [-pos], *AmE also* crosspatch, (old) crabbie, glumpot, vinegarpuss, Adam Sourguy [Calamity Jane].

Zwiefache *m* -n/-n *mus.* "double trouble", gay Bavarian dance music involving alternation between 2/4 and 3/4 time; surprise changeovers for those unfamiliar with the particular tune often cause them to lose step, thus providing extra merriment for all concerned.

Zwieseler Fink *m* - -en/no pl. *mus.* a major choral event inaugurated by Paul Friedl, a regional poet of Zwiesel, in 1947: "Zwiesel Finch", **1.** a folkmusic competition, in some ways comparable to the Welsh eisteddfod [aɪsˈteðvəd], held annually at one town or another in the Bavarian Forest. - **2.** the challenge trophy which rests with the winning choir for one year.

Appendix

A Correspondences and Disparities of Diction

B Poetic Vignettes Englished

For further translations of pieces of Bavarian prose and poetry, see pp. 11, 12, and the Glossary, esp. pp. 29, 45, 84, 88, 94, 129, 169, 170, 181, 185.

Analogues of Proverbial Lore:
Dialect Gleanings from Old Bavaria and Highland Scots

A proverb is a short saying that offers advice or warning, and is widely taken up by the common people. In the process, its source becomes blurred, and so do the lanes along which such wisdom travels. Questions of origin and dissemination apart, however, we should not forget that "men are more like than unlike one another". We can always count, therefore, on people of different nationalities and tongues coming up with identical or near-identical sayings although they have never really been in contact with each other. Let us, for instance, invite Bavarians and Scots to bear unwitting testimony to the phenomenon. Very few isolated instances apart, there have really been no major contacts between the two countries until after the Second World War, and yet a good many age-old parallels in proverbial lore abound.

Because of these striking similarities in content, glossing the Highland dialect (which here is chiefly that of Aberdeenshire) can be kept at a minimum:

D' Schuastaweiba und d' Schmiedsroß genga barfuß.
The shaemakker's wife an the smith's meer 's aye warst shod.

Deandln, de pfeifn, und Henna de krahn,
sollt ma all zwoa an Hals umdrahn.
Fustlin maidens an craain hens
should aa get their necks thraan.

Nix wia naus, was koan Hauszins zahlt!
Better an empty hoose nor an ill tenant.

Liabar an Magn varrenkt als am Wirt was gschenkt.
Better belly rive (*burst*) nor gweed mait (*food*) be connached (*spoiled*).

Wer koan Kopf hat, muaß Füaß habn.
Little wit in the heid maks muckle traivel tae the feet.

Wia da Herr, so sei Gscherr.
Sic mannie, sic horsie.

Auf oam Weg, wo viel gfahrn wird, wachst koa Gras.
Ower sair bett (*sorely beaten*) a roadie niver grows corn.

Wann der Bettlmann aufs Roß kommt, kann er's nimmer derhalten.
Set a beggar on horseback, and he'll ride a gallop.

Liabar an Augenblick feig als a Lebm lang tout.
Better a livin cooard nor a deid hero.

Kommt der März wiar a Wolf, dann geht er wiar a Lamm.
If Mairch comes in like a lion it'll gang oot like a lamb.

I zoag da, wo der Zimmamann 's Loch glassn hat!
I'll lat you see the hole the mason left.

Is guat für d' Mülla, daß d' Säck net redn kinna.
It's aye kent the mullert (*miller*) keeps fat hogs, bit naebody kens
faa feeds them.

Der hat lauta Daumen.
His fingers is aa thoombs.

Drum is 's Geld rund, daß 's rollt.
Money's made roon tae gang roon.

Da Kessl hat vor da Pfanna nix voraus, weil's alle zwoa schwarz san.
Pottie canna cry black airsie tae the pannie.

Das Messa da schneid't das kalte Wassa bis am Bodn.
These scissors widna clip butter though it wis meltit.

Willst dein Sach habm recht, mach dein eigna Knecht.
Gin ye want a thing doon well, Stoop an do it aa yersel'.

Schwarze Küah gebm a weiße Milch.
A black hen lays a white egg.

Wann d' Maus satt hat, is 's Mehl bitta.
As the soo fills, the draff soors.

*D' Nußbaam und d' Weiba, de muaß ma schlagn,
daß s' üba 's Jahr wieda guat tragn.*

A woman and a walnut-tree,
The mair ye ding' em the better they be.

Aus am Schweinern kannst koa Rindfleisch macha.
Fit d' ye expect fae a soo bit a grumph?

Alls hat oa End, nur die Wurscht hat zwoa.
Athing has an end bit a pudden has twa.

Landlubbers and Seafarers:
Bavarian and British Metaphors Compared

The mind of man concerning elemental things in life is much the same the world over, and the present lexical study bears this out to no small degree. However, there are limits, and sometimes even remarkable differences. The geographical position of our respective countries is one of those factors that make for idiomatic heterogeneity. Bavaria is land-locked, and Britain sea-girt; and while many English phrases are quite obvious in their nautical origin (often having duly passed, with metaphorical signification, into the speech of Britons on land), Bavarians fall back upon their own terrain, on their mountains and meadows and fields, on their favourite pastimes, or on general phenomena to colour their everyday utterances with.

Here are just a few of such disparities of vision encapsulated in language:

A vague hope for a favourable turn of one's fortune is couched in the words

wann's amal bei mir Dukaten reg-net, or *wenn ich einmal einen Haupttreffer im Lotto mache*

when my ship comes in (*or* home).

A placidly resigned person, when confronted with an awkward or difficult situation, says

macht nix, es sollt' nix Ärgeres (or *Schlimmeres*) *passieren!*

never mind, worse things happen at sea.

Of a scheming person, who makes a small gift or concession in the hope of obtaining a large one, we are told

des is oana, der schmeißt d' Wurst nach 'm Sausack

he's one to throw out (*or* set) a sprat to catch a mackerel (*or* herring, *or* whale).

And let us remember, in this connection, two kindred vows of modesty:

Lieber ein Spatz in der Hand als eine Taube auf dem Dach

A trout in the pot is better than a salmon in the sea.

Here is a word of comfort for a bashful young man whom a girl unexpectedly refused to marry after having promised to do so:

andere Mütter haben auch schöne Töchter

there are as good fish in the sea as ever came out of it.

On the other hand, someone who thinks of himself as a singularly important person is rightly given to understand,

hinterm Berg san aa no' Leut'

you're not the only pebble on the beach.

A room or a building which has cold air flowing through it may well make the squeamish protest

da ziagst's wia in am Voglhäusl,   there's a draught like on a
or *wia durch an Bahnhof*   raft in the open sea.

The anxious is overheard asking whether there is not someone around who might interfere:

ist (denn) die Luft rein?   is the coast clear?

A course of action without any difficulties readily evokes the picture of

a gmahts Wiesl   plain sailing.

Graphic comparisons also come to one's mind at the sight of someone acting out his excessive nervousness,

herumfahren wia a Fuder Muckn   jumping about like a herring
nach 'm Gebetläuten   on a hot griddle,

or when hearing a stout person breathe noisily after having run for some distance,

schnaufen wiar a Bierdimpfl,   breathing (*or* puffing, *or*
or *wia da Igl im Birnhaufn*   wheezing) like a grampus.

The grampus is a kind of whale; and "whale" itself figures in an English maritime idiom (for the otherwise truly Bavarian concept of having 'a hugely enjoyable time'),

eine Mords- or *Pfunds-* or   a whale of a time.
Riesengaudi

The other end of the emotional scale is reached when somebody is thought gullible enough to believe a fraudulently newsy item; he is then likely to burst out into a scornful

das kannst du deiner Großmutter   tell that to the Marines (*or*,
verzählen!   the Horse Marines)!

The latter variant would be more in the spirit of the gibe since the Marine Corps is a sea-going force in which horses are but a figment of the imagination.

Farmers and sailors are equally aware of the need to keep a weather eye open, for an opportunity lost may not present itself again so soon:

heugn muaß ma,   hoist your sail
wann's Heuwetter is   when the wind is fair.

And we gladly take comfort from the thought that on earth, when in straits, there are companions in need but also companions to lighten our burden:

wir sind alle in der gleichen Gassen   we're all in the same boat.

KARL STIELER

Beim Michael

Beim Michel geht's aufs letzte End,
As Wei steht da und woant und flennt
Und jammert halt, was 's jammern kann.
Denn schaug, er war a guater Mann.
„Gel, Weibei", schnackelt er so hin,
„Gel," sagt er, „bal i gstorben bin,
An Mann, den brauchst ja dengerscht - und -
Na heiratst - halt an - Sepp von Gmund."
„O mei," flennt sie, daß sie 's ganz z'sprengt,
„An den da han i aa scho denkt!"

At Michael's

With Michael, life drains soft away,
His missus bawling through the day;
And bawl and moan is all she can
For, mind, he was a right good man.
"Look, wifey, please," his voice, near fled,
Comes halting, slow, "Please, when I'm dead
A man you'll be in need of, though ...
You could - och - marry Lake-End Joe."
"Oh my," and fast her tears forth well,
"That's one I've thought of, too, mysel'."

EUGEN ROTH

Das Ferngespräch

Ein Mensch spricht fern, geraume Zeit,
Mit ausgesuchter Höflichkeit,
Legt endlich dann, mit vielen süßen
Empfehlungen und besten Grüßen
Den Hörer wieder auf die Gabel -
Doch tut er nochmal auf den Schnabel
(Nach all dem freundlichen Gestammel),
Um dumpf zu murmeln: „Blöder Hammel!"
Der drüben öffnet auch den Mund
Zu der Bemerkung: „Falscher Hund!" ...
So einfach wird oft auf der Welt
Die Wahrheit wieder hergestellt.

The Telephone Call

A man's been phoning quite a while,
Polite and suave, his gentle style
Holds rich civilities in store;
And at long last, "goodbyes" galore.
The phone's now hushed, no longer spills
The purly voice soft murmerings.
But now, and how, that mouth's agape
With muffled growls of "Stupid ape!"
The other, too, his teeth unlocks
To hiss a spiteful "Tricky fox!" ...
This world does simple means contrive
To make amends, thus Truth can thrive.

A Long Dozen of Chatter Ditties*

Is ma lusti und froh,
mag da Herrgott oan scho,
aba wuiseln und reahrn,
mag er gar nit gern hörn.

Gin ya grin wi' guid cheer,
God 'll think y'are a dear;
But He 'll sin change His min'
Gin ya whimper an' whine.

Was nutzt oan des Grantln,
was nutzt oan des Sorgn?
's Le'm geht ja eh grad
von heut bis auf morgn.

Now why do folks worry,
Why grumble and groan?
Life that 's today
Will tomorrow be flown.

Hast an Juhschroa im Herzen,
nur außa damit!
Graunzt hat die Welt gnua,
aber gjuchazt no nit!

If yer heart feels like yodellin',
Come on, let it out!
It 's cheer the world's needin',
Too many folks pout.

I woaß nit, i hab
mit da Oawat koa Freid,
denn grad mit da Oawat
versamt ma die Zeit!

For work, let me tell you,
I don't care as such,
For work is the thing
Cuts me out of so much.

I kénn scho dein' Brauch
und a wó ma di' findt:
im Wirtshaus ganz vorn,
in da Kirchn ganz hint.

I know all your likes
And what places you mind -
In the pub, right up front;
In the church, way behind!

Und es bleibt scho beim Altn,
es bleibt scho beim Brauch:
wann der Schoaß draußn is,
ja da gfreit si' der Bauch.

Here 's a time-honoured custom
We'll keep without doubt:
'Tis the belly's delight
When the fart thunders out.

De ratschatn Leut,
dene schick i an Gruaß:
sie sollnt si erst waschn,
san selba voll Ruaß.

To mud-slinging gossips
I give this salute:
"Use soap on your own mouths,
Look there for the soot!"

Das Oansiedlalebm, *das geht mir nit ein,* *i wollt' scho viel liaba* *a Zwoasiedla sein.*	A hermit's existence I wouldn't pooh-pooh Were hermits allowed each A hermitess, too!
Wia höcha da Berg, *wia höcha da Wind,* *und wia schöna das Deandl,* *wia kloana die Sünd.*	The higher the mountain, The cosier the inn; The sweeter the lassie, The smaller the sin.
Hat oaner a schöns Deandl, *na hat a sei Freid,* *und dawischt er a schiache,* *is' eahm néamad net neid.*	A beauty on your arm Is a nice thing to win; But there's nobody jealous If she's ugly as sin.
Mei Deandl is sauba *von d' Fiaß bis zum Hals;* *do' léida des Gsicht,* *des verschandlt dann alls.*	My lass is a beauty, From shoes to her shawl. Too bad there's her face, Though - which damages all.
Mei Deandl hat a Ding, *is net schwaar und net gring,* *is net eng und net weit,* *is a Ding, des mi gfreit.*	My sweet one sports a spot, Not too cold, not too hot, Not too broad, not too tight: 'Tis a thing of delight.
Geh weg vo' meim Stadl, *geh weg vo' meim Bett:* *du könnst ma was machn,* *was Händ' und Fiaß hätt'.*	Boy, stay from my quarters, Stand clear of my bed: You might make a third set Of legs, arms, and head!
Jetzt pfüat enk Gott, Leut, *packts z'samm und gehts ham.* *So schön und so jung* *kemma net wieder z'samm!*	Good-bye, folks, farewell, Our songs are now sung! We won't meet again Quite as fair and as young.

*Further *Schnadahüpfln* can be found in the body of the Glossary, on pp. 72, 84, 169, and 170.

Hints for Further Reading

ANON. "Haberfeld Treiben in Upper Bavaria", *The Cornhill Magazine* (London), Vol. 16 (1867), pp. 667-76.

ARNOLD, GUY. *Down the Danube from the Black Forest to the Black Sea.* London: Cassell, 1989. [Bavarian impressions to be found in four chapters: Munich, pp. 5-10; The Danube and War, pp. 41-48; Ingolstadt and Munich again, pp. 49-53; Neustadt to Regensburg, pp. 54-59.]

ASHWORTH, ALISON J. "Brass Bands in Bavaria and Lancashire: Stereotypes and Realities", *Bavarica anglica*, Volume One: *A Cross-Cultural Miscellany Presented to Tom Fletcher* ([Forum anglicum, ed. OTTO HIETSCH, Vol. 8] Frankfurt am Main, Bern, Las Vegas: Peter Lang, 1979 [hereafter quoted as: *Bavarica anglica*]), pp. 178-82.

—, and JEAN RITZKE-RUTHERFORD. "Mirrors of Modern Sadness: Leaves from the Pages of a Bavarian Poetess", *Bavarica anglica*, pp. 141-45. [On translating two of Erika Eichenseer's lyrics.]

BAKER, SUZANNE ST. BARBE. *A Wayfarer in Bavaria.* London: Methuen & Co., 1930.

BAUER, BÄRBEL. *Deutsche Abtönungspartikeln und ihre englischen Entsprechungen: Eine sprachvergleichende Untersuchung unter besonderer Berücksichtigung umgangssprachlicher und mundartlich gefärbter Partikeln des Bairischen.* Thesis for the Higher Teachers' Diploma in English Linguistics, University of Regensburg [unpublished], Autumn 1973.

BÖKER, UWE. "English Visitors to Oberammergau: Amelia M. Hull, Jerome K. Jerome, Graham Greene", *Bavarica anglica*, pp. 205-24.

BOURKE, JOHN. *Baroque Churches of Central Europe.* London: Faber and Faber, 1978 (^{2}1962; ^{1}1958).

BUCKETT, ANNA M. "The 'Discovery' of Bavaria by British Travellers and Minor Novelists, 1830-1860", *Language and Civilization: A Concerted Profusion of Essays and Studies in Honour of Otto Hietsch*, ed. with the assistance of Teresa Kirschner, Donald Gutch and Judith Gilbert by Claudia Blank (Frankfurt-on-Main, Berne, New York, Paris: Peter Lang, 1992 [hereafter quoted as: *Language and Civilization*]), Vol. 1, pp. 335-80.

BURGSCHMIDT, ERNST, and DIETER GÖTZ. *kontrastive linguistik, deutsch/englisch: theorie und anwendung.* München: Max Hueber, 1974.

CHANNON, HENRY. *The Ludwigs of Bavaria.* (Collection of British and American Authors, Vol. 5126.) Leipzig: Bernhard Tauchnitz, 1934.

DOZAUER, RUDOLF. *A Phonology of the Dialect of Bergstetten.* Ann Arbor: University of Michigan Press, 1967.

EICHENSEER, ADOLF. "Yorkshiremen and Bavarians: A Cultural Encounter at the Harrogate Music Festival", *Bavarica anglica*, pp. 172-77.

FINKENSTAEDT, THOMAS. "Drei englische Reisende in Augsburg", *Language and Civilization*, Vol. 1, pp. 323-34, 2 illus. [Thomas Nugent, Thomas Frognall Dibdin, Frances Trollope.]

GLEISSNER, REINHARD. "Middle English *-ind-* > *-ing-* ? and Bavarian *-ind-* > *-ing-*: A Note", *Bavarica anglica*, pp. 53-60.

—. "English Language Interference in the Letters of Archabbot Boniface Wimmer O.S.B. (1809-87) to King Ludwig I of Bavaria (1786-1868)", *Language and Civilization*, Vol. 1, pp. 474-529, 3 illus.

GÖLLER, KARL HEINZ. "Sir George Etherege in Regensburg", *Bavarica anglica*, pp. 185-204.

—, and JEAN RITZKE-RUTHERFORD. "St. Oswald in Regensburg: A Reconsideration", *Bavarica anglica*, pp. 98-118.

GRUBER, HEINRICH. "*A Holiday in Bavaria*: Ein viktorianischer Reisebericht", *Language and Civilization*, Vol. 1, pp. 406-27, 11 illus.

GUTCH, DONALD "Bavarians and Others: Jerome K. Jerome's View of Germany", *Bavarica anglica*, pp. 225-46.

—. "Linking and Intrusive *r* in English and Bavarian", *Language and Civilization*, Vol. 1, pp. 555-611 [A detailed discussion of present-day usage, but also shedding new light on past developments (before 1800).]

HAAS, RENATE. "Fortunatus: A Bavarian Literary Hero in England", *Bavarica anglica*, pp. 119-38.

HIETSCH, OTTO. "Folk Tune Reworded: A Dozen Bavarian Dainties in English", *Bavarica anglica*, pp. 146-71, with musical notations.

—. "Die Sprache des Niederbayern: Gleiches und Vergleichbares aus der Sicht des Anglisten", *Niederbayerisches Kern- und Wurzelholz* ([Straubinger Hefte, No. 32] Straubing: Johannes-Turmair-Gymnasium, 1982), pp. 121-47, 3 illus.

—. "'Allerweltskirta' und 'Zwieseler Fink' auf englisch: Ein kleiner Beitrag zum zweisprachigen Kulturverständnis des ostbayerischen Raumes", *Heimat Ostbayern* (Grafenau), Vol. 7 (1992), pp. 28-34, illus.

—. "Waldlerisches im englischen Widerhall: Ein zweisprachiges Glossar zu Sprache und Brauchtum einer Landschaft", *ibid.*, Vol. 8 (1993), pp. 104-15, illus.

—. "A Grab-Bag of Chatter Ditties: Österreichisch-bairische 'Schnadahüpfeln' in englischem Gewande", *Neuphilologische Nachlese* (Schriftenreihe der Zeitschrift *Moderne Sprachen* [Vienna], ed. ERWIN REINER), No. 22 (1993), pp. 54-61.

—. "Alpenländischer Humor im englischen Widerhall", *ibid.*, No. 28 (1994), pp. 5-6.

HOWITT-WATTS, ANNA MARY. *An Art-Student in Munich*. 2 vols. London: Thomas de la Rue, ^{2}1880 (^{1}1853).

KASTENBERGER, PETER. *Bayerische Spracheigentümlichkeiten im Englischunterricht.*

Thesis for the Higher Teachers' Diploma in English Linguistics, University of Regensburg [unpublished], Spring 1976.

KELLER, THOMAS L. *The City Dialect of Regensburg*. Hamburg: Helmut Buske, 1976.

LARSEN, EGON. *Munich.* (Cities of the World, No. 6.) London: Phoenix House, 1967.

LEHMAN-IRL, DEBORAH. "Some Aspects of Language Interference in the English of German-American Children", *Language and Civilization*, Vol. 1, pp. 530-42, 1 illus.

MACDONELL, ARTHUR A. *Camping Voyages on German Rivers*. London: Edward Stanford, 1980. [The Main, pp. 132-65; The Danube, pp. 185-260.]

MACGREGOR, JOHN. *A Thousand Miles in the Rob Roy Canoe on Rivers and Lakes of Europe.* London: Sampson Low, Son, and Marston, 1866.

MANSFIELD, ROBERT BLACHFORD. *The Water Lily on the Danube: Being a Brief Account of the Perils of a Pair-Oar during a Voyage from Lambeth to Pesth.* London: John W. Parker and Son, 1853.

—. *The Log of the Water Lily (Thames Gig) during two Cruises in the Summers of 1851-1852, on the Rhine, Neckar, Main, Moselle, Danube and Other Streams of Germany.* (Collection of British Authors, Vol. 294.) Leipzig: Bernhard Tauchnitz, 1854.

MARKMILLER, FRITZ. "A Votive Tablet Commissioned by Scottish Clerics for the Pilgrimage Church near Ottending, Lower Bavaria", *Language and Civilization*, Vol. 1, pp. 286-90, 1 illus.

MITCHELL, JEROME. "Bryant in Bavaria", *Language and Civilization*, Vol. 1, pp. 381-90, 3 illus.

MOWAT, J.L.G. *A Walk along the Teufelsmauer und Pfahlgraben*. With a Map of the 'Limes Imperii' from the Danube to the Rhine. Oxford: privately printed, 1885.

PHILLIPS, JOHN A. S. *Ein Engländer in Bayern: Skurrile Erlebnisse eines Zugereisten.* Pfaffenhofen: W. Ludwig, 1986.

RADLOF, J[OHANN] G[OTTLIEB]. "Verwandtschaft der bayerischen Mundart mit manchen nordischen, besonders der ängelländischen", *Teutschkundliche Forschungen und Erheiterungen für Gebildete* (Berlin), Vol. 3 (1827), pp. 54-61.

RAITH, JOSEF. "Linguistics in the English Lesson, or, Are the English Descended from the Lower Bavarians?", *Bavarica anglica*, pp. 27-34.

REYNOLDS, JAMES. *Panorama of Austria, with Glimpses of Bavaria and Switzerland.* New York: G.P. Putnam's Sons, 1956.

RIEDERER, INGEBORG. *Mundartbrücken: Parallelen zwischen dem Bairischen und dem Englischen.* Thesis for the Higher Teachers' Diploma in English Linguistics, University of Regensburg [unpublished], Spring 1975.

ROSE, HANS. "München und das Englische", *Die Gabe: Dichtungen und Aufsätze. Wilhelm Hausenstein zum 50. Geburtstag* (Munich, 1933), pp. 66-78, 1 illus. [On British influence on local art and architecture in the nineteenth century.]

ROWLEY, ANTHONY "Tyke and Bavarian: A Comparison of Two Dialects", *Bavarica anglica*, pp. 35-52. [The author draws his illustrations from the speech of West Yorkshire.]

ROWSE, A[LFRED] L[ESLIE]. "Munich under the Weimar Republic", *A Cornishman Abroad* (London: Jonathan Cape, 1976), pp. 69-91.

SEIDL, HELMUT A. "Health Proverbs in Britain and Bavaria: A Sampling of Parallels", *Bavaria anglica*, pp. 71-97.

SELLAR, ALEXANDER CRAIG. *The Passion-Play in the Highlands of Bavaria.* Edinburgh and London: Blackwood, ³1871.

STEINBERGER, HERMANN. "Bayerische und englische Ortsnamen", *Der Zwiebelturm* (Regensburg), Vol. 1950, No. 2, pp. 45f. [A brief survey of correspondences.]

THIELECKE, ALISON M. "Bringing up Children Bilingually: A Progress Report", *Language and Civilization*, Vol. 1, pp. 543-54.

TYLOR, CHARLES. *Historical Tour in Franconia in the Summer of 1852.* Brighton: R. Folthorp; London: Longman & Co., 1852.

UHDE-BERNAYS, HERMANN. *Nuremberg.* London: A. Siegle, 1904. [Describing "the art treasures of the old Imperial city."]

WADLEIGH, HENRY RAWLE. *Munich: History, Monuments, and Art.* London: T. Fisher Unwin, 1910.

WHITLING, HENRY JOHN. *Pictures of Nuremberg; and Rambles in the Hills and Valleys of Franconia.* 2 vols. London: Richard Bentley, 1850.

WICKHAM, CHRISTOPHER J. "Dialekt im Phonetikunterricht", *Forum Phoneticum* (Hamburg), Vol. 5 (1977-78), pp. 105-18. [The author, a former lector in Bavaria, recommends basing English phonetic drill on the pupils' regional dialect.]

—. *Modern German Dialect Poetry as a Linguistic, Literary and Social Phenomenon: The Case of Bavarian and Austrian.* Ann Arbor: University of Michigan Press, 1982.

WILBERFORCE, EDWARD. *Social Life in Munich.* London: William H. Allen, 1863. Trans. (after cutting the text by one third), with copious notes, by GERHARD WIESEND: *Ein Snob in München: Die erstaunlichen Beobachtungen des Mr. Edward Wilberforce in München anno 1860.* Munich: Ehrenwirth, 1990.

ZEHETNER, LUDWIG. "'Bairisches Englisch': Muttersprachlicher Dialekttransfer im Fremdsprachenerwerb am Beispiel regionalspezifischer Schwierigkeiten und Möglichkeiten für den Englischunterricht im bairischen Dialektraum", *Neusprachliche Mitteilungen aus Wissenschaft und Praxis* (Berlin), Vol. 35 (1982), pp. 150-61.

ZEHNDER, HERMAN F. *"Teach My People The Truth!": The Story of Frankenmuth, Michigan.* Bay City, Mich.: privately printed, 1970.

ZINTL, JOSEF. "Prosodic Influences on the Meaning of 'Leck mich am Arsch' in Bavarian", *Maledicta* (Waukesha, Wis., U.S.A.), Vol. IV, No. 1 (Summer 1980), pp. 91-95, 1 illus.

Abbreviations Used

abbr.	abbreviation	*diet.*	dietetics
adj	adjective	*dim.*	diminutive
admin.	administration	*Du*	Dutch
adv	adverb		
agr.	agriculture	*E*	English
AmE	American English	*eccles.*	ecclesiastical
anat.	anatomy	*econ.*	economics, economy; economic
apprec.	appreciative(ly)		
approx.	approximate(ly)	*educ.*	education
archaeol.	archaeology	*e.g.*	exempli gratia (L, for instance)
archit.	architecture; architectural		
arith.	arithmetic	*el.*	(compound) element
attrib.	attributive(ly)	*e-m*	einem
AusG	Austrian German	*emot.*	emotional; emotive
AustralE	Australian English	*ent.*	entomology
		e-s	eines
bak.	baking	*esp.*	especially
BavG	Bavarian German	*euphem.*	euphemistic(ally)
bev.	beverage		
bot.	botany; botanical	*f*	feminine
BrE	British English	*F*	French
brew.	brewery	*fig.*	figurative(ly)
ca.	circa (L, about)	*G*	German
CanE	Canadian English	*garm.*	garment
civ. eng.	civil engineering	*gastr.*	gastronomy
colloq.	colloquial(ness)	*gen.*	general(ly); genitive
com.	commerce; commercial	*geog.*	geography
comest.	comestible	*geol.*	geology
comp(s).	compound(s)	*Germ.*	Germanic
concr.	concrete(ly)	*Goth*	Gothic
contp.	contemptuous	*Gr*	Greek
cp.	compare		
cul.	culinary art	*her.*	heraldry
curl.	curling	*hist.*	history; historical
		hum.	humour; humorous(ly)
d.	died	*hunt.*	hunting
decl.	declension	*husb.*	husbandry
dial.	dialect; dialectal	*hyd. eng.*	hydraulic engineering

ibid.	ibidem (L, in the some place [i.e., in the book just quoted])	*numis.*	numismatics
		OBav	Old Bavarian
Icel	Icelandic	*obs.*	obsolete
ichth.	ichthyology	*OE*	Old English
i.e.	id est (L, that is)	*OF*	Old French
IE	Indo-European	*OHG*	Old High German
imit.	imitative	*opp.*	opposite
indus.	industry	*ornith.*	ornithology
interj	interjection	*orogr.*	orography
IrE	Irish English		
iron.	irony; ironic	*PaG*	Pennsylvania German
It	Italian	*phr.*	phrase(s)
		phys.	physics
j-m	jemandem	*physiol.*	physiology
j-n	jemanden	*pl.*	plural
joc.	jocular	*poet.*	poetical
journ.	journalism	*Pol*	Polish
jur.	jurisdiction	*polit.*	political
		p.p.	past participle
L	Latin	*pr.t.*	present tense
ling.	linguistics	*prec.*	preceding
lit.	literature; literally	*pred.*	predicative(ly)
		prob.	probable; probably
m	masculine	*pron.*	pronounced; pronunciation
math.	mathematics	*prov.*	proverb(s); proverbial
ME	Middle English		
mech. eng.	mechanical engineering	*R*	Russian
med.	medicine; medical	*R.C.*	Roman Catholic
MedL	Medieval Latin	*relig.*	religion
meteor.	meteorology		
MHG	Middle High German	*sarc.*	sarcastic
mil.	military	*scil.*	scilicet (L, [to be] understood or supplied)
ModE	Modern English		
ModHG	Modern High German	*ScotE*	Scottish English
mot.	motoring	*sg.*	singular
mount.	mountaineering	*sl.*	slang
mus.	music; musical	*s.o.*	someone
myc.	mycology	*sobr.*	sobriquet
		SouBrE	Southern English
n	neuter	*SouG*	Southern German
NorBavG	Northern Bavarian	*Sp*	Spanish
NorBrE	Northern English	*stand.*	standard
NorG	Northern German	*StandE*	Standard English

StandG	Standard German	*viz.*	videlicet (L, namely)
s.th.	something	*v/refl*	reflexive verb
Sw	Swedish	*v/t*	transitive verb
		vt/i	verb used both transitively and intransitively
tech.	technology		
theat.	theatre		
		vt/refl	verb used both transitively and reflexively
UK	The United Kingdom (of Great Britain and Northern Ireland)		
		vulg.	vulgar
		VulgL	Vulgar Latin
UpG	Upper German		
usu.	usually	*WelshE*	Welsh English
vet.	veterinary	*Yid.*	Yiddish
v/i	intransitive verb		
vinic.	viniculture	*zo.*	zoology

<	is derived from	*	the asterisk (1) marks a deduced, and therefore undocumented, word form; and (2) serves as a warning, before whole sentences, that in the absence of a close equivalent in English the wording offered is an idiomatic, but only more or less literal translation
>	develops, morphologically or semantically, into		
→	(1) see; (2) the sense develops to		
[ ]	square brackets (1) contain etymological information; (2) vary, and thus stand within, round brackets; and (3) indicate free variations in model sentences, e.g. boys [girls]		
<>	angle brackets enclose individual letters (or graphemes)	:	the colon, after due definitory preliminaries, is the curtain raiser for the exact and concise equivalent of the headword; if non-standard, the headword here finds its match on the proper non-standard level (colloquial, slang, vulgar, etc.)
~	the swung dash stands for the headword; when its initial letter changes from a capital to a small letter, or vice-versa, a superscript ^{x} is added:^{x}		

"O cor, it's all o'er!" *"Don't be sore there's no more."*
[A topical *and* local variant in English of the Bavarian (to be found on p. 70).]

Bayerische Autoren im ADV

Gerd Maier
Wos wirklich zäiht
Heitere und besinnliche Geschichten und Gedichte
in einfühlsamer Mundart

Marzell Oberneder
Und immer wieder Sonnenschein
Biographie eines bewegten Lebens

Marzell Oberneder
Von Weltenburg bis Passau
Ein literarischer Spaziergang entlang der Donau

Gunther Zorn
Das gläserne Haus
Amüsante Erzählungen aus einer reichen Kindheit

Der Andreas Dick Verlag bedankt sich
für den Kauf des Buches.
Wir wünschen Ihnen viel Freude beim Lesen.

Andreas Dick Publishers thank you
for having bought the present title.
They wish you many lucky dips and browses,
and much enjoyable reading.

If you have any suggestions for further items to be included in future editions, or in a second volume, of *Bavarian into English*, please send them to the author direct, at Gumpelzhaimerstrasse 5b, D-93049 Regensburg. We greatly appreciate your co-operation.